UNDERSTANDING THE CLASSICAL
MUSIC PROFESSION

This book is dedicated to musicians past, present and future in the hope that barriers of genre, hierarchy and perception can be gradually eroded and holistic practice valued.

The task is not so much to see what no one yet has seen, but to think what no body yet has thought about that which everyone sees.

Arthur Schopenhauer

Understanding the Classical Music Profession

The Past, the Present and Strategies for the Future

DAWN BENNETT
Curtin University of Technology, Australia

ASHGATE

Published by
Ashgate Publishing Limited
Gower House
Croft Road
Aldershot
Hampshire GU11 3HR
England

Ashgate Publishing Company
Suite 420
101 Cherry Street
Burlington, VT 05401-4405
USA

www.ashgate.com

British Library Cataloguing in Publication Data
Bennett, Dawn Elizabeth
   Understanding the classical music profession : the past,
   the present and strategies for the future
   1. Music – Vocational guidance
   I. Title
   780.2'3

Library of Congress Cataloging-in-Publication Data
Bennett, Dawn Elizabeth.
   Understanding the classical music profession : the past, the present and strategies for the future / by Dawn Elizabeth Bennett.
      p. cm.
   Includes bibliographical references (p.   ).
   ISBN 978-0-7546-5959-4 (alk. paper)
   1. Music–Vocational guidance. I. Title.

   ML3795.B45 2008
   781.6'8023–dc22

                                                                           2007049837

ISBN 978-0-7546-5959-4

bound in Great Britain by
s Ltd, Bodmin, Cornwall.

Contents

List of Figures and Illustrations

Figures

Illustrations

List of Tables

Foreword

It is widely recognized that the survival of all living things on this planet depends largely on their ability to adapt to environmental changes. It is also acknowledged that plants nurtured in a hot house (also known as a conservatory!) do not always survive when transplanted into the open air.

Classical musicians are no different, and if they are to avoid extinction they need to develop the diverse skills required to survive in our present-day multicultural, economic rationalist and computer-dependent society.

There is an urgent need, therefore, for musical conservatories to change from their traditional 'hot house' concentration on the exclusive training of performers and instead develop a more flexible and realistic curriculum to cater for a wider range of careers involving music and music-making.

For many years music educators have expressed concern regarding the antiquated nature of typical tertiary music institutions (for example, Graham Bartle, Doreen Bridges as well as myself in Australia) but perhaps because they were music *educators* rather than *performers*, very few of the institutions themselves paid heed to their warnings.

However, tertiary institutions will find that the clear messages of *Understanding the Classical Music Profession* can no longer be ignored, for they are drawn from data collected from musicians who were trained as performers. But Dawn Bennett goes further than describing the evolution and threatened extinction of the classical musician; she offers practical, yet thoroughly researched suggestions for the transformation of music conservatories into more relevant institutions for the training of musicians. I therefore recommend that this book be essential reading for all musicians in the hope that their survival can be secured.

Helen Stowasser

Preface

I am a musician. As a child, being a musician meant being a performer: a soloist, or (failing that) a member of a string quartet, orchestra or chamber ensemble. Teaching was a second-rate occupation upon which one would embark only if performance opportunities were insufficient. This meant that one's attention should focus on the acquisition of an elite level of technical skill and a repertoire that could be played from memory at a minute's notice. How different was the reality that I faced as an adult. I was fortunate in that performance work was plentiful; however, nobody prepared me for a life away from home and the long-term isolation of travel and hour upon hour of individual practice. Later, as an orchestral musician, I discovered a much-needed collegiate; but I was unprepared for a life devoid of artistic decisions and my own creative identity. What is more, I quickly found a love of teaching, arts management and research. I resisted telling fellow performers about these newfound passions as though I were having a secret affair! In a way, I was; the new activities offered variety, independence, creativity, a sense of identity and a whole new perspective on my life in music.

Almost twenty years later, I came to realize that the hierarchy of music careers inhibits today's new graduates just as it did my own generation. The hierarchy contributes towards much of the angst experienced by intending performers who feel an agonizing sense of failure when non-performance roles are required to keep the bread on the table or to meet the responsibilities of having a family. This sense of failure contributes to attrition from the profession, and it contributes greatly to the unfortunate perception of music teachers as lesser beings. It occurred to me that the term *musician* is still used to mean *performer*. Thus used, where does it leave the majority of musicians, whose professional identity is far more diverse and complex?

To sustain their careers, musicians have to meet the challenges of an increasingly complex and competitive cultural environment. Musicians are not simply performers: a musician is someone who works within the music profession. Is success the achievement of a top solo career? To some people, absolutely; however, that does not define success for the profession. Success as a musician is marked by the achievement of sustainable practice, which requires musicians to break down attitudinal and hierarchical barriers. Success should be based upon personal career satisfaction rather than a pre-conceived hierarchy of roles, and the possibilities are endless.

I am a musician. I play, research, teach and enjoy music. No one task is more worthy than another, and I look forward towards many more years of discovering what else the profession of music has to offer.

Dawn Bennett

Acknowledgements

Books are not written alone, and I would like to acknowledge the many people who have contributed their wisdom, experience and support.

Colleagues such as Graham Seal, David Tunley and Tom Stannage have provided a wealth of experience and insight. Nina Divich (editor extraordinaire) formatted the references and turned some rather unusable figures into professional-looking ones. Graphic designer and musician Ashley Doodkorte took my illustration ideas with the instruction to be 'quirky', and produced the wonderful illustrations. Many other colleagues around the world have added their own perspectives and have generously shared their research, stories and materials. Friends, especially Jan, Kate and Theresa, read chapters or the whole book and gave me honest feedback and ideas.

Many wonderful musicians and artists responded to questionnaires and gave of their time to attend interviews or focus groups, often volunteering much more time and information than I could have hoped. People shared their stories and their words brought tears on several occasions. The quotation or epigraph at the start of each chapter of this book represents or directly quotes these participants. Several musicians went out of their way to encourage others to participate, and I am particularly grateful to the musicians who publicized my work amongst colleagues.

Finally I would like to acknowledge my family. To Martin for your unconditional support, love, encouragement and belief in me from the very beginning, and to my parents Ann and Ken, parents-in-law John and Fran, and children Simon, Beckie and Emily, whose musical activities are such an integral part of their lives and who remind me that music-making is far from being a job: it is both a pleasure and a passion.

List of Abbreviations

ABC	Australian Broadcasting Corporation
ABO	Association of British Orchestras
ABS	Australian Bureau of Statistics
ACLC	Australian Culture and Leisure Classifications
ACM	American Conservatory of Music
AEC	European Association of Conservatoires
ANZSIC	Australia and New Zealand Standard Industry Classifications
CAE	Colleges of Advanced Education
CBT	Cognitive Behavioural Therapy
CCD	Community Cultural Development
CEPROM	Commission for the Education of the Professional Musician
CIRAC	Creative Industries Research and Application Centre
CMC	Cultural Ministers Council
CMCSWG	Cultural Ministers Council Statistics Working Group
CMS	College Music Society
CoP	Community of Practice
CPD	Continuing Professional Development
GAIN	Gateway Arts Industry Network
GDP	Gross Domestic Product
GST	Goods and Services Tax
HEFCE	Higher Education Funding Council for England
ICT	Information Communications Technology
IPM	Institute for Popular Music
ISME	International Society for Music Education
ITP	Industry Training Package
LIPA	Liverpool Institute for Performing Arts
MUSKE	Musikkiyrittäjyyden Kebittämisbanke
NACHTMUS	The National Council of Heads of Tertiary Music Schools
NASM	National Association of Schools of Music
NCCRS	National Centre for Culture and Recreation Statistics
NEA	National Endowment for the Arts
PALATINE	Performing Arts Learning and Teaching Innovation Network
PRI	Playing-related Injuries
QTS	Qualified Teacher Status
RCM	Royal College of Music
TAFE	Technical and Further Education

UK	United Kingdom
UNS	Unified National System
UNESCO	United Nations Educational, Scientific and Cultural Organization
US	United States of America

Chapter 1

What Lies Ahead

'Music is my hobby, my job and my passion'

Introduction

I once set out to write the 'ultimate curriculum' for the education and training of aspiring classical musicians. I looked up the term *musician* in music dictionaries, and it was significant in its absence. I turned to government statistical data and found them to be fragmentary and incomplete. I read economic reports and learned that the writers agree with the sorry state of the statistics; in fact, economists have been calling for improved data collections for the past 30 years. I turned to the literature on the cultural industries and discovered that no-one has yet agreed what they are. And so it was that my research changed direction, and I have since spent my time trying to put together the pieces of what it is to be a musician.

Musicians in the twenty-first century require a broad and rapidly evolving suite of skills on which to build and sustain their careers. Adopting multiple roles that change according to both personal and professional needs, musicians constantly look beyond their training and experience to forge new opportunities. The key here is the word 'opportunities'. Whilst globalization, emerging technologies, and creative and cultural industries can be perceived as threats, dilemmas or barriers, they present wonderful opportunities to explore, challenge and diversify one's practice when they are positively portrayed alongside changes within the general populace such as an ageing population and an increasing focus on recreation and leisure time.

Opportunities within the wider cultural industries are much more than the means to make ends meet, or a 'fall-back position' in the absence of a full-time performance career. Holistic practice enables musicians to create and sustain intrinsically satisfying careers with the flexibility to meet changing personal and professional needs. Whether these realities are greeted by fear of the unknown or with excitement and preparedness is largely determined by informal and formal training experiences. However, the education and training of classical instrumental musicians is an unenviable task, occurring without a clear understanding of what it is that musicians do. How do musicians spend their time? Do they change roles, and if so, why, and how often? How much do they earn? Are music careers different for women and men? Is performance the only, or the ultimate, mark of success?

Holistic practice is not as new as some would suggest; one has only to consider the working lives of Telemann or Borodin, or the use of itinerant musicians as spies, to realize that musicians have historically earned at least some of their income outside of music. However, today's musicians, more than perhaps ever before, practice beyond traditional boundaries. Musicians are part of a growing sector of the workforce within which casualization and multiple employments are rife. In fact, the cultural workforce as a whole pre-empts employment trends in many Western countries. The traditional linear career model has little relevance to the cultural sector, wherein people self-manage their careers in what have been described as 'protean' careers (so-named after the mythological sea god Proteus, who was able to change form at will).

Protean careerists expand their work behaviours, competencies and connections in search of success that is determined not in the eyes of others, but in terms of self-identity, psychological (intrinsic) success and the satisfaction of personal and professional needs. Fascinating (and exciting) though it is to plan and engage with a protean career, the concept also highlights immediate problems for musicians given the common usage of the term *musician* to mean *performer*. Asked 'What do you do?' the response 'I am a musician' invariably leads to the query, 'What do you play?' Consequently, self-identity is paradoxical for the majority of musicians, whose activities contradict the traditional image of the musician as performer.

Psychological success is paramount to career satisfaction, and whereas a performance career may mean success to one musician, others will find success within an abundance of potential roles such as teaching, arranging, management or audio engineering. What, then, is a musician?

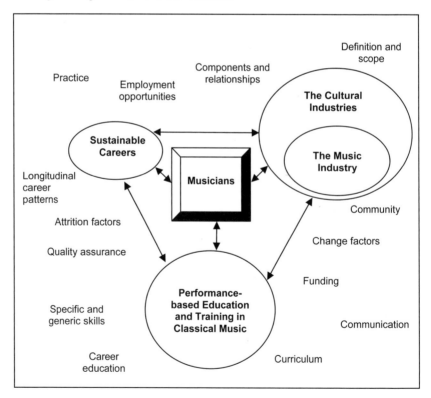

Figure 1.1   Initial Conceptual Framework

Conceptual Framework

To view non-performance careers as a failure to reach the elusive peaks of performance success is both unrealistic and self-defeating. Rather, this text will argue that success is the achievement of a sustainable career within which intrinsic satisfaction is found and self-identity established. This requires a fresh new look at the key elements: the musician, the cultural industries and performance-based education and training.

Anselm Strauss and Juliet Corbin's description of theory development is particularly helpful when considering the comparison and classification of concepts and their relationships without necessarily relating the concepts to each other. Even though multiple concepts are included in the initial conceptual framework, they are not aligned with a single key concept so that relationships can emerge rather than being pre-supposed. The initial conceptual framework is shown as Figure 1.1. For those who like to read the last page of a book before the middle, you can find the final conceptual framework at the start of Chapter 7.

Research Method in Brief

Interpretive (qualitative) design is 'a commitment to some version of the naturalistic, interpretive approach to its subject matter and an ongoing critique of the politics and methods'.[1] Qualitative research is based on the notion that reality is subjectively created rather than objectively defined. Bill Ticehurst and Tony Veal describe how researchers strive 'to uncover meanings and understanding of the issues they are researching ... This enables qualitative researchers to match their methods to the research problem, thus providing a flexible approach that contrasts with the structured approaches found in many positivist studies'.[2] Normative (quantitative) research, on the other hand, assumes that the social domain is an absolute reality; nevertheless, 'qualitative and quantitative research can complement each other by playing the respective roles of discovery and confirmation'.[3]

Strauss and Corbin advocate the integration of qualitative and quantitative methods within research: 'the qualitative should direct the quantitative and the quantitative feedback into the qualitative in a circular, but at the same time evolving, process with each method contributing to the theory in ways that only each can'.[4] In the doctoral study and in my subsequent work, the two paradigms have been combined in an integrative approach, using different methods for different aspects

---

1   Norman K. Denzin and Yvonna S. Lincoln, *Handbook of Qualitative Research* (Thousand Oaks, CA, 2000), 2nd edn.

2   G. William Ticehurst and Anthony J. Veal, *Business Research Methods: A Managerial Approach* (Sydney, NSW, 2000).

3   Meredith D. Gall, Walter Borg and Joyce P. Gall, *Educational Research: An Introduction* (New York, 1996), 6th edn.

4   See Anselm Strauss and Juliet Corbin, *Basics of Qualitative Research* (Thousand Oaks, CA, 1998), 2nd edn; and Gretchen Rossman and Bruce Wilson, 'Numbers and Words: Combining Quantitative and Qualitative Methods in a Single Large-Scale Study', *Evaluation Review*, 9/5 (1984): 627–43.

of the study to provide increased opportunities for analysis and, as a result, a richer detail of data. The normative and interpretive paradigms interacted as illustrated by Matthew Miles and Michael Huberman:[5]

QUAL[itative]   QUANT[itative]   QUAL[itative]
(exploration) ————————▶ *(questionnaire)* ————————▶ *(deepen, test findings)*

Qualitative methodologies assisted with the identification of a representative sample by providing background data in the design stage, and were utilized throughout the study. Survey methodology was useful in combining the normative and interpretive paradigms as considered appropriate for the three phases of the study: survey instruments included questions that would yield both quantitative and qualitative data. Quantification acted as a means of summarizing qualitative data into categories reflective of emergent themes.

The study utilized three distinct, but interrelated data collections within three sequential research phases. Identification of the key concepts as illustrated in the initial conceptual framework led to a pilot study comprising twenty-three interviews, the data from which informed the development and implementation of a survey. A subsequent set of interviews provided the basis for two in-depth focus group interviews within which significant evolving themes were further pursued. Smaller sets of interviews were conducted between each phase to clarify initial results and enlarge upon emerging themes.

For the pilot study (Phase I), interviews were conducted with 23 practitioners from within the cultural industries. Stage 1a interviews were conducted with participants (N=13) drawn from throughout the cultural industries, and Stage 1b encompassed a sample (N=10) of performers and non-performers within the music sector. The samples resulted in two discrete sets of data from which comparisons could be drawn. The interview was selected for the pilot study as it 'can provide a greater depth of data than the other types, given its qualitative nature'.[6] A semi-structured format was chosen to incorporate the formulation of open questions based upon the initial conceptual framework and the review of literature, at the same time encouraging participants to provide a depth of information on issues that they perceived to be of relevance and importance.

The survey (Phase II) was designed to yield information pertinent to the research questions, to test the revised conceptual framework developed from the pilot study, and to identify potential participants for the focus group interviews planned in Phase III of the study. The survey was answered by 152 musicians. Development of the survey instrument was further enhanced by two interviews conducted at conservatories with representatives who were instigating curricular change, and who had a depth of experience within the profession as performers and teachers. I should note that I use the term *profession* because of the inclusivity that it offers musicians who engage in a myriad of different roles. I do not use it as a signifier of success or to

---

5   Matthew B. Miles and A. Michael Huberman, *Qualitative Data Analysis* (Beverley Hills, CA, 1994), 2nd edn.

6   Denzin and Lincoln, *Handbook of Qualitative Research*.

describe someone who earns an income from music. In each case the change process employed by the institution had included representation from within the profession, and was thus determined to be of particular relevance.

Informed by the results of Phases I and II of the study, Phase III comprised two in-depth focus group interviews with groups of musicians. Focus groups were selected for the final phase in order to encourage 'interactions among the participants [that would] stimulate them to state feelings, perceptions, and beliefs that they would not express if interviewed individually'.[7] In addition, focus groups provided the opportunity to observe the interaction/discussion process of the group. With validity and reliability in mind, focus groups enabled participants to validate the initial results and to enlarge upon given themes. The research design and methodology is illustrated as Figure 1.2.

Understanding the Classical Music Profession investigates the careers of classically trained instrumental musicians; how they spend their time, the skills and attributes required to develop and sustain their careers, the environment in which they work, and the relevance of existing education and training. The text reinforces that musicians are much, much more than performers, and that success as a musician should be measured not by the number of recitals and recordings, but by the ability to build a sustainable career with a variety of different roles that satisfy both personal and professional needs.

Chapter 2 introduces the cultural environment within which musicians work, with an overview of the cultural industries and a non-hierarchical look at the enormous variety of activities pursued by cultural practitioners. Chapter 3 considers historical aspects of life as a musician, followed by the employment characteristics of the present-day musician including gender issues, attrition and injury. Chapter 4 explores performance-based education and training, and examines the extent to which the realities of professional practice are reflected within existing performance-based programmes. Chapter 5 asks whether the characteristics of practice within other artforms reflect the practice of musicians, and whether musicians could draw upon opportunities within the wider cultural industry for employment, training, funding and networking. Chapter 6 looks at the destination of performance graduates: painting a picture of the performance positions available to orchestral instrumentalists and comparing the allocation of musicians' time with the core components of Australia's undergraduate curricula. The chapter goes on to define the skills and personal attributes crucial to musicians and artists in the achievement of sustainable careers. The final chapter suggests that similarities between the practice of musicians and other artists offer the potential for the collaborative delivery of initial and ongoing education and training more reflective of the eclectic nature of musicians' work, and illustrates a non-hierarchical view of cultural practice that clearly indicates the potential for an exciting diversity of holistic practice.

---

7   See Gall et al. For more information on interviewing as a research methodology, see Louis Cohen, Lawrence Manion and Keith Morrison, *Research Methods in Education* (London, 2001), 5th edn; and Ticehurst and Veal, *Business Research Methods: A Managerial Approach*. Whyte's hierarchy of interview questions is particularly useful, and is found in the latter book.

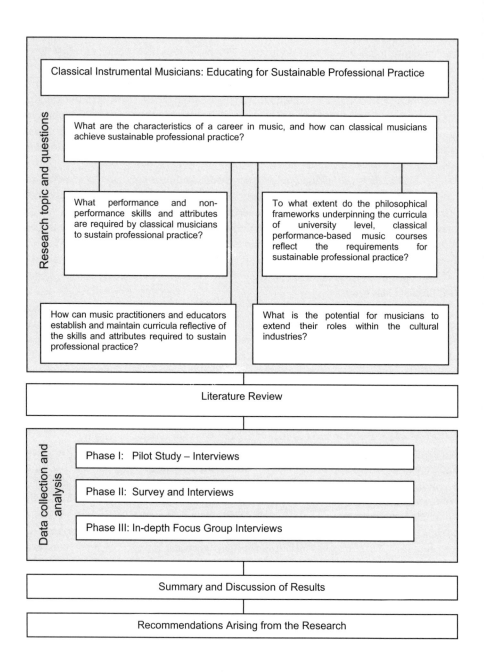

Figure 1.2   Research Design and Methodology

Suggestions for Further Reading

The extent to which classical, performance-based music education and training reflects the careers of its graduates has gained heightened exposure at the same time as higher education institutions become increasingly accountable for the employability of graduates, and yet much of the available literature has only tangential relevance and there remains a shortage of literature relating to the complex area of music.

Consideration of the wide-ranging elements that impact on musicians' careers has necessitated the deliberation of a diverse range of subjects with which no one person could be the expert. The aim is to provide a picture of what it is to be a musician, and I encourage others to engage in the numerous possibilities for further research. Principal issues relating to this area of research include cultural practice, employment trends, self-identity, the music, cultural and creative industries, cultural policy, pre-tertiary music education and training, and tertiary education and training. Sources of information include academic journals, industry generated literature, government and non-government reports, published and unpublished employment data, documentation pertaining to music curriculum and related philosophical frameworks, and media articles. Research into creative or cultural practice is a burgeoning field, and there is an increasing amount of research on the education and training of musicians. Three of the initiatives concerning music are the International Society for Music Education (ISME) Commission for the Education of the Professional Musician[8] (CEPROM), which meets bi-annually prior to the ISME World Conference, the Polifonia Project[9] from the Erasmus Thematic Network of the European Union, which looked at professional music training and practice in Europe and reported in 2007, and PALATINE (Performing Arts Learning and Teaching Innovation Network): the UK higher education subject centre for dance, drama and music.[10]

Terminology

It is important to clarify the meaning of terms that appear frequently throughout the book. Some, such as *business practices* are terms used by musicians to describe the administrative side of their practice. Some terms require explanation because they are Australian, and others are defined for the benefit of those readers not familiar with the intricacies (and acronyms) of music practice and training.

Business Practices

The term *business practices* is defined by musicians as administrative tasks such as marketing, funding applications, financial management, interpersonal skills,

---

8   For more information, see <http://www.isme.org/en/education-of-the-professional-musician/education-of-the-professional-musician-ce.html>.

9   For more information, see http://www.polifonia-tn.org/Content.aspx?id=58.

10 PALATINE has researched the creative labour market with respect to performing artists. See <http://www.palatine.ac.uk/>.

professional ethics, arts law, human resource management, time management, public relations, negotiation and information communications technology (ICT).

Career Education and Experience

Career education and experience refers to career preparation through a range of activities such as real and simulated experience, mentoring, career planning and industry studies.

Classical Music

Classical music is used to describe traditions of European art music evolving from medieval sacred and secular musical practices.

Composite Careers

Please see protean careers.

Conservatorium

Traditionally, a music conservatorium is a music school that is independent of a college or university, and which provides specialized training in classical music performance. In the twenty-first century, conservatories are usually affiliated with colleges or universities. An increasingly diverse range of degree and non-degree courses includes music performance in multiple genres, musicology, composition, conducting and music education: sometimes in combination with each other or with non-music disciplines. The European term for conservatorium is *conservatoire*, and in the United States the term *conservatory* is often used. An overview of the history and philosophy of music conservatories together with an analysis of selected programmes is included in Chapter 4.

Core Studies

Core studies are the compulsory units of study within a formal course and typically include units in performance, history, keyboard skills, musicianship and theory of music.

Cultural Industries

The cultural industries are described in Chapter 2. I deliberately avoid the term *creative industries*, which emphasizes the act of creating rather than the holistic practice that is most likely to result in a sustainable career. I use the term *cultural industries* in its most holistic sense. The term *creative industries* has been popular for the past 10 years; hence literature concerning cultural industries and creative industries, cultural practice and creative practice, is all critical to research in this area.

Instrumental Pedagogy

Instrumental pedagogy refers to the principles and practice of teaching an instrument.

Multiple Careers

Please see protean careers.

Music Technologies

Music technologies refer to technological software and hardware relating to music performance, composition, teaching and learning, and recording.

Musical Genre

A musical genre is a category or style of musical work such as classical or jazz.

Performance Psychology

Primarily practised in the field of elite athletics, performance psychology pertains to psychological factors that affect the acquisition, execution and retention of performance skills. Associated with this is the development of effective practice methods.

Portfolio Careers

Please see protean careers.

Protean Careers

Protean careers are defined as careers in which multiple roles are undertaken. Protean careers are also commonly described as 'portfolio', 'multiple' or 'composite' careers. Protean careerists self-manage their careers and adapt their practice as necessary to meet personal and professional needs.

Technical and Further Education (TAFE)

The term Technical and Further Education (TAFE) has been used in Australia since the 1970s.[11] TAFE providers deliver vocational programmes in a wide variety of industry sectors including music. Although TAFE study has traditionally been at a level below university study, TAFE colleges increasingly provide courses that overlap with undergraduate degree programmes, and growing numbers of university graduates are turning to TAFE for vocational skills and practical training.

---

11 Australian Committee on Technical and Further Education, *TAFE in Australia* (No. ACOTAFE 1974) (Canberra, ACT, 1974).

Tertiary

The tertiary education sector in Australia refers to post-compulsory education and training such as that undertaken at a university or other accredited facility.

Concluding Thoughts

Of crucial importance to this book are the stories of musicians and artists, who are quoted throughout the text. Their experiences are the single best source of information about the realities of cultural practice, and I hope that their words will be valued and respected by all who read them.

Chapter 2

The Cultural Industries

'It's all very well having a bean-counter mentality, but the person counting the beans has to know the value of the beans in order to assess their worth'

Achieving a sustainable career most often requires artists to pursue a diversity of roles within and outside of their discipline, and it is within the broad context of the cultural industries that the majority of potential roles can be found. Thus, the cultural industries constitute the environment within which musicians conduct much of their practice. This text does not seek to provide an economic analysis. Rather, I provide an outline of the factors that impact on cultural practice: considering first the cultural industries and how practitioners and their activities fit into them, and then the relationships between governments and the arts. As such, the chapter is written from the perspective of the arts practitioner, and much of the discussion concerns artists in general rather than focusing on musicians. I have included links for those who wish to further investigate the fields of cultural economics and policy. These links will also enable readers to update statistical data, which are continuously renewed.

Performing artists are the least likely to consider the potential for a diverse range of employment options beyond those associated with their artform. Take the example of a musician. Most music students intend to pursue a career in performance, conducting or composition; however, academics and students are aware of the low probability of achieving such a career. Although performance is a fundamental part of a musician's life, for many this engagement will be primarily through teaching, ensemble direction, technology and management. The reality is that musicians sustain their careers within an increasingly complex and competitive cultural environment. Despite this, few institutions introduce students to the potential for employment throughout the cultural industries and there is insufficient professional development available to help musicians broaden their practice.

Culture

Originally relating to the cultivation of soil, culture became synonymous with good taste, manners and education. Harry Chartrand reflects that culture in the nineteenth century was defined as '"high culture", that is the cultural forms and activities of the educated elite. Both cultural diplomacy and cultural relations tended to be exclusively concerned with prestige and influence'.[1] In the twenty-first century, culture, in the sense of artistic and social pursuits considered within social policy includes a much wider cross section of the community who access a variety of cultural pursuits including books, music and film. In its broadest sense, culture is 'the whole way of life of society, the intellectual development of the population and the practice of the arts'.[2] The United Nations Educational, Scientific and Cultural Organization (UNESCO), which has played a key international role in cultural development, defines culture as something that is 'not limited to a particular set of activities connected with heritage and arts, but encompasses all those activities which define the identity of a particular human society or group'.[3] Given that definition, it is hardly surprising that the concept of global culture has proven somewhat problematic!

In a move away from the more usual definitions of category or product, Helsinki's City of Culture Foundation defines culture in terms of process: 'culture is the space or degree of material and spiritual development achieved over time with all its phenomena', which Robin Trotter considers to encapsulate a significant move towards the function of cultural theory within cultural practice.[4] In recent times, a more purposeful view of culture has been adopted in terms of economic and productivity measures, social capital and cultural heritage. Economic and public policies have therefore become intertwined. There are both positive and negative outcomes arising from the blending of economic and public policies. The move towards economic measurement of cultural activities has had an acute impact on the arts, which cannot expect to be measured purely upon aesthetic interest, or on cultural social capital gained from the entrustment of core societal values to future generations. The products of culture have an economic value leading to the need to measure both tangible and intangible values of culture against economic principles. Taking a more optimistic stance, arts competencies are increasingly marketable given the economic shift from manufacturing to service and, most recently, to information or knowledge-based economies.

The results of economic measurement are also felt at the individual level. As one musician said, 'it's all very well having a bean-counter mentality, but the person counting the beans has to know the value of the beans in order to assess their worth'.[5] There is currently little agreement on the value or definition of cultural beans. A US report by the RAND Corporation reiterates the difficulty of measuring the intrinsic value of the arts, which it suggests have been lost within the broad economic discourse concerning social and economic goals. Henry Kingsbury highlights the ironic nature of tangible and intangible values when he cites Karl Marx, who said that 'although a piano maker engages in productive work, a pianist does not'. Kingsbury responds

---

1   Henry Chartrand, 'International Cultural Affairs: A Fourteen-Country Survey', *Journal of Arts Management, Law and Society*, 22/2 (1992).

2   David Throsby, *Economics and Culture* (Cambridge, 2001).

3   See Robin Trotter, 'Cultural Policy', *The Year's Work in Critical and Cultural Theory*, 10/1 (2002): 202–25.

4   Ibid.

5   Dawn Bennett, 'Peas in a Cultural Pod? A Comparison of the Skills and Personal Attributes of Artists and Musicians', *Australian Journal of Music Education*, 1 (2004): 22–5.

that 'a product is truly a cultural product not because it is marketable, but because it is meaningful'. In other words, a piano has value only because someone wishes to buy it for the purposes of making music.[6]

What are the Cultural Industries?

Understanding the environment within which one works is crucial to career planning, development and maintenance. Developing such an understanding, however, is a difficult task given that definitions for the cultural industries vary between different locations and organizations, and are influenced by the objectives of the documents within which they are contained. The lack of an agreed definition for the cultural industries within Australia and internationally impacts the effectiveness of data collections that inform funding, education, training, policy and advocacy. Advocacy has the potential to increase the efficiency of funding for education and professional practice, as well as advocating the social and economic value of culture. Unfortunately, a united voice for the cultural industries requires the definitional agreement that is currently lacking. It also inhibits effective research into the needs and circumstances of artists. As decision makers struggle for understanding of the requirements for sustainable practice within parameters that are unclear, many artists are left floundering with little long-term, practical support.[7]

Although many artists resist the notion of the economic term *industry*, there is potentially great strength in the united voice of the cultural industries, which in Australia are worth over Aus$31 billion in goods and services each year. Representing approximately 2.5 per cent of Australian gross domestic product, the cultural industries are as big as the education, health services, road transport and residential building industries.[8] Almost three million people work in Australia's 'arts and related industries'.[9]

In considering a definition for the cultural industries, Create Australia suggests there to be 'no right or wrong answer ... [however] it would be impossible to undertake a communication campaign without a comprehensive definition'.[10] Paul Costantoura concurs, writing that 'at present the term "the arts" takes on whatever

---

6   For the RAND report *Gifts of the Muse: Reframing the Debate about the Benefits of the Arts*, see <http://www.rand.org/pubs/monographs/MG218/>. See also Henry Kingsbury's book, *Music, Talent and Performance: A Conservatory Cultural System* (Philadelphia, 1988).

7   A career and education support service exists for the Australian dance sector. See <http:// www.ais.org.au/dance.asp> for more details.

8   See Commonwealth of Australia, *Some Australian Arts Statistics: Supporting and Promoting the Practice and Enjoyment of the Arts* (No. 700.994021) (Canberra, ACT, 2003). Updates are available from the Australian Bureau of Statistics. Ausstats are particularly useful: <http://www.abs.gov.au/ausstats/abs@.nsf/web+pages/statistics?opendocument>. The latest compendium at the time of writing is Music in Australia: A Statistical Overview, published by the CMCSWG in February 2007. See: <http://www.culturaldata.gov.au/__data/assets/pdf_file/58544/Music_in_Australia_A_Statistical_Overview.pdf>.

9   See Department of Foreign Affairs and Trade: <http://www.dfat.gov.au>.

10   Create Australia, *Creating a Position: Education, Training and the Cultural Industries* (Sydney, NSW, 2001).

meaning each individual who uses it chooses to apply'.[11] Hans Hoegh-Guldberg defines the cultural industries as those industries to which copyright is applicable. Similarly, United Kingdom policy developed as part of the knowledge economy initiative is based around activities with the potential to create something that would attract intellectual property rights.[12]

Reflecting Richard Florida's concept of a creative class, David Throsby and Virginia Hollister summarize the emergence of the cultural industries:

> All sorts of creative people are seen as content providers for the information superhighway and as the source of innovative ideas in inventing the future. This has led to the identification of a 'creative class' within society, and of 'creative workers' within the labour force – artists, designers, scientists, researchers and others whose work generates new ideas, new processes and new products. These concepts are associated with the emergence of the economic phenomenon of the 'cultural industries', referring to those sectors of the economy that produce cultural goods and services ranging from poetry to television programs to fashion design.[13]

The search for a definition of the wider cultural industries in Australia arises from the need to conceptualize cultural activity for the purposes of economic analysis and the compilation of data on issues such as participation and productivity, linked for the most part to broader political agendas discussed later in this chapter. Cultural industries as defined by the Australian Bureau of Statistics (ABS) include the traditional cultural activities of creation and expression together with support services and related activities with some cultural content such as newspapers, multimedia and publishing. Multiple terms are used inconsistently to describe elements of the cultural industries, and many of the inconsistencies appear within reports generated by governments or by publicly funded agencies. The terms *applied arts, applied arts and cultural activity, arts, arts and crafts, arts and culture, content, creative, creative arts, cultural, culture and leisure, culture and recreation, entertainment, future-oriented, high arts, leisure, music, performing arts, sunrise,* and *visual arts* are all commonly used in the literature, and more generic terms such as *performing arts* are themselves defined in many different ways according to the parameters of each publication.

The discrepancy regarding definition of the cultural industries is by no means confined to Australia. In Canada, for instance, cultural goods and services such as film and television, literature and publishing, visual, performing and media arts constitute the *arts and cultural industries*. The United States apply the term *arts, entertainment and recreation*. United Kingdom (UK) policy-makers employ the term *creative industries*, which the UK Department of Culture, Media and Sport defines as extensive industry areas including advertising, architecture, the art and antiques market, crafts, design, designer fashion, film and video, interactive leisure

---

11 Paul Costantoura, *Australians and the Arts* (Sydney, NSW, 2000).

12 Department for Culture, Media and Sport, *Creative Industries Fact File* (2002), retrieved 9 February 2005, from <http://www.culture.gov.uk/PDF/ci_fact_file.pdf>.

13 David Throsby and Virginia Hollister, *Don't Give Up Your Day Job: An Economic Study of Professional Artists in Australia* (No. 331.7617) (Sydney, NSW, 2003). See also Richard Florida, *The Rise of the Creative Class* (New York, 2002).

software, music, the performing arts, publishing, software and computer games, television and radio.[14]

The US-based National Endowment for the Arts agrees that differences in how countries define the arts, public arts expenditure, and economic and political systems 'make a comparative analysis of public arts spending a difficult endeavor'.[15] Recognizing the difficulties associated with definition and its potential impact on trade agreements, cultural policy and statistical comparison, UNESCO suggests that

> it is generally agreed that the term [cultural industries] applies to those industries that combine the creation, production and commercialisation of contents, which are intangible and cultural in nature. These contents are typically protected by copyright and they can take the form of goods or services ... The notion of cultural industries generally includes printing, publishing and multimedia, audio-visual, phonographic and cinematographic productions, as well as crafts and design. For some countries, this concept also embraces architecture, visual and performing arts, sports, manufacturing of musical instruments, advertising and cultural tourism.[16]

UNESCO defines ten categories in its Framework for Cultural Statistics: cultural heritage, printed matter and literature, music, performing arts, visual arts, cinema and photography, radio and television, socio-cultural activities, sports and games, and nature and the environment. The UNESCO framework formed the basis for Australia's statistical framework for culture and leisure. Despite this, in 2005 Australia was one of only four countries to abstain from voting on in-principle support for UNESCO's draft Universal Declaration on Cultural Diversity. David Throsby suggests that the Australian government's stance on the cultural diversity conference has given Australia a new-found international image as a 'cultural pariah'.[17]

Australia conducts two key statistical collections: a national census conducted every six or seven years, and monthly labour force surveys. The latter surveys focus in turn upon selected industry categories, including the cultural industries. In addition, the ABS conducts service industry surveys that are of relevance to the cultural industries.[18] Artists are well aware of the frustration or 'lack of fit' when faced with a census form or phone survey about employment and it is due in part to the increasing diversity and multiplicity of roles that artists' work is not accurately reflected in existing data collections. Additional difficulties stem from complex work patterns and changes within the cultural industries such as an increased emphasis on self-management, globalization, and new technologies.

---

14 For US data, see the United States Census Bureau. Canadian statistics are found at the Department of Foreign Affairs and Trade. For UK data, see the Department of Culture, Media and Sport, at <http://www.culture.gov.uk/what_we_do/Creative_industries>.

15 National Endowment for the Arts, *International Data on Government Spending in the Arts* (No. Note #74) (Washington, 2000).

16 See UNESCO, *What Do We Understand by Cultural Industries?* (2003), retrieved 21 January 2004, from <http://www.unesco.org/culture/industries/trade/html_eng/question1.shtml#1>.

17 David Throsby, *Does Australia Need a Cultural Policy?* Platform Papers issue 07. See <http://www.currencyhouse.org.au/pages/pp_issue_07.html> for more information.

18 For more information, see <www.abs.gov.au>.

The fact that census data necessarily rely on self-definition as an artist is itself a controversial issue as many artists hold employment outside of the arts. Artists' work is sporadic and is often secondary in terms of income as artists undertake non-arts work in order to remain financially viable. Data collection processes do not allow for such employment patterns, despite the suggestion that the fluidity of employment patterns experienced by artists 'pre-empts a pattern of employment that will become more common in other sectors in the future'.[19] Significantly, if the fluid working lives of artists is a sign of things to come in the general workforce, the inclusion of data on multiple job-holding and new occupational categories is essential to statistical collections. Likewise, it is imperative for graduate destination data to recognize the protean careers in which most musicians and other artists engage.

Attempts in Australia to improve the accuracy of data collections include a new category 'artists and related professionals', which was added to the national census in the 1990s.[20] This was followed by the Australian Culture and Leisure Classifications (ACLC), which were released in 2001 by the ABS to provide a common framework for the collection and dissemination of data relating to culture and leisure: generating more accurate statistical data about employment, expenditure and participation. Recognition of the problem has also resulted in the commission of regular economic reports, four of them under the leadership of economist David Throsby. The first of these – published in 1984 before the establishment of the ACLC – found Australian statistical data to be insufficient, inadequate, fragmentary and 'impossible to obtain'. Despite the recommendations for change, the 2001 report suggested that relevant data remained deficient within Australia and internationally: 'A serious hindrance to the international endeavour to advance the status and understanding of cultural policy is the lack of data and documentation about the cultural industries of various countries, making it difficult to carry out soundly-based empirical research in this field.'

And the latest economic report, published in late-2003 and conducted by David Throsby and Virginia Hollister, reiterates the continued inadequacy of Australian cultural statistics: 'A survey of individual practising artists … is the only workable means for compiling an accurate and comprehensive picture of the living and working arrangements of professional artists in Australia at the present time.'[21]

---

19 Australian Centre for Industrial Relations Research and Training (ACIRRT), University of Sydney, The Working Life of Visual Artists in Australia, Working Paper 9, Visual Artists Industry Guidelines Research Project – NAVA Member Survey 2001, Strategic Partnerships with Industry for Research and Training Project, funded by the Australian Research Council and the Australia Council, 2002.

20 A major contributor was Peter Brokensha, whose work between 1987 and 1990 prompted the establishment of the ABC culture and leisure statistical centre.

21 David Throsby's work is crucial reading, and the reports are designed to be 'readable' rather than 'academic'. Three publications are quoted in this section: D. Throsby, *The Artist in Australia Today: Report of the Committee for the Individual Artists Inquiry* (Sydney, NSW, 1984); D. Throsby, *Economics and Culture* (Cambridge, 2001); and Throsby and Hollister, *Don't Give Up Your Day Job: An Economic Study of Professional Artists in Australia*. See also D. Throsby and Beverley Thompson, *But What Do You Do for a Living? A New Economic Study of Australian Artists* (Sydney, NSW, 1994); and D. Throsby, 'Centenary Article – Public Funding of the Arts in Australia, 1900–2000', *Year Book Australia, 2001* (Canberra, ACT, 2001).

Included in the 2003 report are 43 additional occupations not classified within current government data collection sets, and it is clear that there are still more occupations to include. In fact, it is likely that the number of occupations will increase as casualization of the music workforce continues to grow. In Britain, too, there have been campaigns to improve the effectiveness of data relating to the cultural labour market. The British Musicians Union states that 'in all sectors of music performance the pressure is to move towards more casualization and less employed work. As well as the highest levels of performance skills, British musicians will need more and more sophisticated ancillary and backup skills to support their chosen career'.[22] The statement is supported by the findings of a British labour force survey that reported a rise of 38 per cent between 1981 and 1991 in the number of self-employed musicians.[23]

The Arts Economy 1968–98: Three Decades of Growth in Australia was commissioned by the Australia Council as part of its strategic planning and positioning, and in recognition that the needs and circumstances of individual artists were under-researched.[24] Arts professions and other cultural occupations are defined by the ABS as shown in Table 2.1, and it is from ABS data that the study drew its data. Oddly, as can be seen from the category 'Arts professionals', musicians are classified separately from other performing artists. In addition, private music teachers are classified under the category 'Other cultural occupations' with the result that a musician who reports more of a teaching role than a performance role is in a separate occupational group than that of the performance-based musician.

Table 2.1   ABS Classifications 'Arts' and 'Other Cultural Occupations'

Arts Professions	*Other Cultural Occupations*
Authors	Architects
Designers and illustrators	Librarians
Film, TV, radio and stage directors	Media producers and artistic directors
Journalists	Private art teachers
Media presenters	Private dance teachers
Musicians	Private drama teachers
Performing artists	**Private music teachers**
Photographers	
Potters	
Unidentified (not classified)	
Visual artists, except potters	

22 Metier, *The Music Industry: Skills and Training Needs in the 21st Century* (London, 2000).

23 See Jane O'Brien and Andy Feist, *Employment in the Arts and Cultural Industries: An Analysis of the Labour Force Survey and Other Sources* (London, 1997).

24 See Hans Hoegh-Guldberg, *The Arts Economy 1968–98: Three Decades of Growth in Australia* (Sydney, NSW, 2000). See also Hoegh-Guldberg, 'Statistical Light Dawns on the Music Sector', *Australian Music Forum*, 11/2 (2005), available at <http//www.mca.org. au/index.php?id=38>.

Performing and teaching are the two most common activities for musicians, and the proportion of each is likely to change on a regular basis according to the work that is available. Musicians are therefore likely to move between occupational groups on a regular basis and there is no way for both activities to be recorded in data collections.

Reconciling later census data with their own survey data, Throsby and Hollister conclude that the 2001 census had underestimated the artist population by 21,000, or 46 per cent. Despite this, *The Arts Economy* found that full-time Australian artists account for 1.07 per cent of the total Australian workforce and number three times those recorded in 1976; over six times average workforce growth.

According to *The Arts Economy*, 51 per cent of Australian adults participated in the arts in the year 1997. Some payment was received by 58 per cent of people working 'practically all year' in cultural pursuits, and by 82 per cent of those who worked more than 35 hours in cultural pursuits in any given week. Only 5 per cent of the 209,000 music performers received payment, although this almost certainly reflects the small number of hours worked by many people, the commonality of cash payments prior to the introduction of the Goods and Services Tax[25] and modifications to insurance requirements over the previous decade. Total involvement in the arts was reported to have grown by 6 per cent from 1993 to 1997. Between 1985/86 and 1995/96 there was an annual decline in medium artist incomes of 0.7 per cent, compared to a total workforce decline of only 0.4 per cent. From 1984 to 1994, the annual growth of the Australian arts economy was 4.4 per cent, compared to total economy growth of only 3.1 per cent. The growth in self-employed artists was reported as 10.4 per cent, although it is likely that this figure is exaggerated due to somewhat-improved Australian data collections. Household expenditure on the arts grew over three times faster than average during the same period. For their 2003 study, Throsby and Hollister were able to draw on national census data from the year 2001, and they suggest musicians to be three-and-a-half times more likely to earn over $50,000 per annum if they undertake non-arts work than if they focus on their principle arts occupation. Less than half of the sample of artists believed that they would be able to meet their future financial needs, and 75 per cent of artists were freelance or self-employed. Only 13 per cent of artists were salaried as permanent employees. Of those who were employed rather than self-employed, 88 per cent were casual employees.

The National Centre for Culture and Recreation Statistics (NCCRS) leads the development of Australian statistical data relating to culture and leisure and works closely with two peak bodies: the Cultural Ministers Council (CMC) and the Cultural Ministers Council Statistics Working Group (CMCSWG). The CMC, founded in 1984, established the CMCSWG to enhance cultural policy, decision making and government cultural development through improvement of the quality, scope, accessibility and treatment of cultural statistics.[26] In a move away from traditional activity-based classifications, in 1997 the ABS Time Use

---

25 The Goods and Services Tax was introduced in July 2007 in a move to quash the cash economy.

26 SWG publications can be found at: <http://www.culturaldata.gov.au/home>.

Survey allocated the 24 hours in each day to nine major categories, grouped into four different kinds of activities:

Necessary time	Sleeping, eating, personal care
Contracted time	Paid work and education
Committed time	Housework, childcare, shopping, voluntary work
Free time	Discretionary time – leisure and recreation

Due to their coverage of all industries, the Australia and New Zealand Standard Industry Classifications (ANZSIC) provide necessarily broad classifications. In order to enable greater compatibility of statistics and the inclusion of additional activities, NCCRS in collaboration with Statistics New Zealand developed three economic classifications focusing on: (1) the economic side of cultural and recreational activities; (2) the money that consumers spend; and (3) the funding provided by government.

The previously mentioned ACLC exclude some free-time activities that people may not freely choose to do, and include some free-time activities that are not classified as such: eating out is considered to be 'committed' time because one has to eat whether at home or at a restaurant. A distinction is also made between the main intended use of a product being for culture and leisure or for use elsewhere. The classification refers to the chain of supply: a set designer is involved in the cultural industries, but the manufacture of the materials used to build the set falls beyond the scope of the classification. To facilitate greater compatibility of statistics and the inclusion of additional activities, 461 classes within 48 groups were identified. The three existing economic classifications relate to industry, product and occupation. It is likely that further classifications will follow, starting with an 'activities' classification.[27]

The *Industry Classification* is the first of the three economic ACLC classifications, and concerns the manufacture or supply of goods and services to a client. Australian cultural surveys define cultural industries as those listed within the Heritage and Arts divisions of the ACLC. Groups Two (Arts) and Four (Other Culture and Leisure Industries) are the most pertinent to cultural industries research. The two groups include the following pertinent sub-headings:

- Literature and print media (21)
- Performing arts (22)
- Music composition and publishing (23)
- Visual arts and crafts (24)
- Design (25)
- Broadcasting, electronic media and film (26)
- Other arts (27)
- Community and social organizations (45)
- Other culture and leisure services (46)
- Other culture and leisure goods manufacturing and sales (48)

---

27 For more information, see the Cultural Ministers Council information at <http:// www.culturaldata.gov.au/publications/statistics_working_group/other/aclc_industry_ classification_summary>.

The *Product Classification* categorizes 'goods and services which are considered to be cultural in nature'. The product classification comprises 26 groups in 227 classes, and includes crucial elements of the cultural industries such as arts education, artistic works, musical instruments, live presentation of performing arts, audio and video, venues, and the services of artists.

The *Occupation Classification* was designed to categorize cultural occupations in the arts, sport, recreation and leisure. The scope of occupations is limited to those that are intrinsically creative, and those that enable others to participate. A dance production, for example, incorporates a range of occupations that would be included in the occupation classification of ACLC.[28] Work may be paid or unpaid, but activities that are social or recreational in nature are not included. The inclusion of unpaid activities is an important move as it recognizes the extent and importance of voluntary work within the cultural sector. Hoegh-Guldberg and Richard Letts confirm that existing statistics are insufficient to create a comprehensive picture of the music sector, key components of which would be economic, cultural and social significance. They adopted the term 'music sector' for their report titled '*A Statistical Framework for the Music Sector*' on the basis that *industry* concerns economic inputs whereas *sector* involves individuals and groups. In light of this, they advocate an innovative 'Music GDP', which includes gross value added.[29]

Politics and the Arts

As shown in Figure 2.1, cultural policy as such came into existence after World War II with the overriding theme of cultural democracy, which posits that different cultural traditions will co-exist and not dominate over one another and that participation should be available to everyone within a democratically controlled cultural life.

It is perhaps obvious to state the importance of achieving a balance between economics and culture when forming effective policy; yet culture and the arts historically have been politicized and the difficulty is further compounded considering the intangible nature of much artistic product. A balance is necessary between economic and cultural considerations, and requires careful thought about the objectives of cultural policy in the light of separate agenda such as the institutional allocation of funds for social improvement or for political gain. Subvention has been the topic of many publications nationally and internationally: the Institute for Cultural Democracy suggests that 'many policies with profound cultural impact are made by decision-makers who've hardly given cultural considerations a thought'.[30]

---

28 Occupations in a dance production might include company manager, choreographer, dancer, costume designer, set designer, musical director, musician, artistic director, lighting and sound technicians, ticket collector, venue manager, publicist and agents.

29 Commonwealth of Australia *Statistical Framework Report* (2005), written by Hans Hoegh-Guldberg and Richard Letts. Retrieved 9 November, from <http://www.mca.org.au/index.php?id=37>. A significant new contribution is the Music in Australia Knowledge Base, which incorporates qualitative data in addition to statistical information. The Knowledge Base can be found at <http://mcakb.wordpress.com/>.

30 The Institute for Cultural Democracy, *Webster's World of Cultural Policy*.

Mono-Cultural Access

Access and Participation

1800–1900	Debate about the 'exemplary' person led to an emphasis on education, and consequently to a role for the state
1945	The United Nations (UN) Charter was written
1946	The United Nations Educational, Scientific and Cultural Organization (UNESCO) was formed
1948	The Universal Declaration of Human Rights was written and included the right to cultural participation
1950–1970	The rise of the welfare state led to community and education programmes to address access and equity issues. Heritage conservation and globalization were major foci
1960–1982	UNESCO conferences led to recognition of the importance of culture, and to internationally agreed guidelines for the development of cultural policy. This included the status of the artist (1982)
1968	The Australian Council for the Arts was founded (known as the Australia Council from 1973)
1970 ff	Culture became recognized for its importance in economic and community development including tourism, employment and cultural identity
1975	The Australia Council became a statutory authority
1988–1997	The UNESCO World Decade of Culture emphasized developing countries
1992–1995	The UN World Commission on Culture and Development (WCCD) promoted participation, cultural identity and international cooperation
1998	The first biennial World Culture Report was published by UNESCO to publish and analyse international statistics, and to inform cultural policy-making and development initiatives

Diverse and Inclusive

Figure 2.1 A (Very) Brief History of Cultural Policy Development[31]

Amongst other things, cultural subvention is a crucial part of the agenda to influence relationships within a community, partly because a focus on the intrinsic values of culture has often triggered media attention for being an elitist view that does not consider issues of access.

31 Derived from Deborah Stevenson, *Art and Organisation* (Brisbane, QLD, 2000); The Institute for Cultural Democracy, *Webster's World of Cultural Policy* (2001); and David Throsby, *Economics and Culture*.

The Australian Labor government (1983 to 1996) emphasized the role of culture in bringing together people in Australia's multicultural society. The succeeding government (1996 to 2007), being a coalition, took a geographic stance: moving from ethnicity towards rural and remote community development. The community arts concept of the 1990s led to cultural funding programmes with specific community objectives and related funding opportunities, an increasing number of which call for artists to demonstrate prior Community Cultural Development (CCD) experience. CCD programmes are intended to promote renewed interest in the fabric of community, continued cultural development, and increased engagement in core values and beliefs that will, in turn, result in stronger and safer communities: 'the cultural practices of communities could be effective instruments for prompting social and political change'.[32] CCD funding generally requires artists to visit regional or lower socio-economic areas with programmes that result in a degree of 'up-skilling' for community members. One of the most difficult aspects of CCD for artists is that CCD is about community and not about them: a total change of mindset. As Jon Hawkes writes, 'community cultural development is what communities do: CCD workers help'.[33] In its third term of office, the Coalition government continued the trend towards financial independence for a number of areas including the arts, education and health.

Given that culture represents society's whole way of life, cultural policy has a broad and essential role to play and the arts represent only one dimension; however, rapid and continual change has an inevitable impact on practising artists and arts organizations. The pragmatic use of culture within wider agendas places an immense responsibility upon the shoulders of artists, seen clearly in the previous Labor government's cultural policy paper *Creative Nation*: 'it is the role of arts – artists, writers, musicians, the lot – to enrich, stimulate, educate and provide enjoyment for our society'. Of interest, the same strategy lists as its priorities venues, equitable access for target groups and audience development, rather than the artists upon whose shoulders the responsibility has been placed.[34]

Creative Nation was written in 1994 towards the end of a thirteen-year reign of government, and reflected international trends in calling upon the arts to become more independent of public funding. A wide-ranging statement, the paper positioned the creative industries as vital to Australia's international interests and to economic and employment growth. *Creative Nation* was the first (and remains the sole) national cultural statement recorded by an Australian federal government. It is the closest that Australia has come to the formation of a national cultural policy, although the debate has recently been refuelled by the long-awaited Arts Discussion Paper, which was issued by the Federal Labor Party four months before the general election that brought them back to power in December 2007. The Paper advocates increased overall support for artists in recognition of their 'significant field of endeavour'. In addition to broader issues such as the potential for a national cultural policy, the Paper suggests practical

---

32 Deborah Stevenson, *Art and Organisation*.

33 Jon Hawkes, 'Community Cultural Development According to Adams and Goldbard', *Artwork*, (August 2003).

34 Commonwealth of Australia, *Creative Nation: Commonwealth Cultural Policy* (1994), retrieved 3 July 2003, from <http://www.nla.gov.au/creative.nation/creative.html#intro>.

initiatives such as the development of a 'Social Security and the Arts' policy that would permit artists to produce work whilst receiving welfare payments.

Integral to the trend towards socially driven models for arts practice, the rise in the number of CCD programmes has led inevitably to the need for artists to be more connected to their communities, and to possess demonstrated skills in the facilitation and organization of workshops and similar activities. Similarly, as funding bodies concern themselves with the community relevance of performing institutions, they often require proof of systematic education and community activities. The impact on musicians has been involvement in community education programmes for which many musicians feel inadequately prepared: 'Musicians are increasingly expected to participate in sustained relationships with schools, teachers, and children, and to demonstrate skills of engagement that are developmentally appropriate for learners.'[35]

A noteworthy result of the politicization of culture is that funding initiatives forming part of much larger social initiatives are beyond what can realistically be tackled by an individual artist; hence funding is targeted towards organizations rather than individuals. In addition, funding bodies strive for an equitable division of resources for traditional and contemporary arts, and there is a growing trend towards cross-art and non-arts-specific funding. The impact on the artist is manifold, particularly in that the artistic elements of any grant proposal have to be shrouded in terms of a funding strategy's non-arts objectives. Many artists do not possess the skills and political knowledge to write such proposals, notwithstanding the skills and experience required to manage a programme of social change. Moreover, there is inadequate availability of skills training in requisite community development and social improvement, thus placing many funding strategies beyond the reach of individual artists. Ironically, it would seem that individual artists are not the only ones to struggle; a British survey found that 89 per cent of music institutions require outside, specialist assistance to access funding.[36]

The trend towards institutional allocation of funds has resulted in a growing number of organizations (there was a 400 per cent increase in the number of Australian arts-related organizations between 1970 and 1991) vying for and distributing funds within distinct 'boxes' linked exclusively to criteria such as genre, geography or equity. The result is a duplication of training and research that wastes a vast amount of precious resources and paints a picture of disunity as organizations strive for their own survival rather than working towards a common, coordinated goal. Ralph Smith suggests that 'one might venture the opinion that cultural policy has in fact inspired more creativity in fund-raising than in the making and performing of art'.[37]

---

35 See David Myers, 'Preparing Professional Musicians for Effective Educational Work with Children', in Orlando Musumeci (ed.), *The ISME Commission for Education of the Professional Musician. Preparing Musicians: Making Sound Worlds* (Barcelona, 2004), pp. 149–63.

36 Metier, *AS2K: Arts Skills 2000* (London, 2001).

37 Ralph Smith, 'Reflections about Policy during Troubled Times', *Arts Education Policy Review*, 103/3 (2002): 29–34. The trend is reflected in the US: Kevin McCarthy found that between 1982 and 1997 the number of non-profit organizations in the US had risen by over 80 per cent, and the number of commercial organizations had risen by over 40 per cent. See K. McCarthy, *Change of Scene: Traditional Arts Organizations Need To Update the Plot* (Santa Monica, CA, 2001).

Kevin McCarthy predicts that the number of large and midsized organizations will decrease and professional activity will increasingly be centred within large metropolitan areas and programmed for mass audiences. Community, avocational arts activity will then become more important in meeting community needs outside of the metropolitan areas, and in the areas of innovation and diversity.[38] These issues also impact smaller organizations and individual artists, with the result that artists require a solid understanding of economic and social strategies within the corporatized world of the arts. This is a critical consideration for training institutions. Opportunities for artists in terms of individuality, experience and employment are likely to be greatly reduced and, as the supply of artists outstrips demand, an ever-increasing number of artists can be expected to pursue avocational and semi-professional arts activity. The effects of such funding changes are already apparent in Britain, where funding cuts have impacted acutely on the amount of on-the-job training available to artists.

Culturing: Audience Development

Audience development is a fundamental concern for all of the arts. The Macquarie Dictionary defines *culture* as 'the sum total of ways of living built up by a group of human beings, which is transmitted from one generation to another'. Conversely, *cultured* is defined as 'being artificially nurtured or grown', and there is no doubt that culturing audiences is problematic.[39] The development of new audiences is most effective with long-term investment in cultural participation rather than culturing audiences to meet short-term targets. However, long-term development requires a degree of financial stability enjoyed by very few arts organizations. In contrast, the development of a new audience base is a slow process and one that is difficult to sustain given short-term political cycles and accountancy requirements: the 'tendency for cultural institutions to focus on increasing the rates of participation of existing users rather than attracting new ones is a strong one'.[40] In reality, existing users can be enticed to attend more frequently with the use of subscription deals, coupons and vouchers, 'meet the artist' functions, and other incentives that are simple, effective and, importantly, have almost immediate results.

Commissioned reports on the arts sector are a way of life in most Western countries, clearly marking the need felt by the arts to justify their existence in terms of participation, community benefit and so on: fighting for a slice of the funding pie. Australia is no different and the following section outlines recent reports and a changing environment that is indicative of the situation in other countries. *Australians and the Arts* was commissioned in 1998 by the Australia Council to provide information about 'how Australians see the arts today and how they would like to see the arts tomorrow': ensuring that Australia Council strategic directions were cognizant of public opinion.[41] All Australians were reported to enjoy at least

---

38 Ibid.

39 *Macquarie Dictionary*, 4th edn, available at <www.macquariedictionary.com.au>.

40 Tony Bennett, Michael Emmison and John Frow, *Accounting for Tastes: Australian Everyday Cultures* (Cambridge, 1999).

41 Costantoura, *Australians and the Arts*.

some aspect of the arts; however, geography, finance, education, information and clear communication from the sector were identified as impediments to accessing both creative self-expression and the creative expression of others. The development of new audiences was emphasized as being vitally important to the sector: a call that reflects a great deal of other research. The report found that 'the arts sector is not well-organised when it comes to dealing with the general public outside specific markets. The focus is usually on those market segments which will most likely contribute to the immediate financial viability of individual artistic ventures'.

The people most likely to value and to participate in the arts tend to be female, older (or without children), well educated, in higher-income households, or living in capital cities, and often have been exposed to the arts as children. *Australians and the Arts* author Costantoura suggests that people with some non-English speaking background are more likely to place a high value on the arts, and recommends the development of programmes drawing upon Australia's diverse society. Negative feelings about the arts tend to be allied with 'a sense of social exclusion' that overshadows the association with formal education and places many artforms out of reach. Approximately half of Australians perceive the arts to have 'elitist and pretentious people and practices'. People who are personally involved in the arts are more likely to participate in the arts of others, and a thought-provoking analogy is made with the sporting activities of children, which lead so often to a lifelong love of sport both as a participant and a spectator.[42]

Many people express a desire to be creative, but most are not able to identify ways in which they could become involved in the arts as a social activity, or as 'beginners'. Despite this, 88 per cent of Australians attend at least one cultural event or performance each year.[43] The general public favour a broad definition of the arts, including many day-to-day activities with which most of the populace are involved. In this regard, the findings reflect Christopher Small's observation that financial support received from sites of industrialized power influences the socially constructed perception that classical music is not available to everyone.[44] It may be that a broader definition would overcome some of the strong elitist perceptions that were expressed.

Australia has three tiers of government. The federal government governs the Australian Commonwealth of eight States and Territories and is elected for a three-year period of office, with an average parliamentary life of about two-and-a-half years. Each Australian State and Territory has its own government, which holds office for up to four years, and local governments are elected for a fixed four-year term with half of the seats becoming vacant every two years. Meeting the requirements of these short-term political cycles is unrealistic given the planning timeframes of arts

---

42 For further reading, including the report *Motivations Matter: Findings and Practical Implications of a National Survey of Cultural Participation*, see the Wallace Foundation work on participation building at <http://www.wallacefoundation.org/ KnowledgeCenter/KnowledgeTopics/Arts_Participation/?source=wfgawg0101&adgroup =Arts+Participation+01&kw={keyword}>.

43 See: <http://www.dfat.gov.au/aib/arts_culture.html>.

44 Christopher Small, *Musicking: The Meanings of Performance and Listening* (Hanover, NH, 1998).

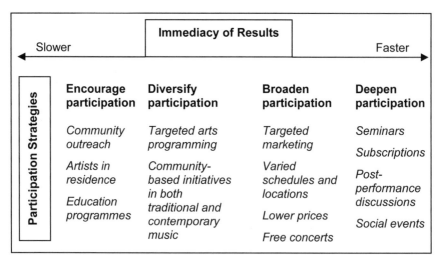

Figure 2.2   Short- and Long-Term Participation Strategies

organizations, many of which have been obliged to alter their accountancy methods in order to demonstrate continuous financial viability regardless of artistic seasons and programming. Kevin McCarthy and Kimberly Jinnett propose a behavioural participation model encompassing stages of individual decision making.[45] Utilizing the participation strategies from that model, Figure 2.2 illustrates the rate with which the results of audience development strategies might be seen.

Ironically, the result of 'culturing' audiences, of rationalization and of corporate sponsorship, in conjunction with policy constraints, is often quite the opposite of what had been intended. Many audience development strategies have taken a necessarily short-term approach, as a result of which there has been increased participation by existing audience members and further marginalization of the public and the subsidised sectors. Programming is another aspect affected by short-term financial pressure, which according to the Symphony Orchestra Musicians' Association leads to orchestras becoming 'more conservative in their programming'.[46] Further, a diminished base for artistic innovation reduces the number of guest artists, and in turn an orchestra's potential to secure engagements with leading musicians and artists. Conservative programming further decreases the opportunities available to new artists, particularly composers, and accentuates the divide between existing and new audiences.

In *The Arts Economy*, Hoegh-Guldberg tables cultural funding made from 1988 to 1997 by federal, state and local governments and by the Australia Council and

---

45 There are many participation models available. This one was designed with the arts specifically in mind. See Kevin McCarthy and Kimberly Jinnett, *A New Framework for Building Participation in the Arts* (New York, 2001).

46 Symphony Orchestra Musicians' Association, *The Australian Government Review of Orchestras* (Sydney, NSW, 2004).

state art authorities.[47] Financial data were converted to 1996–97 to enable direct comparison across the thirty years of the report, and to factor in significant changes made to the statistical framework during that time. Figure 2.3 illustrates the trend towards decentralized patronage. The baseline for funding has been set at $zero.

Donald Adams and Arlene Goldbard suggest that, akin to the blending of economic and public policy, decentralization has both positive and negative results; although important decisions are taken nearer to communities, central protection of rights becomes more difficult.[48]

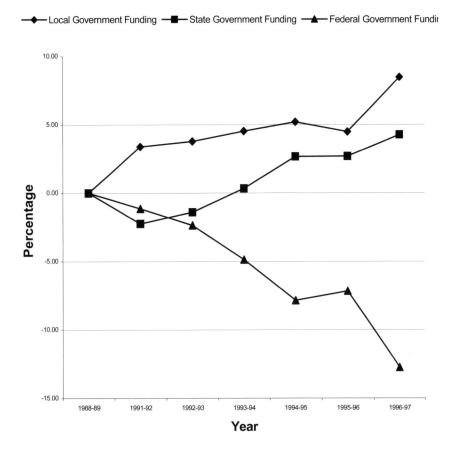

Figure 2.3   Percentage of Total Cultural Funding in Australia from 1988 to 1997[49]

---

47 Hoegh-Guldberg, *The Arts Economy 1968–98: Three Decades of Growth in Australia.*

48 Donald Adams and Arlene Goldbard, 'Cultural Policy and Cultural Democracy', *Crossroads: Reflections on the Politics of Culture* (Talmage, CA, 1990), pp. 107–9.

49 Figures were derived from Heogh-Guldberg, Ibid.

Arts Organizations: The Major Performing Arts

An unremitting issue much reported in Australia (as elsewhere) is the relatively small number of people who appear to benefit from publicly funded arts: particularly the arts known as 'high arts'. Solutions posed by these and many other reports can be categorized into two streams: (1) to educate the population so that people have the skills and knowledge to participate fully in the arts; or (2) to rationalize public funding so that 'high arts' are increasingly funded through corporate and other private forms of sponsorship, thereby removing the pressure to educate the population. However, a Myer Foundation Inquiry suggests that the arts sector earns approximately 85 per cent of its income, and has a proportionately larger cash flow than many manufacturing and sporting sectors.[50]

Parallel to the earlier discussion regarding disunity, Costantoura suggests that 'the arts sector could learn from the experience of other industries and professions which work together to achieve common goals throughout their sectors despite internal competition'.[51] Costantoura notes the distinction between the subsidized and commercial sectors, highlighting the individual and organizational strengths to be found within each, and stressing the need for communication and for unified market development. The effectiveness of current communication within the sector and with the general public is also questioned. Organizations are perceived as out-of date in their views of public needs and attitudes, and lacking in sector-wide interaction, planning, advocacy, sharing of skills and knowledge, and vision. Communication is informal, diffuse and often limited to within artforms, genres or funding types. Further, the marketing skill of those involved is considered inadequate for the sector to compete effectively for public attention and funding. Lack of public understanding and engagement, it is argued, necessitates the 'demystification' of the arts to improve access, participation and the feeling of cultural ownership. Similarly, British research concludes that the arts sector functions within a weak policy framework, and therefore lacks organizational strength and operates within unclear operational boundaries.[52]

The recent history of Australia's orchestras is indicative of the way in which rationalization and corporatization have affected arts organizations. The Australian Broadcasting Corporation (ABC) was founded in 1932, and part of its charter was to establish an orchestra in each Australian state for the provision of radio broadcasts and live concerts for the general public. In 1997 the six ABC orchestras gained operational independence and became subsidiary companies.[53] A seventh company, Symphony Australia, was created to reduce duplication of services and infrastructure, and on that basis it provides a user-pay service to all six orchestras. It also manages artist development programmes including the annual Symphony Australia Young

---

50 Geoffrey Bolton, *The Muses in a Quest for Patronage* (Perth, WA, 1996).

51 Costantoura.

52 See Clive Gray, *The Politics of the Arts in Britain* (London, 2000).

53 West Australian Symphony Orchestra, *About the West Australian Symphony Orchestra* (2003), retrieved 5 April 2004, from <http://www.waso.com.au/waso/std_content.jsp?ident= R9ITUAXT4Y97RQQL048PIC38SZHRTP>.

Performers Awards. At the time of corporatization, all of the regional Australian orchestras (orchestras outside of Melbourne and Sydney) had negative balance sheets. Funded on a 'break-even' basis and with an 'efficiency' dividend that reduces subsequent funding in the event of a profit, much of the debt remains.The final phase of divestment occurred in 2005–2006, at which time the orchestras were reconstituted as public companies limited by guarantee. This coincided with a national review of orchestras to which we will return later.

In line with the other ABC orchestras, the West Australian Symphony Orchestra (WASO) was granted permission in the late 1980s to accept sponsorship providing there were no 'ties', and yet within a decade there were radical advertising campaigns aimed at developing potential audience groups within given timeframes. The infamous example was a compact disc distributed at local railway stations. The CD was titled 'Are you a classical virgin?' and included a free condom. The orchestra furthered its audience development strategy by establishing an ongoing education programme, which helps to meet government funding requirements and enables the orchestra to attract additional funding from organizations such as Healthway, promoting healthy lifestyle education programmes.

In reality, numerous orchestras had established targeted audience development strategies and community programmes prior to political pressure for their involvement to be publicly recognized. It is interesting to note that the substantial contributions made by individual orchestral musicians to their communities in the form of community music-making, chamber music and education are not recognized in the assessment of orchestras' societal contribution. With an uncertain level of funding, most orchestras are hired out for private functions and perform regularly for touring acts to raise their public profiles and to meet costs. Corporate sponsorship has become essential to the survival of orchestras and many other arts organizations, and inevitably involves functions, free tickets and parking, and logos emblazoned on programmes and stages. In return, the involvement of corporate interests on the boards of arts organizations can provide valuable executive and management expertise, although not always expertise that is conversant with the nature of cultural organizations.

The *Major Performing Arts inquiry*, chaired by Helen Nugent and released in 1999, recommended a new funding model for Australia's major performing arts organizations, and as such it has had a far-reaching impact.[54] The final report includes ninety-four recommendations (fifty-three to companies and forty-one to governments) that represent a three-year strategy to address the financial and artistic health of the thirty-one major performing arts companies, twelve of which were financially insolvent at the time the report was commissioned. The report emphasizes the 'severity of the financial challenges facing the companies and the adverse impact on their artistic vitality and accessibility'. A strong consideration is

---

54 Commonwealth of Australia, *Major Performing Arts Inquiry Final Report: Securing the Future* (Government No. DOCITA 44/99) (1999). The report can be downloaded from <http://www.dcita.gov.au/__data/assets/pdf_file/10700/Securing_the_Future_Inquiry_into_the_Major_Performing_Arts.pdf>.

inequitable access to publicly funded 'high arts': the traditional musical activities of opera, theatre, ballet and classical music.

The ABS definition of performing arts is 'opera, musical comedy, theatre in its various forms and various styles of dance'.[55] At odds with that definition, the Australian major performing arts consist of the thirty-one major government-subsidised theatre, dance, music and opera companies, including Australia's fourteen music and opera companies. The report recommended state and federal governments to designate major performing arts companies as *global, Australian flagship, niche,* or *regional flagship* companies using the criteria given below:

Global Companies[56]

- Recognised as internationally competitive
- At least 20 per cent of annual performances are outside of Australia
- Government funding forms less than ten per cent of the international touring budget

Australian Flagship Companies

- Play a leadership role within Australia
- Recognised as internationally competitive
- Present an extensive and broad program each year

Niche Companies

- Focus on one artform or type of work
- Access audiences within and outside of Australia
- Partner major Australian festivals and/or international festivals
- Provide national leadership of product, artist development and education

Regional Flagship Companies

- Maintain a high standard of performance
- Present a broad annual program
- Maintain a regular leadership role with particular emphasis on the development of local artists
- Embark on annual intrastate touring
- Undertake a significant education program

---

55 Australian Bureau of Statistics, *Service Industries: Performing Arts* (January 2002), retrieved 11 November 2002, from <http://www.abs.gov.au/Ausstats/abs@.nsf/94713ad445ff1425ca25682000192af2/7aacl.html>.

56 Australia's Symphony Orchestras cannot become global companies as their size deems touring costs prohibitive, and as a consequence they are unable to meet the criterion for at least 20 per cent of annual performances to be outside of Australia.

Percentage of funding between state and commonwealth was also proposed:

Company Type	Commonwealth (%)	State (%)
Global	90	10
Australian Flagship	80	20
Niche	50	50
Regional Flagship	20	80

As a result of the Inquiry, the fourteen music and opera companies considered by the report were categorized as follows:

Global Company

- Australian Chamber Orchestra (ACO)

Australian Flagship Companies

- Opera Australia (OA) including the Australian Opera and Ballet Orchestra (AOBO)
- Melbourne Symphony Orchestra (MSO)
- Musica Viva Australia (MVA)
- Sydney Symphony

Niche Companies

- State Opera of South Australia (SOSA)

Regional Flagship Companies

- Adelaide Symphony Orchestra (ASO)
- Opera Queensland
- Queensland Orchestra
  (formally Queensland Philharmonic and Queensland Symphony Orchestras)
- Tasmanian Symphony Orchestra (TSO)
- West Australian Symphony Orchestra (WASO)
- West Australian Opera (WAO)

Orchestra Victoria (formally the State Orchestra of Victoria) remains unclassified. The review recommended the orchestra to merge with the state orchestra (MSO); however, as neither orchestra wanted the merger, the Victorian government agreed that they would remain independent. Orchestra Victoria now dedicates approximately 50% of its time to its community programme, and its concertmaster is also the artistic director.

Taking into account earning potential and size of population, increases in total funding were sought from the commonwealth (70%) and state (30%) governments. Responding to the Nugent report, Music Council of Australia's Executive Director Richard Letts suggested that the burden of the proposed funding strategy on a state such as Queensland, which has only regional flagship companies, could result in the demise of some companies.[57] He was right.

Companies were encouraged to showcase and commission new works, and to link with Australian and overseas festivals. Company personnel were advised to become more expert in marketing and development, including the development of private sponsorship. Suggestions for widening access included regional touring, the use of technology and mentors, and programmes targeted specifically at youth and non-English speaking audiences. Cooperation between companies was also encouraged in the form of holding companies, joint ventures, increased sharing of resources, and 'communities of musicians' working between two branded organizations to reduce the number of required artistic and administrative positions. Companies were to work with unions towards more flexible work practices and enterprise agreements, and to reduce barriers that limit the hire of international artists. Logically, the Inquiry recommended that the funding for touring companies through 'Playing Australia' should become tri-annual to enable a greater planning timeline; however, no other recommendations were made to address the difficulties of short-term financial reporting.

Since the report's publication, the two Queensland orchestras have combined to create the Queensland Orchestra. In the twelve months to April 2004, four of the six remaining full-time orchestras experienced the resignation of their General Manager and in two cases also their Artistic Advisor. In the 2004/2005 financial year, the eight symphony and pit orchestras in Australia received a total of Aus$56m; 56 per cent of the major performing arts funding, which in 2007 consists of 28 companies.[58]

The Inquiry recommended funding to be governed by the Australia Council's Major Performing Arts board – although funding levels would be set by the federal government – and suggested that companies should be permitted to build reserves of up to 20 per cent of their funded amount without subsequent loss of funding. Following the report, the Australia Council adopted a new structure by splitting the Major Performing Arts board into smaller boards relating to specific artforms such as music, and created a Major Organizations (later key organizations) board to meet the needs of the flagship organizations. The federal government reviewed the new funding model in 2003 and again in 2006. In 2004, indicative of the continued uncertain climate, the Australian orchestras contracted an audit of Symphony Australia. A further Australia Council restructure in 2005 saw the abolition of the boards in Community Cultural Development (CCD) and New Media Arts in favour of a holistic approach that situates CCD at the centre of activities within all artforms. The restructure has the potential to remove much of the expertise in new media and CCD, both of which are complex and developing areas.

Nugent recommended a further review of Australia's orchestras three years after the publication of the report, and in 2005 the Federal Government contracted an outside agency to conduct the review. The Review of Orchestras was chaired by James Strong and was hailed by the Minister for Arts and Sport (Senator Rod Kemp)

---

57 Richard Letts, 'The Nugent Rescue', *Australian Music Forum*, 6/3 (2000): 3–5.

58 See information available from Symphony Orchestra Musicians' Association such as the response to the Nugent Report; and from the Australian Major Performing Arts Group, <http://www.ampag.com.au/2index.asp>.

as an 'opportunity for orchestras and governments to work to improve the long-term sustainability of the sector'.[59] From a business perspective, Strong assessed the efficiency of the orchestra network: the six state orchestras, two ballet and opera orchestras and Symphony Australia. He also considered the role of Australia's two part-time orchestras: the Darwin Symphony Orchestra and the Canberra Symphony Orchestra. At the time of the Review, Australia's eight orchestras carried a debt of Aus$7 million.

Unlike previous reviews, which had resulted in substantial amounts of additional funding, this one resulted in only $25m over four years to pay for conditional one-off payments, redundancies and debt relief. The reason for this is apparent in the Review's terms of reference, which stipulate that each state was to retain its orchestra and that no additional federal funding would be made available. Queensland Liberal senator George Brandis criticized the terms of reference as generating a review that assessed only whether each orchestra was financially viable, rather than seeking workable solutions. Of most concern was the recommendation that the Tasmanian, Adelaide and Queensland Symphony Orchestras should be reduced in size, resulting in the loss of 42 jobs (or 7.5 per cent of all full-time orchestral positions). This was described by Adelaide orchestral manager Rainer Jozeps as artistic suicide; however, it was just about the only option open to Strong given the terms of reference. The Review report was leaked just prior to its planned release and there followed an unprecedented political reaction: twelve speakers spoke in parliament in opposition to the proposed cuts, and there was a media frenzy. By the end of that week the Federal Government pledged not to downsize the orchestras and provided additional funding to maintain player numbers, but the concessions ended there.

The Review recommended rigorous workplace reforms such as the removal of non-playing calls from a musician's call count, better financial accountability and board governance, and full independence from the ABC. The debate about which of the recommendations should be implemented, and the distribution of orchestral funding across different levels of government, commenced even prior to the report's official release. Despite the more contentious recommendations, Strong acknowledged the substantial societal contribution made by orchestral musicians to the 'continuing vitality of music in its various forms':[60] a contribution rarely acknowledged in official reports.

A welcome element of the Review was the recommendation for relief from the 'efficiency dividend', which Strong estimated to have removed $570,000 in funding from the orchestras in 2004 alone, and which Jennifer Bott (General Manager of the Australia Council) said had cost Australia's major performing arts companies over Aus$10m between 1995 and 2005. Federal funding for all government departments is increased annually at a pre-determined rate, and under the efficiency dividend the base rate is reduced by 1 per cent to ensure that organizations demonstrate

---

59 The review was published by the Department of Communications, Information Technology and the Arts, as *A New Era – Orchestras Review Report 2005*. It is available at <http://www.dcita.gov.au/arts_culture/publications_and_reports/inquiries_and_reviews/orchestras_review_2005>.

60 Ibid.

efficiencies. In many cases, efficiencies can be made with the use of new technologies and staffing reductions. The greatest cost of an orchestra is people, and it takes the same number of people to perform an orchestral work now as it did when the piece was composed. The dividend had kept funding to a little over 1 per cent each year at the same time as the cost of employment rose annually by 4 per cent.

Concluding Comments

The cultural industries are significant, and they continue to grow in size as leisure time increases and the population ages. Together, the cultural industries have the potential to advocate the tangible and intangible values of culture and to help practitioners meet their economic and creative needs. Unfortunately, there is a continued reliance on economic studies rather than improving national data collection processes and gaining better intelligence about the way in which artists live and work. The NCCRS reports that although valuable data on Australian culture and recreation are collected by governments, industry and other organizations, the nature and existence of the data is not generally known. The same can be said in the US and the UK. If data were widely communicated, they would make a substantial contribution to policy and funding, and they would assist practitioners and curricular designers to better understand the complex environment of cultural practice. In short, there is much work ahead before the cultural industries can find a collective voice, and before data collection is sufficiently accurate to inform and support those working within the cultural sector.

Understanding the cultural environment is paramount to identifying potential sources of funding, opportunities for employment, sources of professional development, networks and other resources. Practitioners and educators would do well to plough ahead regardless of the statistical and definitional shortcomings described in this chapter: keeping their 'fingers on the pulse' of the cultural industries and watching (but not waiting) for much-anticipated change.

Chapter 3

The Musician

Musician *n.* a person who plays a musical instrument, esp. professionally[1]

Surprisingly, specialist music dictionaries including *The New Grove Dictionary of Music and Musicians*[2] don't include the word 'musician'. General English dictionaries provide definitions that indicate a traditional view of a musician as one who performs: *The Budget Macquarie Dictionary*[3] defines a musician as 'one skilled in playing a musical instrument', and *The Oxford Reference Dictionary* describes 'a person who plays a musical instrument, esp. professionally, or is otherwise musically gifted'. Conversely, Lionel Salter's 1963 guide to careers in music suggests that the term musician 'can cover a number of quite different fields: interpretative – performers (both instrumental and vocal) and conductors; creative – composers and arrangers; educative – professors, teachers, lecturers, examiners and adjudicators; and those of scholarship, writing, criticism and various other activities'.[4] More recent career guides reflect a similarly broad view of the diverse opportunities available within the music profession; however, the perception of a musician as a performer persists.

Leopold Mozart offers several suggestions as to the etymology of the word *music*. These include a Greek word meaning to seek industriously and scrutinize, Egyptian words referring to water and to science, and a Hebrew word signifying 'an excellent and perfect work, conceived and invented to the honour of God'.[5] It is interesting also to consider the derivation of the word 'artist'. According to James Allen, the English word 'art' 'derives from the Latin word *ars*, the term for technical skill in making things or performing difficult tasks, and *ars* originates in the Greek word *ararisko*, for fitting something together'. *Ars* relates to *arts-techne*, which describes the skill and rules involved in making something, and to *poiein*, which refers to making something happen and from which comes the term 'poetics'. Allen points out that the arts were considered craft until the eighteenth century, at which time the so-called 'fine arts' were separated and the word 'aesthetic' was coined. Prior to

---

1   Judy Pearsall and Bill Trumble (eds), *The Oxford English Reference Dictionary* (Oxford, 1996), 2nd edn. The quote below the chapter heading is taken from this definition.

2   Stanley Sadie and John Tyrrell (eds), *The New Grove Dictionary of Music and Musicians* (London, 2003), 2nd edn.

3   Macquarie, *The Budget Macquarie Dictionary* (Sydney, NSW, 2000), 3rd edn.

4   Lionel Salter, *The Musician and His World* (London, 1963).

5   Leopold Mozart, *A Treatise on the Fundamental Principles of Violin Playing*, trans. E. Knocker (Oxford, 1971), 2nd edn (original work published 1756).

the aesthetic labelling, arts had been considered a part of the social fabric of society incorporating morality, education and leisure.[6]

Despite being at the heart of the cultural industries, little is known about visual and performing artists. The majority of research on careers in the arts concerns the broad visual and performing arts sector, or the still broader cultural industries. Likewise, little is known about the working lives of classical musicians: a lack of research acknowledged internationally. Classical music performance is a specialist field that demands exceptionally high levels of skill and commitment in preparation for a career that is unlikely to offer participants rewards commensurate with effort. The requirement for musicians to have a broad base of skills has been widely accepted for some time; indeed professional musicians have always engaged in multiple roles to remain financially viable, or for increased job satisfaction. Defining the composition of such a base of skills, though, requires understanding of the performance and non-performance roles of musicians and the extent to which music-related activities occur or are supported within the wider cultural environment.

In Chapter 2 we contemplated the environment in which musicians conduct the majority of their work, and later we will examine education and training. This chapter considers general characteristics of the musician. First we look at historical aspects of life as a musician including employment, roles, status and salary. This is followed by an overview of general employment characteristics of the present-day musician, in which we address issues relating to gender, attrition and injury.

Chronological History of the Professional Musician

It is frequently implied that musicians' careers were historically less broad than they are today. Although aspects of globalization and technology impact musicians more than ever before, multiple employments are characteristic of musicians' careers from the Middle Ages to the present day: 'The environment in which art is made has always been "commercial" and "product-driven" and this needs to be acknowledged.'[7] Carl Weber (1726–1826) was so concerned about the realities of forging and sustaining a freelance career in music that he began a guidebook for musicians in which he included information about travel routes, useful contacts, profitable seasons and dates, expenses and venues.

Musicians in the Middle Ages and the Renaissance (c. 1000–1600AD)

In the mid to late Middle Ages professional musicians were often civil watchmen: known as *pifferi* in Italy, *turmer* in Germany and *waits* in England and Scotland. Typically, a German *turmer* lived in the town tower and used his instrument (often a shawm because of the large amount of noise it could generate) to warn the townspeople of fire, approaching strangers or impending catastrophe. He would also

---

6   James Sloan Allen, 'The Morality and Immorality of Art', *Arts Education Policy Review*, 104/2 (2002): 19–24.

7   Helen Lancaster, 'Leading Musicians: Succession', *Australian Music Forum*, 10/3 (2004): 41–4.

ring the church bells as required and would sound the town bells or play music to signal each hour. The *turmer* was assisted by apprentices whom he trained to be musicians whilst they boarded with him and worked as servants. *Waits* also began as night watchmen; however, they increasingly became professional performers who provided entertainment and gave concerts in addition to their civic duties.[8]

From the twelfth century, musicians' guilds were founded to protect the rights of their members and would fight to maintain their respective performance monopolies. Claudio Monteverdi famously found himself in the midst of one such dispute and had his beard pulled by angry city musicians. Itinerant musicians of the eleventh and twelfth centuries such as *jongleurs* and minstrels, were unable to secure guild membership or employment; along with their children they were perceived as dishonourable and were without legal rights. Such was the stigma of itinerant musicians that applicants to trade guilds were required to provide proof that they did not descend from a musician. As court and royal patronage of musicians grew so did the disdain with which itinerant musicians were held, to some extent fuelled by court and civic musicians who jealously guarded their positions. Musicians satisfied the need for entertainment as required, and the majority lived outside of the social class system until partial integration in the late Middle Ages.

Unlike the members of other guilds, musicians' official duties often did not generate sufficient salary; consequently, they would subsidise their salary by providing music for weddings, funerals and other social occasions. Salaries for court musicians varied from alms given to the poorest musicians, to feudal tenure awarded the most respected of court musicians. Itinerant musicians were often paid in the form of gifts rather than with money, despite the obvious need for money to meet their daily needs. Many performing musicians were separated from the nobility by a curtain behind which they performed. One of the ways in which musicians achieved sufficient income or a higher social status was to undertake non-music work as scribes, spies, teachers and servants (see Illustration 3.1).

The formation of court music ensembles in the fourteenth century enabled musicians to achieve civil servant status; hence the availability of more secure and non-mobile employment became increasingly attractive. Nonetheless, civic positions still were preferred because civic musicians were appointed for life and enjoyed greater security than could be found in a position at court. Civic musicians also had the advantage of close contact with the church and the court as well as their interaction with the municipality.

It was in the fourteenth century that Canterbury Cathedral in England established an instrumental group for inclusion in the music for services. This was a significant move because the use of instruments in the church had been hotly debated for some time. By the fifteenth century, England hosted guild chapels where services were sung, resulting in increased employment for musicians and the potential for a freer style of music than would have been acceptable in churches and cathedrals.

Employment for seventeenth-century musicians commonly took the form of a director of school music, church organist, or musician for a court or municipality.

---

8 Christopher Headington, *The Bodley Head History of Western Music* (London, 1980), 2nd edn.

Illustration 3.1   Musicians Have Always Worked in Multiple Roles

From the later seventeenth century there were also many military posts for musicians, most of whom were without military obligations and who formed part of standing armies. Many town pipers took up the fashionable *hautbois* in the mid-seventeenth century as it offered the potential for more lucrative and prestigious employment, and because the *hautbois* was easier to blow than the cornet! *Hautboists*[9] were amongst the most respected performing musicians of the time; court *hautboists* were often paid as master musicians from a separate budget, with a salary higher than they would previously have received from the military. Typically, *hautboists* were exempted from numerous duties of the regular court musician and were only obliged to follow the directives of the court conductor during court performances. *Hauboists* also came from traditional systems of training such as that offered to English and Scottish *waits*.[10]

Social status also differed between wind and string instrumentalists: trumpets were considered the instrument of the elite or ruling classes, and wind players were able to charge considerably more for their performances than were their string counterparts. Organists were thought to be lower class if playing portable organs, which were often used for dance and street music. Conversely, church organists could achieve a relatively high social status due to the ecclesiastical nature of their work.

---

9   The *hautbois* was the precursor to the modern oboe.
10   Manfred Bukofzer, *Music in the Baroque Era* (London, 1978), 4th edn.

Musicians from the Eighteenth Century to the Present

The career of the instrumental musician from the eighteenth century onwards is marked by a diminution of ecclesiastical and court control, the popularity of virtuoso instrumentalists and the emergence of the concert orchestra. The dismissal of many eighteenth-century court musicians enabled numerous noblemen to maintain their own orchestras. It became a hallmark of social status to maintain one's own orchestra inclusive of the prestigious wind instruments: 'at no other time did so many court orchestras exist ... It is said that around 1780 some 400 musicians were employed in the service of the nobility in Vienna'.[11]

There were immense variations in the salaries of eighteenth-century musicians. Table 3.1 demonstrates the variation in salaries for musicians at the court of Dresden in the year 1711. Included are examples of Italian operatic musicians who were generally paid much higher salaries than instrumental musicians and who on occasion attained 'superstar' status.

Table 3.1   Salaries of Eighteenth-Century Musicians in Italy and Dresden[12]

Position(s)	Noted examples	Fee (taler)
Italy 1717		
Kapellmeister and first singer	Lotti and Stella	10,500
Singer (castrato)	Senesino	7,000
Dresden 1711		
Kapellmeister	Schmidt	1,200
Master of concerts	Woulmyer	1,200
Court composer	Veracini	1,200
Chamber musician	Weiss	1,000
Court accompanist/organist	Pezold	400
Violinist (probably principal)	Pissendel	400
Contre Basse	Selencka	350
Violist (rank and file)		100
Copyist		50

It was common practice in the eighteenth century to delay – sometimes for several years – the payment of salaries and allowances to court employees. This caused inevitable hardship to employees and their families; Richard Petzoldt[13] cites the petition of German violinist Kastner, who appealed that he had fulfilled the role of the

---

11 Werner Braun, 'The "Hautboist": An Outline of Evolving Careers and Functions', Herbert Kaufman and Barbara Reisner (trans.), in Walter Salmen (ed.), *The Social Status of the Professional Musician from the Middle Ages to the 19th Century* (New York, 1983), pp. 123–59 (original work published 1971).

12 Richard Petzoldt, 'The Economic Conditions of the 18th Century Musician', H. Kaufman and B. Reisner (trans.), in W. Salmen (ed.), *The Social Status of the Professional Musician from the Middle Ages to the 19th Century* (pp. 161–88).

13 Ibid.

deceased first violinist for almost six years and was still awaiting his pay rise! The lavish festivals and excessive funding of the time provided many opportunities for music making; however, musicians were at the mercy of the ducal budgets: following the death of the German Duke Christian, who reigned from 1712 to 1726, an imperial decree demanded that balance be restored to the budget. The response of Christian's successor, Duke Adolph II, was to reduce costs by dismissing the entire orchestra.

Georg Philipp Telemann was typical of an eighteenth-century musician who sought multiple employments in order to secure a reasonable income. His diaries and writings include mention of a number of concurrent roles including director of church music, secretary of the Frauenstein Association, Chairman of the Tabakskollegium, and composer for wealthy citizens and the church.[14] Multiple roles were quite usual for eighteenth-century musicians who gave music lessons, produced concerts, organized and performed with freelance groups, sold musical equipment and copied manuscripts.[15]

Well into the nineteenth century the uncertainty of court appointments led many musicians to seek the security of municipal roles, to form an alliance with the wealthy middle class or to established businesses such as retail and publishing houses. Musicians would also have considered a court's claim to intellectual property created by the musician during a period of service, and the difficulties associated with obtaining permission to travel other than as required by the court. Writing about British musicians between 1750 and 1850, Deborah Rohr suggests that musicians 'often combined both relatively low social and economic conditions with direct dealings with wealthy patrons'.[16]

The designation of ecclesiastical states to secular control following the Congress of Vienna in the early nineteenth century led to the further dissolution of court orchestras throughout Europe.[17] Over one hundred states in Germany alone lost their independence; hence many court establishments became commercial and public concerns and a paying audience became essential to the survival of each venture. Loss of power amongst the lesser aristocracy resulted in significantly less patronage than had previously been available and, as more musicians worked as freelance musicians, the position of music director became less prestigious.[18]

---

14 Richard Petzoldt, *Georg Philipp Telemann*, trans. H. Fitzpatrick (London, 1974) (original work published 1967).

15 Klaus Hortschansky, 'The Musician as Music Dealer in the Second Half of the 18th Century, H. Kaufman and B. Reisner (trans.), in W. Salmen (ed.), *The Social Status of the Professional Musician from the Middle Ages to the 19th Century*, pp. 191–218 (original work published 1971).

16 Deborah Rohr, *The Careers and Social Status of British Musicians, 1750 – 1850: A Profession of Artisans* (Cambridge, 2001).

17 The Congress of Vienna, held in 1814–1815 following the downfall of Napoleon, aimed to create peace in Europe by re-establishing a balance of power. The changes were profound and resulted in peace for almost 40 years.

18 For more information on the social circumstances of musicians, see Henry Raynor, *A Social History of Music from the Middle Ages to Beethoven* (London, 1972); and *Music and Society since 1815* (London, 1976). A position of Director of Music was much sought after

Virtuoso and Freelance Musicians   Marc Pincherle describes a virtuoso as 'a skilled performer, but one limited to the practice of his instrument'.[19] Its origins, however, suggest a much broader definition as an adjective derived from the Italian word *virtu* or the Latin word *virtus*. *Virtu* relates to goodness of soul and to superior skill or talent in the theory or practice of the fine arts. Used also to describe visual artists, the term has been applied most commonly to musicians. Ancient Rome was dazzled by visiting virtuosi who were rewarded with riches, property and influence; and Greek aulos players of around 600BC gave glittering performances often for great reward. Virtuosi came back into prominence in the mid-eighteenth century when public concerts grew in popularity, printing made more music available, and travel increased between cultural centres. The travels of Wolfgang Amadeus Mozart as a child prodigy exemplify the trend towards European tours.

In the nineteenth century, freelance virtuosi and composers became increasingly common as did the trade in printed music. Virtuosity such as that displayed by Paganini, Liszt and Chopin was one of the ways in which to succeed quickly as a soloist; however, success was not attributed solely to performance skill. All three of the aforementioned instrumentalists combined brilliance in performance with a variety of income streams such as teaching, composition and the sale of publications. Likewise, composers such as Beethoven, Schubert, Brahms and Berlioz sustained freelance careers.

Family background, patronage and personal wealth were important factors in a musician's ability to pursue a musical career. Philanthropy was often crucial for the less financially fortunate, and it was accompanied by routine obligations that required an unwelcome additional interface with the real world. As stated by Franz Schubert, the desire for independence encompassed a desire not to be concerned with the more mundane aspects of life: 'the artist prefers to be left to himself [sic] and desires to be freed from reality'.[20] Inevitably, however, the reality of a freelance existence included dealers and the public, whose favour was required for economic security; hence total separation from the mundane was rarely achieved. Support from the state was not free of obligations either: travel was often restricted, the demand for compositions and performances was high, and times of revolution and political turmoil could necessitate the composition of numerous anthems and patriotic songs.

The Rise of the Concert Orchestra   The publication of music sparked interest in the performance of existing popular repertoire and contributed to growing numbers of freelance composers. Another important change was the nineteenth-century trend from private to public ownership, which was epitomized by the emergence of opera houses. These factors had a radical impact on the status and role of the instrumental

---

until the decline of the nobility. See *kapellmeister* in Germany, 'chapel master' in England, *maître de chapelle* in France, and *maestro di cappella* in Italy.

19 Marc Pincherle, *The World of the Virtuoso*, trans. L.H. Brockway (Toronto, Ontario, 1963) (original work published 1961).

20 Walter Salmen, 'Social Obligations of the Emancipated Musician in the 19th Century', H. Kaufman and B. Reisner (trans.), in W. Salmen (ed.), *The Social Status of the Professional Musician from the Middle Ages to the 19th Century*, pp. 265–81.

musician, and on the interface of musicians with audiences and directors. Music ceased to be an intimate social necessity and became 'a remote, esoteric delight thundered out by vast orchestras or dispensed by virtuoso players and singers. It became increasingly the pleasure of a cultured *elite* rather than an immediate communication between men and women'.[21]

Orchestral salaries in the nineteenth century display similar variations to those in the preceding century. Salaries from both court and state orchestras were largely insufficient to meet musicians' daily needs, with the result that musicians were forced to take additional employment such as teaching in order to survive. Henry Raynor quotes Hallé's description of the dire situation in which many musicians found themselves when the wealthy students on whom they depended were scattered due to the French Revolution of 1848: 'A first violin at the Opera was lucky if he [sic] earned 900 francs a year; he lived by giving lessons. It is hardly to be supposed that he could have saved on a very brilliant scale. Now their pupils have gone, what is to happen to such people?'[22] In line with Table 3.1, Table 3.2 includes for comparison the details of salaries awarded to operatic musicians.

Table 3.2   Salaries of Nineteenth-Century Musicians in Dresden and Leipzig[23]

Position(s)	Noted examples	Fee (Taler)
Operatic musicians (c1821 – Dresden)		
Kapellmeister	Moracchi and Weber	1500
First soprano		5000
Second soprano or tenor		2000
Additional female singers		1500
Opera orchestra musicians (1820 – Leipzig)		
Concert master		400
Section leaders		200
Rank and file players		150
Casual players		150

In the post-war period of the mid-nineteenth century, numerous amateur and semi-professional orchestras, choirs and associations were formed, and many musicians travelled extensively to give concert tours. Public concerts originated – and remained particularly popular– in cities that did not contain opera houses. In cities with opera houses, operatic orchestras employed professional musicians and tended towards a much higher standard than their amateur counterparts. The operatic orchestras had very busy schedules: the Leipzig orchestra played each year for 110 opera performances and a similar number of plays. Accordingly, despite the potential for difficulty with the technical demands of new works, amateur concert orchestras provided a vital source of exposure for composers and soloists.

---

21 Raynor, *A Social History of Music from the Middle Ages to Beethoven*.
22 Raynor, *Music and Society since 1815*.
23 Ibid.

Professional musicians from the remaining court orchestras began to organize concerts in addition to their regular duties. Nineteenth-century concert orchestras such as that of the London Philharmonic Society and the semi-professional Gewandhaus orchestra, which was amalgamated with the Leipzig opera orchestra, increasingly performed larger scale works with a conductor and at a much higher standard than previously heard. Figure 3.1 illustrates a selection of the semi-professional and professional concert orchestras founded from the mid-1800s, most of which were either linked to an opera company or were limited to an annual season.

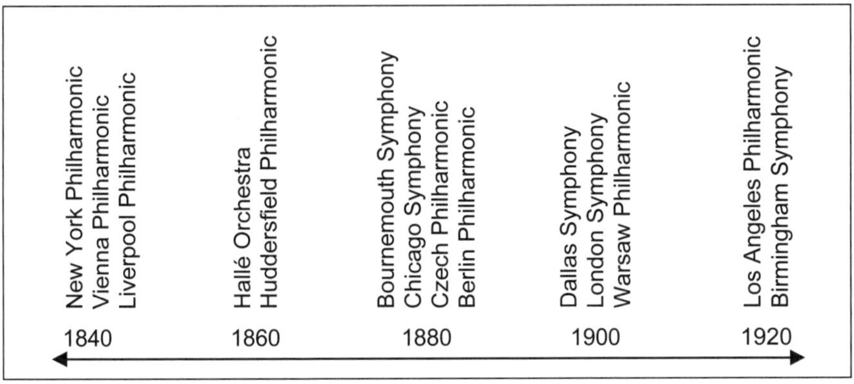

Figure 3.1   Sample of Symphony Orchestra Establishment from 1840–1920

Performance work for musicians was also to be found in pit orchestras, choral festival orchestras and at the theatre. Until 1840, theatres in London were permitted to produce only works that included music; consequently music in theatres was a source of regular work for musicians and heralded many singing actors. Intervals provided opportunities to perform concert works: conductor Franz Lachner scheduled Beethoven symphonies during intervals at the Vienna court opera theatre from 1830 until 1834 and Otto Nicolai – conductor of the Kärntnertortheater from 1841 to 1847 – directed symphonic works with an orchestra comprising the instrumentalists from the Vienna state opera. Initially headed The Philharmonic Academy, the orchestra is known today as the Vienna Philharmonic. Similarly, The Philharmonic Society in London was founded in 1813 by a group of professional musicians. Rather than maintain its own orchestra the Society contracted musicians from the opera, and tickets were affordably priced to encourage attendance regardless of social class. Later concert societies in Europe brought with them a social elitism incorporating formal dress, preferred seating and committees dominated by businessmen.

The first salaried full-time orchestra in England was the British Broadcasting Authority Philharmonic (known now as the BBC Philharmonic Orchestra), which was founded in 1930. Australia's first full-time orchestra was founded with the support of the government of New South Wales by the first Director of the Sydney Conservatorium of Music, Henri Verbrugghen, in 1916; one year after the conservatorium's foundation. Titled the Conservatorium Orchestra, its players comprised salaried players and conservatorium students.

Employment Characteristics of Today's Musicians

To the observer, the world of a professional musician may be somewhat romantic; comparable to that of athletes and actors, the superstars of stage, screen and track. High earnings of the 'superstars' create an unrealistic picture of average earnings, and the superstar image serves to inspire naïve interest in the profession, motivating the next generation of musicians. The reality of the musician's working life, however, is rather different: 'performing artists face more difficult employment circumstances than do other professionals'.[24] The British Musicians' Union reports that 'in all sectors of music performance the pressure is to move towards more casualisation and less employed work. As well as the highest levels of performance skills, British musicians will need more and more sophisticated ancillary and backup skills to support their chosen career'.[25] It is rather disheartening to see Richard Petzoldt reflect that 'the world of difference between the *bierfidler*, dependent upon tips, and the internationally known castrati of the eighteenth century still would exist. In general, little has changed in this respect to the present day'.[26] Gerald McDonald concurs, observing that orchestral salaries are not substantial and that non-tenured orchestral players in particular depend on income from additional activities such as teaching.[27]

As prefaced in Chapter 2, engagement with the performance of music is a fundamental part of life as a musician; yet for many musicians this engagement will be primarily through teaching, mentoring, directing, technology, business and management. Although numerous musicians would prefer to focus solely on performance, the reality is that musicians have to be conversant with the role of business manager and operate their practice within a market that is ever more global, diverse and digital, and increasingly concerned with localized identities. Further, performance itself has changed over time as musical scores have become on the whole much more prescriptive, and as technology has enabled audiences to grow to a size where the intimacy between performer and audience is difficult to capture. Socio-cultural, economic and political dimensions of globalization all impact the musician. Richard Letts highlights the global and changing market: 'music, more than almost any other commodity, has lent itself to globalisation. And globalisation is upon it'.[28]

A survey of 100 British arts organizations reveals the prevalence of multiple job holding and workforce casualization: the organizations employed approximately 7,500 people, of whom 3,500 (47 per cent) were casual employees and 920 (23 per cent) worked on a part-time basis. Volunteers comprised an additional 1,600 workers. Data expose the growing trend towards casualization and an ensuing need for effective business skills:

---

24 Kevin McCarthy, Arthur Brooks, Julia Lowell and Laura Zakaras, *The Performing Arts in a New Era* (Santa Monica, CA, 2001).

25 Metier, *The Music Industry: Skills and Training Needs in the 21st Century* (London, 2000). Similarly, a British labour force survey reported a rise of 38 per cent between 1981 and 1991 in the number of self-employed musicians.

26 Petzoldt, 'The Economic Conditions of the 18th Century Musician'.

27 Gerald McDonald, *Training and Careers for Professional Musicians* (Surrey, 1979).

28 Richard Letts, '(More than) 100 Ways Globalisation Affects Music', *Australian Music Forum*, 6/5 (2000): 1–16.

A large majority (over 70 per cent) [of participants] believe that the number of freelance and short-term contracts is going to rise and that there is going to be more competition in securing work. Allied to this is a trend towards increasing 'portfolio' careers and a recognition of the necessity of multi-skilling.[29]

A previous Metier music sector study found that 81 per cent of musicians hold a secondary occupation, and 41 per cent hold more than two.[30] A survey of Royal College of Music (RCM) alumni also notes a significant trend towards casualization, data from which is shown in Table 3.3.

Table 3.3   Percentage of RCM Alumni Holding Portfolio Careers[31]

Employment characteristics	1979 (%)	1995 (%)
Single job	71	28
Multiple employment	29	72

Attrition

Typically, careers in music are intense and short-lived, and factors contributing to attrition include family commitments, low and irregular salary, sporadic work, unsociable hours, prolonged periods of travel, managing multiple employments, and injury. Goodman suggests that many musicians leave the profession soon after entering it, and implies an 'average professional life expectancy of just less than seventeen years'.[32] Pierre-Michel Menger describes attrition as occurring typically in the mid-thirties or forties at which time career mobility declines.[33] Many musicians leave for more stable employment outside of the music sector. They pursue their artistic interests avocationally and contribute to the plethora of amateur arts organizations.

Performing artists are more likely than other artists to undertake work in low-skilled service industries, a factor that contributes significantly to a low average income. According to the RAND report, musicians and composers in the United States earn half the amount received by actors and directors, even though they work an average of 48 weeks each year and have only 4 per cent unemployment.[34] However, low rates of unemployment can be misleading. Taking into account that 75 per cent of performing artists earn at least part of their income in non-arts employment, the rate of unemployment calculated in terms of arts-related employment alone would be much higher.

---

29 Metier (2001a), *AS2K: Arts skills 2000*. London: Metier.

30 Metier, *The Music Industry: Skills and Training Needs in the 21st Century*.

31 Janet Mills and Jan Smith, 'Working in Music: Becoming Successful', paper presented at the Musikalische Bebabung in der Lebenzeitperspektive, University of Paderborn, 2000.

32 C.J. Goodman, 'Will the Next Mozart Please Step Forward: A Progress Report on the Singular, Expensive Business of Training America's Best Musicians' (California, 1970).

33 Pierre-Michel Menger, 'Artistic Labor Markets and Careers', *Annual Review of Sociology*, 25/1 (1999): 541–74.

34 McCarthy et al., *The Performing Arts in a New Era*.

One-third of performing artists cease work as artists within two years of joining the labour force and in general the artists who remain are those who work contractually and who pursue a number of different interests. Low salaries and irregular income are contributing factors: 'more [people] want to get in than there are places for. So employers can pay less than the job warrants. People get to 35, want to marry and have kids, and can no longer afford to stay in the theatre'.[35] The influence of inconsistent income is reflected in a book compiled from the statements of Australian musicians: 'there's no average income when you're freelance. You get a good week and then you get a bad week ... we can't exist on my precarious income'.[36]

Higher levels of performance success equate to longer periods of travel, resulting in difficulties with the management of family responsibilities and meeting the commitment of non-performance roles that demand regular attendance. The impact of irregular hours on personal relationships can be compounded as artists respond to the demands of family commitment: 'I go off to work at seven o'clock at night when my husband is home so he can look after the children. The night work when you work five or six nights a week is killing ... It's soul-destroying.'[37]

Orchestral Musicians

In a letter written in 1911, Ferruccio Busoni describes orchestral players as akin to 'a suppressed crowd of rebels ... Routine gives their playing the varnish of perfection and assurance. For the rest, they loathe their work, their job and, most of all, their music'.[38] Robert Faulkner's 1973 survey of orchestral musicians suggests that most become 'anchored in their organization, experience no or little mobility and, unless they feel entrapped, adjust and become committed to their work in a stable work setting'.[39] Walter Salmen describes much the same lack of mobility for eighteenth-century orchestral musicians: 'Only when there was no opportunity for employment in one's own court did one make the decision, generally with the permission of the local ruler, to seek employment away from home.'[40] Musicians tended to remain within the jurisdiction of a particular ruler, and it was unusual for an orchestra to employ musicians from other countries. The exception, of course, was the virtuoso or 'super star' musician for whom travel was the norm.

A 2001 British survey of 498 orchestral players concludes that orchestral work 'can be spiritually exhausting ... all but the most devoted tend to become increasingly disenchanted with their lot ... Under [circumstances] such as these the orchestral musician's life becomes a series of dull chores'.[41] For today's orchestral musician, the routine existence of life within an orchestra together with a lack of

---

35 Metier, *AS2K: Arts Skills 2000* (London, 2001).

36 Stephen Smith and John Robinson, *Working Musicians* (Fremantle, WA, 1990).

37 Ibid.

38 Ferruccio Bonavia (ed.), *Musicians on Music* (London, 1956).

39 Robert Faulkner, 'Career Concerns and Mobility Motivations of Orchestral Musicians', *Sociological Quarterly*, 14 (1973): 334–49.

40 Salmen, 'Social Obligations of the Emancipated Musician in the 19th Century'.

41 Metier, *Orchestral Research Final Report: First Draft*.

career mobility, lack of personal practice time and irregular hours can contribute to dissatisfaction with the role. This dissatisfaction is described by an orchestral musician who contributed to Stephen Smith and John Robinson's study: 'there are in most symphony orchestras long periods of frustration. I don't think that any orchestra, no matter how great the conductor, can provide anyone with a continuously stimulating and exciting experience'.[42] The sentiment is highlighted by Louis Yffer in his bibliographic account of life as an orchestral musician: 'out of perhaps 150 concerts a year, the number that were truly enjoyed by the players on account of an inspiring conductor can be counted on the fingers of one hand'.[43] One musician told me that it is 'hard to produce inspired performances when working 20–24 hours per week: it starts becoming routine, unless you have incredible passion'. Another musician had reduced the amount of time spent performing, and commented: 'I perform less often but with quality instead of a full-time job.'

In general, research on orchestras raises concerns about effective organizational communication and the lack of individual creativity for performers. These concerns are indicative of the comments made by musicians who participated in the studies from which this book is derived. They describe 'dirty, sleazy politics'; 'totalitarian workplace dynamics, appalling management … too little respect'; and a 'lack of artistic input'. Musicians also draw attention to the negative results of long periods of orchestral playing, which takes 'the spirit out of performance', and which led one musician to confess: 'I lost my love of music.' In fact, new orchestral musicians describe disillusionment soon after starting orchestral work: 'I found my first year in the orchestra supremely disillusioning.' By far the most frequently reported reason for orchestral attrition was an absence of opportunities for individual creative and strategic involvement: '[I was] dissatisfied with the lack of opportunities for thinking creatively.' Unsociable hours were described as being 'incompatible with growing family commitments'.

Orchestral musicians pursue a diverse range of roles outside of the orchestral setting, and report an initial lack of the skills required to manage orchestral and other roles. Many musicians integrate orchestral roles as part of protean careers that include teaching, business and community work, and many hold formal qualifications in a myriad of other professional fields. The involvement of orchestral players in a wide range of activities beyond their orchestral roles is evidenced in the British survey of orchestral musicians, which reported players' concerns about insufficient skills in areas such as instrumental pedagogy, taxation and copyright, marketing, law and small business management.[44] These secondary roles are important not only to subsidize income, but to fulfil artistic and creative needs; however, a chorus's or orchestra's average call time of around 24 hours each week necessitates many hours of private practice commitment prior to the first rehearsal of each week's new works, and the irregular nature of orchestral rosters makes it difficult for musicians to meet the obligations of other work.

---

42 Smith and Robinson, *Working Musicians*.

43 Louis Yffer, 'The Investigation Proceeds', in *Music Is the Victim* (Melbourne, Vic., 1995), pp. 1–40.

44 Metier (2001), *Orchestral Research Final Report: First Draft*.

The societal role of the orchestra has evolved, and the change has had a profound effect on orchestral musicians. According to Mira Crouch and Jenny Lovric:

> the ideology of 'economic rationalism' which appears to have dominated public discourse in the last few years has often, in the musicians' view, meant that artistic considerations and standards have been subordinated to the drive towards visibly 'increased productivity' imposed upon them by their organizations.[45]

It is essential as orchestras take on more of a community and education role that players are equipped with the skills that will enable successful interaction with those programmes. It would seem to be the position of many organizations that the resources for such training are not made available. Sustainable business depends on steady development and investment in personnel, and Catherine Wichterman suggests that orchestras have 'neglected to provide ongoing professional development for musicians'.[46] Initiatives in other areas of the arts and in sport are the envy of musicians. For example, the Australian Ballet Company has a professional development scheme for dancers who have been with the company for five or more years. Dancers, known increasingly as dance artists in recognition of broader practice, can access funding for education and training towards their post-performance careers.

Christopher Latham, a former violinist with the Australian Chamber Orchestra, predicts that orchestras in the future 'will be a whole bunch of musicians who can do different things ... The orchestra will become a much more fluid organisation, multi-faceted'.[47] Although many orchestral musicians are satisfied with their performance role, the involvement of musicians in the operational side of orchestras would add to the stimulation of the performance role and to the skills and knowledge of both players and management; thus the participation of musicians in artistic and strategic planning, educational and community programmes has the potential to benefit both the organization and the musicians themselves. Musicians are independent, self-motivated thinkers with skills far beyond their performance expertise, and the potential for contracted musicians to play a greater role in their organizations is gradually gaining recognition. Mirroring the move by several London orchestras who function as self-managed organizations with musicians partially responsible for artistic and strategic management, the musicians of the St Paul Chamber Orchestra accepted cuts in pay in May 2003 in return for a new organizational structure that places central artistic decisions in the hands of a new artistic vision committee rather than with an artistic director. The committee draws on the expertise of musicians to facilitate concert programming and orchestral management. The orchestra's managing director, Bruce Coppock, suggests that 'one of the key frustrations for musicians, typically, is they are not engaged, other than playing, in the real artistic planning and

---

45 Mira Crouch and Jenny Lovric, *Paths to Performance: Gender as a Theme in Professional Music Careers. A Pilot Study of Players in Two Orchestras* (Sydney, NSW, 1990).

46 Catherine Wichterman, *The Orchestra Forum: A Discussion of Symphony Orchestras in the US* (New York, 1999).

47 Harriet Cunningham, 'Let Me Entertain You', *State of the Arts* (January–March 2004): 30–40.

development of an orchestra'.[48] In 2007 the orchestra's eclectic programme featured all nine Beethoven symphonies alongside a chamber music series including a world premier by Fred Lerdahl. Members of the orchestra regularly appear as soloists alongside some of the world's top-ranking artists.

Performing arts organizations such as orchestras recruit artists after they have been trained, and most have little involvement in education and training. Musicians consider effective ensemble training to be lacking in most performance degrees, and suggest the solution to be a 'focus on experience'; 'you learn more on the job than you do at university'.[49] Arts organizations and educational institutions would benefit from understanding the way in which each other operates, and collaborative effort towards shared goals would foster productive and mutually beneficial relationships.

Physical and Psychological Injury

There is a higher rate of injury amongst musicians than athletes; hence injury prevention strategies should be of paramount importance to musicians and educators. Musicians have long been acknowledged to be susceptible to physical and psychological injury, with particular susceptibility during periods of intensive conservatorium training, competition preparation and prolonged orchestral work. Susan Harman identifies music injury literature published as long ago as Bernadino Ramazzini's *Diseases of Tradesmen* (1713), followed by Poore's 1887 research into musician's cramp. Carl Philipp Emanuel Bach's *Essay on the True Art of Keyboard Playing*, first published in 1753, warns of the hazards of repetitive bass lines during which the left hand can grow stiff and the muscles remain contracted. Bach also warns of the psychological strain associated with prolonged periods of performance: 'assuming that one were hardened to such labor, even the most dependable musician would begin eventually to waver drowsily and unwittingly through fatigue'.[50] One of the first books dedicated solely to musicians' injuries is Kurt Singer's (1932) *Diseases of the Musical Profession: A Systematic Presentation of their Causes, Symptoms and Methods of Treatment.*[51]

The rate of injury among professional musicians is high: at least 60 per cent of all orchestral musicians in Australia carry an injury at any one time.[52] The Symphony

---

48 See the St Paul Chamber Orchestra website, at <http://www.thespco.org/>. The Andante.com article relating to the change in orchestral management was by written by Matt Peiken and published on 30 May 2003. See 'St. Paul Chamber Orchestra Musicians Take Pay Cut in Return for More Say', retrieved 31 August 2003, from <http://www.andante.com/article/article.cfm?id=21060>.

49 Dawn Bennett, 'The Classical Music Profession: Educating for Sustainable professional Practice', unpublished PhD thesis, The University of Western Australia, Perth, 2005.

50 Carl Philipp Emanuel Bach, *Essay on the True Art of Playing Keyboard Instruments*, trans. W.J. Mitchell (London, 1974) (original work published 1753).

51 Susan Harman, 'Odyssey: The History of Performing Arts Medicine', *Maryland Medical Journal*, 42/3 (1993): 251–3.

52 Susan Archdall, 'Strains of Music That No Musician Wants', *Adelaide Advertiser* (2 July 2002), retrieved 2 July 2002, from <http://www.andante.com/article/article.cfm?id=17526>.

Orchestra Musicians' Association suggests that part of the blame lies in orchestral programming: 'musician injury levels are exacerbated with unduly heavy work schedules'.[53] Australian injury statistics reflect those of other countries: a Spanish study of 1,613 performing musicians found that 79 per cent of musicians suffer from a physical problem related to their profession, as do 90 per cent of musicians between 30 and 40 years of age: 'knowledge about anatomy, physiology, ergonomics and postures appears to be essential in order to change the musicians' attitude'.[54] A 1997 survey of 57 orchestras worldwide reported that 56 per cent of musicians experienced pain whilst playing during the previous year, and 19 per cent suffered pain so acute that they could no longer perform.[55] In fact, numerous studies cite high incidents of injury leading to complete cessation of performance activities: 'potentially career-ending occupational injuries among musicians include hearing loss, overuse syndromes, entrapment neuropathies, focal hand and lip dystonias, and other musculoskeletal and neuromuscular conditions'.[56]

Orchestral musicians attribute injury to ineffective rehearsal techniques, uninformed programming, and the performance of contemporary orchestral music 'designed for machines and not human beings'.[57] Musicians also note a lack of empathy amongst orchestral colleagues and management who are 'completely unsympathetic to the concept of [a] graduated return to work'. Injury prevention strategies have enjoyed success in many parts of Europe but are not available to the vast majority of Australian orchestral players. The importance of prevention is encapsulated in a statement made by one conductor: 'I think of critical importance is for musicians to have regular access to physical support, massage therapy, physical therapy. That's now standard European practice.' The participant, who is an orchestral conductor of international standing, emphasized that many such programmes have more than paid for themselves in a reduction of working time lost to injury.[58]

Since the early 1990s there has been a gradual shift in the focus of performing arts medicine research from the treatment of existing injuries towards strategies for injury prevention. As well, there has been increased recognition of the physiological or cognitive aspects of musicians' injuries; a survey of 2,212 orchestral musicians in the United States determined a marked association between stress and the incidence

---

53 Symphony Orchestra Musicians' Association. (2004), *The Australian government review of orchestras*. Sydney, NSW: Symphony Orchestra Musicians' Association.

54 Jaume Rosset i Llobet, 'Musicians' Health Problems and Their Relation to Musical Education', in O. Musumeci (ed.), *The ISME Commission for Education of the Professional Musician. Preparing Musicians: Making Sound Worlds* (Barcelona, 2004), pp. 195–209.

55 Ian James, 'Survey of Orchestras', in Raoul Tubiana and Peter Amadio (eds), *Medical Problems of the Instrumental Musician* (London, 2000), pp. 195–201.

56 Kris Chesky, George Kondraske, Miriam Henoch, John Hipple and Bernard Rubin, 'Musicians' Health', in R. Colwell and C. Richardson (eds), *The New Handbook of Research on Music Teaching and Learning* (New York, 2002), pp. 1023–39.

57 I have interspersed many quotations throughout the book from musicians and artists who have contributed to the research.

58 Bennett, 'The Classical Music Profession: Educating for Sustainable Professional Practice'.

of physical and physiological injuries amongst players.[59] Dianna Kenny investigated cognitive, behavioural and cognitive-behavioural interventions that include foci on changing dysfunctional behaviours using mental imagery techniques; altering thinking patterns from unproductive to productive; and combinations of educational and psychological interventions. These were grouped as cognitive behavioural therapy (CBT). Despite the apparent plethora of related literature, Kenny's exploration of current treatments concluded that literature relating to music performance anxiety is patchy and contradictory, making firm conclusions difficult to reach.

Important foci of injury prevention have been: (1) increased physiological and psychological awareness from the earliest stages of musical development; (2) availability and affordability of treatment and advice; and (3) the necessity for musicians to become more physically and psychologically aware. Research also highlights: (4) a general lack of pedagogical training amongst instrumental tutors at every level, and the potential role of tutors in reducing the incidence of playing-related injury; (5) the role of conservatories in promoting healthy work practices for students and in providing suitable professional development for instrumental staff; (6) the need for proactive measures such as the development of a fitness regime; and (7) the role of professional organizations in promoting healthy workplaces.

Increasing recognition of the role of conservatories in preventing physical and psychological injury is highlighted in a directive from the US-based National Association of Schools of Music (NASM) that all music schools include injury-awareness and prevention in their curricula. As a result, research and practice centres prepare 'kits' that will enable NASM schools to meet their injury prevention obligations, although it is too early to test the results of this necessarily impersonal approach.

The British Association of Performing Arts Medicine report that over 70 per cent of students seen by them since 1992 presented with non-structural, performance-related problems that could be overcome by effective performance and practising. Aaron Williamon criticizes the lack of injury prevention strategies in conservatories: 'the education and training of performers fail to incorporate the advice to students on care of the body, prevention of injury and psychological well-being'.[60] Williamon's work forms part of an initiative at the Royal College of Music (RCM) that provides performance students with six hours of seminars on physical and psychological issues. Key strategies include a mental skills programme using relaxation and mental imagery techniques adapted from successful programmes used with elite athletes, a neuro-feedback programme enabling participants to observe and then to redress brain activity, and an exercise and lifestyle programme that targets physical fitness using key concepts of exercise science.

59 Martin Fishbein, Susan Middlestadt, Victor Ottai, Susan Straus and Alan Ellis, 'Medical Problems among ICSOM Musicians: Overview of a National Survey', *Medical Problems of Performing Artists Journal*, 3/3 (1988): 1–8.

60 Aaron Williamon, 'Healthy Body, Healthy Mind, Healthy Music: Practice-Based Research Leading to Research-Based Learning', in O. Musemici (ed.), *The ISME Commission for Education of the Professional Musician. Preparing Musicians: Making Sound Worlds* (Barcelona, 2004), pp. 257–70.

The attendance of staff at the RCM sessions is optional, which is a pity as it is crucial for instrumental teachers to be equipped with the skills and knowledge required to implement injury prevention strategies. The majority of instrumental teachers do not have the knowledge to offer effective advice to students: Kelly Barrowcliffe's survey of 231 music faculty members in Canada found that university music teachers are not knowledgeable about specific areas of playing-related injuries (PRI) including focal dystonia, thoracic outlet syndrome and carpal tunnel syndrome, despite the fact that 60 per cent of them had experienced a PRI. A sizeable 80 per cent of the teachers reported having students with a PRI.[61] Chesky concurs, suggesting that 'few students benefit from prevention because music educators are generally unaware of these issues'.[62] And how could they be, when the majority train in the conservatorium system where the incorporation and injury awareness and prevention strategies remains on the periphery.

Women in Western Classical Music

In the current climate of industrial reform, it is interesting to review women in their traditional roles as supporters of the arts; as the player rather than the concertmaster, as the teacher and not the professor, and as avocational player and organizer. Feminist research in music is comparatively recent, and is therefore mostly third-wave or reflective research; the third-wave component addressing the 'lived' experience of women who 'juggle jobs, kids, money and personal freedom in a frenzied world'.[63] Although the music profession is years behind many others in this respect, it benefits from the plethora of research now available from within other disciplines.

Writing about women in music from a historic perspective, Diane Jezic cites Emil Naumann's 1882 history of music, in which it is written that 'all creative work is well-known as being the exclusive work of men'.[64] Historically, women in the Middle Ages were excluded from guild occupations and consequently performed with itinerant musicians whose social status was very low. Writing about music in the nineteenth century, Walter Salmen suggests that women 'shared the economic uncertainties of the profession with their male colleagues, yet were usually paid less and treated with more disdain'.[65] Educational opportunities in music were also quite different for men and women: it wasn't until the foundation of music conservatories in the 1880s that women performers were able to access advanced level music education and training, and few conservatories accepted women composers.

---

61 Kelly Barrowcliffe, 'The Knowledge of Playing-Related Injuries among University Music Teachers', unpublished Master's thesis, University of Western Ontario, London, Ontario, 1999, available online at <http://www.collectionscanada.ca/obj/s4/f2/dsk1/tape9/PQDD_0003/MQ42049.pdf>.

62 Chesky et al., 'Musicians' Health'.

63 Sidra Vitale, 'The 3rd WWWave: What's All This, Then?' (1999), retrieved 23 April 2003, from <http://www.3rdwwwave.com/display_article.cgi?144>.

64 Diane Jezic, *Women Composers: The Lost Tradition Found* (New York, 1994), 2nd edn.

65 Salmen, 'Social Obligations of the Emancipated Musician in the 19th Century'.

Women were not permitted to receive a degree in music from Oxford University until 1921, despite the fact that Elizabeth Stirling passed the examinations in 1856. Men were also able to undertake training in the armed forces, which was an option not available to women until after World War II.

Jutta Allmendinger and J. Richard Hackman describe orchestras as 'relatively elite and traditionally male organizations'.[66] The exclusion of women from professional orchestras led, in the late nineteenth century, to the formation of many all-women orchestras, and opposition to women's involvement in mainstream orchestras continued well into the twentieth century. In line with the workforce in general, the rise of women in orchestras has historically been the result of external factors such as the loss of male musicians due to war: in 1942 the number of women musicians in the Sydney Symphony Orchestra rose to 32 from a pre-war total of 20. The exception to the rule regarding women in orchestras came conventionally in the form of the harpist, described by Ethel Smyth as 'this solitary, daintily-clad, white-armed sample of womanhood among the black coats, as might be a flower on a coal dump'.[67] As late as 1969, applications from women musicians for a position in the Berlin Philharmonic were returned with the answer: 'Following an old tradition, the Berlin Philharmonic does not accept any women musicians.'[68] The Berlin Philharmonic first accepted women in 1982.

In 1997, female harpist Anna Lelkes became a full member of the Vienna Philharmonic Orchestra following several years of work under temporary contracts. It was the first time since the orchestra's foundation in 1842 that a woman had been admitted, and was the same year in which the Czech Philharmonic Orchestra admitted women for the first time. The Vienna orchestra's reposition followed constant lobbying by women's groups and a directive from the German Chancellor, who threatened to stop state subsidies. There were also warnings of boycotts and demonstrations during the orchestra's next major tour, scheduled to begin the week following the historic decision, and a more sceptical observer would note a dire shortage of male harpists! Elena Ostleitner, professor at the male-dominated Vienna conservatory, described the admission of women to the orchestra as a 'difficult and delicate issue … as if the Pope were going to be a woman'.[69] The move to admit women was so significant that it was announced in the Austrian parliament; however, at the New Year's concert Anna Lelkes' name was omitted from the programme and she was permitted to have only her hands uncovered. Since Lelke's appointment, no other women have been admitted as members of the orchestra.

---

66 Jutta Allmendinger and Richard J. Hackman, 'The More, the Better? A Four-Nation Study of the Inclusion of Women in Symphony Orchestras', *Social Forces*, 74/2 (1995): 423–60.

67 Sophie Fuller, 'Dead White Men in Wigs', in S. Cooper (ed.), *Girls! Girls! Girls!* (London, 1995).

68 Eva Rieger, '*Dolce Semplice?* On the Changing Role of Women in Music', H. Anderson (trans.), in G. Ecker (ed.), *Feminist Aesthetics* (London, 1985) (original work published 1976).

69 Hugh Eakin, 'Women Are as Scarce as Change at Vienna Orchestra', *New York Times* (4 June 2003).

The past twenty years has seen an increase in the number of women within the fields of performance, management and composition as women have competed with their male counterparts for available positions. In 1977, Margaret Hillis became the first woman to conduct in Carnegie Hall when, hours before the concert, the orchestra's scheduled conductor was unable to perform. In 1994, Melbourne-born Nicollette Fraillon became the first Australian woman to conduct an Australian Broadcasting Corporation (ABC) orchestra, and the first woman to be chief conductor of a major European symphony orchestra. Another Australian, Simone Young was the first woman to conduct in the opera houses of Paris, Munich, Berlin and Vienna, and in 2005 she became the first woman in 50 years to conduct the Vienna Philharmonic.

Despite an increase in participation at all levels of the profession, however, women continue to experience less opportunities to forge careers in music and are less likely than men to audition for positions in traditionally male-dominated orchestras; particularly for wind, brass and percussion positions. A contributing factor is that musical instrument preference is gendered: fewer girls choose to play instruments perceived as instruments for boys. When trombonist Megumi Kanda won the principal position with the Missouri Symphony Orchestra, only seven of the 76 applicants were women.[70]

Men dominate leadership roles such as the orchestral conductor or section leader. There have been a number of lawsuits triggered when women musicians secured principal roles during 'blind' auditions – where the audition is conducted behind a screen to preserve anonymity – only to be demoted once the director realized her gender. The ethnicity of musicians has led to similar legal action. David Throsby and Virginia Hollister's analysis of Australian artists unearths that female artists earn appreciably less than men in all categories of income. They report 'a long history of disadvantage experienced by women artists', and suggest the financial support of a spouse to be more important for women artists and that 'a substantially larger proportion of females than of males believe that caring for children restricted their careers as artists'.[71] The lack of women in leadership positions would in part explain the salary difference between male and female musicians indicated by several recent economic studies.

Gendered terminology is widely used in music: the term *concertmaster* is applied irrespective of whether the principal violinist is male or female. The adoption of non-gendered terminology would lessen the barriers faced by women, and the use of female mentors is essential to encourage women to pursue positions of leadership and non-gendered instrument selection. The presence in leadership roles of females such as composers Peggy Glanville-Hicks and Elena Kats-Chernin, and conductor Simone Young, is facilitating a change in the traditional image of composers and conductors as bewigged old men;[72] however, one is unlikely to find a poster of a female composer or conductor on a classroom wall.

---

70 Elaine Schmidt, 'MSO Trombonist Didn't Just Slide into Her Spot', *Milwaukee Journal Sentinel* (15 June 2003): 1E, 6E.

71 David Throsby and Virginia Hollister, Don't Give Up Your Day Job: An Economic Study of Professional Artists in Australia (No. 331.7617) (Sydney, NSW, 2003).

72 Sophie Fuller, 'Dead White Men in Wigs'.

Concluding Comments

It would seem that musicians' practice has historically encompassed much more than performance, and that the apprenticeship system of training had much to offer in terms of preparation for the 'real world'. Students learning in the conservatorium tradition are unlikely to be immersed in the cultural environment or exposed to its complexities and opportunities. In terms of career preparation and maintenance, it is crucial to redefine the term *musician* to encompass the broad range of roles that create sustainable careers. Meeting one's personal and professional goals is perhaps the only way to find intrinsic satisfaction and, therefore, success.

Chapter 4

Performance-based Music Education and Training

'Students go into music because of passion. The trick for institutions is to help retain and encourage that passion whilst informing students of the profession'

How does performance-based music education and training relate to professional practice as a musician? What are the characteristics of such training? How has it altered over time, and what can we expect to see in the future? Chapter 4 considers the history and contemporary provision of performance-based education and training with a predominantly western classical music focus, and identifies some of the pertinent issues facing educators and students. The chapter begins with an historical overview of performance-based music education, and next considers some of the current issues confronting practitioners and educators. An outline of the philosophies underpinning existing programmes in Australia is followed by analysis of curricula in terms of structure and content, and includes for comparison several non-classical programmes. The ensuing section concerns graduate destination and employment, professional development and curricular change. Returning to the opening questions, the chapter illustrates the allocation of time within the core units of Australia's performance-based undergraduate degrees. A comparison of musicians' work and their education and training is featured in Chapter 7.

The Past

The term 'conservatorium' is derived not from the verb to conserve but from the Italian word 'conservatorio', and dates back to sixteenth-century Italian orphanages at which musical training occurred. Musical standards at many institutions were high, and by the seventeenth century many orphanages were maintained and enhanced by a Maestro di Capella who was usually attracted to a municipal position as a result of the increasing uncertainty of positions at court. The contributions of the conservatoria were valued not least because church congregations were noticeably larger on occasions when music played a prominent role in the services! Ironically, many of the most accomplished female graduates contracted good marriages and consequently climbed the social ladder. As public performance was sociably unacceptable for a married woman, the majority of married women ceased to perform.

The apprenticeship system of musical training described in Chapter 3 was the most common approach to instrumental musical training until the eighteenth century:

conservatorio schools were relatively rare, and focused most often on vocal training.[1] Training in the apprenticeship system was steeped in tradition, to the disadvantage of graduates who, from the late 1500s, found that amateur or non-guild musicians more in tune with popular musical tastes were able to secure performance work and to undercut official rates of pay.[2] This situation will sound very familiar to freelance performers working in the twenty-first century. For those interested in instrumental and general music training, private training occurred for the most part with musician parents and with other working musicians. From the late Renaissance, this musical training frequently incorporated performance proficiency on the violin and violoncello (or their forerunners) with the result that qualifications became much more difficult to obtain. On average it took between three and ten years of training to qualify as a musician, and the standard shortcut was to marry the master's daughter.

Town pipers' associations (*stadtpfeiferei*) provided another important source of musical training and led to orchestral work in the court system. Admission to *stadtpfeiferei* was open to anyone who could prove honourable status as the descendent of an artisan, and students were generally middle class. The social status of orchestral musicians was determined by income and by prestige according to their position within the social system. Consequently, higher social status could be achieved through career advancement.

By the twelfth and thirteenth centuries, European universities delivered a liberal arts curriculum consisting of grammar, dialect, geometry, arithmetic, astronomy and music. For the most part, universities were aligned to the church; accordingly the advancement of music scholarship and composition occurred most often at institutions such as Oxford, Cambridge and Eton, which were less constrained by diocesan control. In the sixteenth century, for example, Oxford and Cambridge offered a higher degree in music and operated distinct music faculties. As illustrated by the decree of 1340 at Queen's College in Oxford, which stated that the number of students should be equal to the number of choristers, music was considered an essential component of university life.

At the same time, an increased emphasis on performance skill prompted the inclusion of individual music tuition at some European universities such as that at Notre Dame, which employed notable musicians who served at the cathedral. In order to meet financial obligations, seventeenth-century conservatories admitted fee-paying students and employed additional teachers to cater for the increased demand, thus creating an early conservatorium model. Demand for musicians in the eighteenth century rose as a result of the popularity of secular music concerts; hence, universities began to supplement the output of the apprenticeship system and took on the role of trade schools.

---

1   Cynthia M. Gessele, 'Conservatories III(2) up to 1790: Other Countries', in *The New Grove Dictionary of Music and Musicians* (London, 2001), pp. 314–15, 2nd edn.

2   Henry Raynor, *A Social History of Music from the Middle Ages to Beethoven* (London, 1972); and *Music and Society since 1815* (London, 1976).

Academies specializing in voice provided a limited education to 'young ladies of a good family' from about 1800.[3] Whereas male students received a comprehensive education, the majority of conservatories permitted women to study only voice, harp and piano within a specially modified academic curriculum. With the addition of orchestration and composition classes in the 1870s, it became increasingly common for women to select a major in composition or score reading rather than in the traditional areas of performance and teaching.

Significant growth in conservatorium training occurred in the latter half of the eighteenth century, at which time many church music schools closed and the continued popularity of musical performances resulted in a demand for technical prowess. The rise of the bourgeoisie following European industrial revolutions was a contributing factor: it was a primary objective of the Paris Conservatoire (Conservatoire Nationale) to educate musicians who would uphold the values of the French Revolution. Conservatories founded in the late eighteenth and early nineteenth centuries include those in Paris (1795), Prague (1811), Vienna (1817), Milan (1824), Leipzig (1843) and Berlin (1850); and the Royal Academy of Music in London (1822). Performances by conservatorium ensembles were an integral part of many European cities from the early nineteenth century. In contrast, Australia's first classical music concerts were held prior to the establishment of conservatories, with concerts recorded in Hobart and Sydney in 1821 and 1826 respectively. Australia's first conservatorium was the Elder Conservatorium of Music, which was founded in South Australia in 1885. It was followed in 1895 by the Melbourne University Conservatorium and in 1915 by the New South Wales Conservatorium (now known as the Sydney Conservatorium of Music).

Conservatories in the nineteenth century delivered predominantly diploma-level training with a curricular focus on performance, harmony, ear training and sight reading. Students with vocational or avocational intentions – and often from a young age – studied together at most institutions until the twentieth century, when formalized education and training became increasingly common for musicians. Academic music studies were mostly undertaken at universities, which delivered both undergraduate and postgraduate degree courses. In Europe this remained largely the case until 1999, at which time European Ministers of Education signed the Bologna Declaration in a significant move designed to amalgamate academic and vocational training.

The Present

The place of universities in society has come almost full circle. Universities in much of the western world began as institutions in which students acquired skills and knowledge relevant to the requirements of their respective societies. Whereas the nineteenth century saw a shift towards the individual, since the late twentieth century universities have been under increasing pressure to meet the political, social

---

3   Eva Rieger, *Dolce Semplice?* On the Changing Role of Women in Music', H. Anderson (trans.), in G. Ecker (ed.), *Feminist Aesthetics* (London, 1985) (original work published 1976).

and economic demands of society through the provision of courses with more vocational or societal relevance. In contrast with these themes and reflecting the financial difficulties of many conservatories, 'social objectives have been replaced by economic ones in policy and decision making, the demands of which are often met by increasing commercial activities'.[4] There is global debate concerning the effectiveness of performance-based education and training in music, but music programmes are not the only courses to have faced criticism in recent times; when reporting on the university sector in general, the US-based National Centre for Postsecondary Improvement cites 'neglected issues at the heart of higher education's societal obligations'. In particular the report refers to weak links with primary and secondary schools, inadequate engagement of community, underdeveloped definitions of what constitutes educational quality, outdated educational practices, and an increasing lack of community involvement by college graduates. The report calls for institutions to gather data on graduate destinations, and for the data to be used to inform and improve quality.[5]

Criticism of conservatories often recognizes the difficulties of preparing graduates: 'it is not entirely clear how to achieve a balance between education and job training within the traditional educational environment'.[6] However, it has also been acknowledged that many institutions have been reluctant to act on the need for change: Douglass Seaton, President of the College Music Society in the US, suggests that 'colleges, universities, and conservatories must deal with the real world of musical experience, not withdraw from it into ivy [sic] towers'. The National Association of Schools of Music (NASM) was created in 1924, and with more than 550 member schools it is the agency responsible for the accreditation of music curricula in the US. NASM describes the competencies, standards, guidelines and recommendations for Bachelor of Music degrees as follows: 'The Bachelor of Music in Performance is the initial professional degree in music. It emphasizes development of the skills, concepts, and sensitivities essential to the professional life of the musician.'[7] Unfortunately, there has previously been no formal identification of those skills, concepts and sensitivities; consequently the task of designing and maintaining vocationally relevant curricula is an unenviable task.

Peter Renshaw, previous director of the Guildhall School of Music in London, admits that arts training institutions 'are precariously poised between conserving

---

4   Helen Lancaster, 'Leading Musicians: Context', *Australian Music Forum*, 10/1 (2003): 26–9.

5   Patricia J. Gumport, Peter Cappelli, William F. Massy, Michael T. Nettles, Marvin W. Peterson, Richard J. Shavelson and Robert Zemsky, *Beyond Dead Reckoning: Research Priorities for Redirecting American Higher Education* (Stanford, CA, 2002). Reprinted 2003 in *International Higher Education*, 30 (Winter): 19–21. Reprinted 2003 in *Higher Education Digest*, 46 (Summer): 1–11.

6   Kevin McCarthy, Arthur Brooks, Julia Lowell and Laura Zakaras, *The Performing Arts in a New Era* (Santa Monica, CA, 2001).

7   For information about NASM, see <http://nasm.arts-accredit.org/>. See also Janet Poklemba's 1995 thesis, 'Career Education: An Integral Part of the Education of the Undergraduate Music Performance Student?', unpublished Master's thesis, The American University, Washington.

the past and being swamped by the increasing constraints of public accountability'.[8] His list of eight key questions for music training institutions includes graduates' preparedness for diverse careers, wide-ranging artistic practice, collaboration across the cultural industries, accessible professional development and advanced-level training, strategic partnerships, and diversity of courses: 'basically, the training sector, working together with the music sector and other cultural institutions, has to realign its priorities if it is going to meet the needs of this changing world'.[9] The link between the practice and education of artists is summarized by Paul Costantoura:

> The arts sector needs to establish how it can most effectively deliver educational opportunities directly to Australians and how it can work with education professionals … to bring this about … Success as a professional artist in Australia involves at least the same suite of skills expected of any person who chooses to set up a small business.[10]

Rafaele Marcellino and Harriet Cunningham warn that 'in so many ways, if the tertiary music institutions fail to address current demands of music as it exists outside of the University, then they themselves will fail'.[11] Warnings such as this have led to the formation of various initiatives designed to address the dilemma of educating musicians. The seven commissions of the International Society for Music Education (ISME) include a Commission for the Education of the Professional Musician, which first met formally in 1974. The changing priorities of the Commission are indicative of the increasing pressure on conservatories to meet the needs of graduates. The initial objective of the Commission includes reference to the 'unknown future' facing professional musicians:

> to develop direct ties and exchanges between music education institutes of different countries and regions and to collect and disseminate information on new ways in which educational institutions and curricula could better reflect and answer the needs of professional musicians in today's society, and to provide them with the skills and insights for an unknown future.[12]

Prior to 1986 the Commission focused largely on international mutual recognition of qualifications in music and music education. Since 1986 the Commission's research, discussion and activities have prioritized interactions between conservatories and the profession, technological and economic facets of training, the role of music

---

8   See Douglass Seaton, *Music and American Higher Eucation* (1997), retrieved 14 July 2003, from <http://www.music.org/InfoEdMusic/HigherEd/SumSeaton.html>. Peter Renshaw's comments were made at the CONNECTing With conference in 2002. The editorial summary is available at <http://www.gu.edu.au/school/qcgu/Connecting/content01_editorial_summary.html>.

9   Peter Renshaw, 'Remaking the Conservatorium Agenda', *Music Forum*, 8/5 (2002), retrieved 18 March 2004, from <http://www.mca.org.au/mf2008renshaw.hml>.

10   Paul Costantoura, *Australians and the Arts* (Sydney, NSW, 2000).

11   Raffaele Marcellino and Harriet Cunningham, 'Australian Tertiary Music Education', *Sounds Australian*, 60 (2002): 3–34.

12   Marie McCarthy, *Toward a Global Community: The International Society for Music Education 1953–2003* (Perth, WA, 2004).

competitions, the musician's role and place in global and changing contexts, reflective practice, and course content and objectives. Reinforcing its broader agenda, in 1996 the Commission adopted a new mission, namely to

> foster the recognition of the many modes of educating and training musicians, as those modes exist in various societies and cultures; and emphasize ways in which to enable present and future educators to employ modes of preparing musicians that reflect an awareness of the continually changing role of the musician in various societies and cultures.[13]

The Commission comprises practitioners and educators from six continents with experience in a wide variety of music and includes performers, composers, music scholars, educators, administrators and managers. Delegates debate and report research relating to the recognition of musical heritage, innovations in technology, and economic, social and political structures. The 1996 summary report states that

> to bring about change in a tertiary institution, the institution as a whole—leadership and teaching staff, decision makers and funders—as well as the public must recognise the need for change .... Educational institutions ... should at all times take the responsibility for establishing a process of adjusting educational policies, goals and structures to the world in which future musicians will work.[14]

Change

Conservatories have not failed to change; in fact, they have changed considerably in response to both internal and external influences. As recently as the 1960s diplomas in music focused primarily on performance in western classical music, baccalaureate degrees were comparatively rare and formal postgraduate study was still less common. As conservatories reacted to change and as many amalgamated with universities, curricula broadened to include subjects such as composition, pedagogy, musicology, jazz, contemporary and world musics; and the academic study of music became still more prominent in the latter half of the twentieth century with the advent of state-funded university education. This can be seen in the establishment of music as a standard university discipline in places such as North America. At the same time, competition between conservatories – particularly in Europe – led to the development of specialist courses in areas such as early music and ethnomusicology.

Principals of the seven music conservatories in England, all of which specialize in classical music performance, agreed in the 1990s on a range of initiatives to broaden the education of musicians. The results of these initiatives can be seen in projects such as the education programme run by the Royal Northern College of Music in conjunction with Manchester Metropolitan University, and orchestral placements offered by orchestras in collaboration with conservatories. Similar fieldwork initiatives can be found around the world in the form of conducting,

---

13 Giacomo M. Oliva (ed.), Preface, *The ISME Commission for the Education of the Professional Musician. The Musician's Role: New Challenges* (Lund, 1996), pp. 5–8.

14 Maria Aguilar, 'Education of the Professional Musician' (1998), retrieved 2 July 2002, from <http://www.mca.org.au/r18300.htm>.

teaching and performance placements. Several conservatorium projects have attempted to increase the level of business skills for musicians: for example, the 'Musikkiyrittäjyyden Kebittämisbanke' (MUSKE) project was founded by the continuing education centre at the Sibelius Academy in Sweden to develop entrepreneurship in music business. Recognizing the potential for a depth of experience and contact, the Mälmo School of Music brought together the non-performance demands of the music profession under a project-based, sequential series of units headed 'music communication'. The undergraduate music degree at Mälmo also includes a research unit that spans all three years of study, in which students conduct small studies relating to the sector and to their own and their peers' professional practice. The programme was found to provide a motivational platform for students to explore the profession, and provides an example of how curricula can be structured to facilitate self-discovery through situated or active learning: students' 'initiative and complete responsibility for the music in their study may cause a greater motivation than tasks set by teachers'.[15]

Ian Horsbrugh, previous principal of the Guildhall School of Music, advocated an innovative community music programme to develop students' communication, teaching and ensemble management skills. In 1990 Guildhall introduced a compulsory teaching module for performance students, and a community development project followed in 1995. Guildhall later attracted funding from the National Foundation for Youth Music to take music into low socio-economic suburbs in East London. Sean Gregory described the activities as enabling Guildhall to 'redefine its role in the community without compromising its reputation for excellence', although in the same year he described the performance and communication skills of trained musicians outside of the concert hall as 'second rate'.[16] The eclectic philosophy demonstrated by these initiatives is typical of the move towards a more multi-faceted curriculum. The reality, though, is that only a very small proportion of conservatorium students are exposed to the broader course options.

The system of individual tuition has been at the forefront of conservatorium curricula since the nineteenth century, but is currently under scrutiny. Conservatorium performance teachers are employed because of their reputation as performers, and most have no teacher qualifications or training. Roland Persson conducted case study research with instrumental teachers at a British university, and reported a lack of progressive and developmental teaching strategies and planning due to insufficient knowledge of individual learning and teaching: 'to be a formidable artist and a formidable teacher may well be the attributes of the same individual, but the two invariably describe different roles as well as different skills in different contexts'.[17]

---

15 Cecelia Hultberg, 'Instrumental Students' Strategies of Learning in Making Music', in O. Musumeci (ed.), *Preparing Musicians: Making Sound Worlds* (Barcelona, 2004), pp. 91–102.

16 Sean Gregory, 'Collaborative Approaches: Putting Colour in a Grey Area', paper presented at the CONNECTing With conference, Queensland Conservatorium, Brisbane, April 2002.

17 Roland Persson, 'Brilliant Performers as Teachers: A Case Study of Commonsense Teaching in a Conservatoire Setting', *International Journal of Music Education*, 28 (1996): 25–36.

Arguing for wider access to instrumental and vocal expertise, Helena Gaunt suggests that 'a wider spread of teachers is likely to mirror the increasingly diverse range of practices with which students will come into contact within the profession'.[18]

Pre-tertiary Education and Training

Change within pre-tertiary music training and experience is a global concern for conservatories: for example, changes in the Zimbabwean education system resulted in a recommendation to 'consider admitting applicants who are able to demonstrate talent in, say, computer music skills, but who may not have all of the formal academic and music performance pre-requisites that have been the norm up to now'.[19] Similarly, fundamental changes to Australian pre-tertiary music education have increased uncertainty about the appropriateness of tertiary music structure and content for incoming and graduating students. Future students will enter tertiary music education with vastly different skills and knowledge than ever before as a result of amendments to upper-high school curricula and the implementation of new pre-tertiary courses.

Australia has an enviable system of Technical and Further Education (TAFE). Training is most commonly delivered by TAFE Colleges; however, growing numbers of Australian high school students have the opportunity to graduate with a recognized qualification such as a certificate in hospitality, business or music. In reality, school-based delivery of an entire training package is difficult given the limited human and physical resources, particularly in a rural or regional area. Collaborative programmes between schools and TAFE providers are an inevitable and welcome consequence, and are increasingly common.

An industry training package (ITP) is a collection of resources intended to address industry training needs.[20] Training packages comprise a series of agreed qualifications made up of nationally endorsed competency standards for which have been developed assessment guidelines, materials, and learning strategies including curricula. First endorsed in 1997 as a result of the Australian federal government's training reform agenda, by 2006 almost 140 industry training packages had been developed for industry areas as diverse as metalliferous mining and graphic design.

Many aspects of training packages could be adopted for use in the development of new tertiary curricula. Unlike traditional music performance courses, the Music ITP

---

18 Helena Gaunt, 'One-to-One Relationships: A Case Study of Teachers' Perspectives on Instrumental/Vocal Lessons in a Conservatoire', in O. Musumeci (ed.), *The ISME Commission for Education of the Professional Musician. Preparing Musicians: Making Sound Worlds* (Barcelona, 2004), pp. 55–69.

19 Dumisani Maraire, 'The Task of Preparing Future Musicians in a Once Colonized Developing Country', in G.M. Oliva (ed.), *The ISME Commission for the Education of the Professional Musician 1996 Seminar. The Musician's Role: New Challenges* (Lund, 1996), pp. 35–51.

20 Australian National Training Authority, *Standards for Registered Training Providers* (Melbourne, Vic., 2001). Training packages also come with toolboxes of resources. The music tools are at <http://www.ntis.gov.au/?/trainingpackage/CUS01http://search.resourcegenerator. gov.au/search.ashx?search=noted&term=CUS01>.

places equal importance on practical skills in music performance or composition, the application of technology, and skills in business and management. A training package is designed to be flexible in structure, enabling students to create a package of units relevant to their vocational needs. In addition, the structure encourages students to become multi-skilled by facilitating specialization in one stream at the same time as they develop skills in others. There is extensive use of real and simulated work experience, and existing competencies are recognized so that students can apply for course credit and can focus their attention instead on other areas of their development. Students can also customize their course by importing units from other training packages. Training packages are also appropriate for professional development, although in reality it is very difficult – at least in music – to secure places for part-time study. In 2003 an ITP for the music sector replaced with a common curriculum the existing courses at all TAFE institutions. Standardization of courses into a single ITP is designed to facilitate the portability of qualifications across Australia, such that all providers are obliged to mutually recognize and give credit for students' current competencies and prior learning.

The Music ITP was developed in consultation with practitioners; thus the content of vocational-level courses (from Certificate IV to the Advanced Diploma) reflects the skills and knowledge identified by those within the profession as necessary for building sustainable careers. In line with the consultation process employed during their development, the courses were reviewed in 2004 to ensure currency and to reflect the feedback of practitioners and educators. Units within the ITP are categorized as core (compulsory), key elective, and unit bank (portable units from the music and other training packages).

Articulation pathways between TAFE and university have continued to gain importance within a highly competitive sector. Universities offer TAFE graduates up to two years' credit for an Advanced Diploma, although few have embraced the potential for collaborative programmes and seamless articulation. Analysis of the nine core units within the four ITP performance courses, using the same categories of study as earlier defined, reveals that the core (compulsory) units belong to the categories 'business studies' (six units) and 'experience and industry awareness' (three units). The units include the study of occupational health and safety, industry knowledge and negotiation skills: generic skills that are absolutely vital to the careers of all musicians. Specialist studies such as those in performance are included as elective units for selection according to students' career aspirations and potential.

The international trend is towards diversification of university courses, and recent Australian survey data (2004) indicates a growing trend towards collaborative and combined degree programmes that offer a much more diverse choice of course options for informed applicants. The same survey indicates that the number of pre-tertiary courses operating within universities and outside of the TAFE system increased by 500 per cent between 2002 and 2004.[21] In part this reflects the perceived contemporary music focus of the music ITP together with a reduction in the number of funded places available for TAFE study in non-priority areas such as music.

---

21 Helen Lancaster, *Post-Secondary Music Education Guide* (August, 2004), retrieved 22 October 2004, from <http://www.amcoz.com.au/education.htm>.

In the high school system, Western Australian university entrance courses (Courses of Study) were formed as a result of the Post-Compulsory Education Review. Complementing curricular modifications within the TAFE sector with the adoption of a much broader scope, the new Courses of Study are indicative of similar reviews in other Australian states and territories.[22] Designed to meet the needs of all students through the inclusion of general and vocational education, workplace learning and university experience, recommendation 28 of the Review advised

> that the Curriculum Council undertake negotiations with universities, the Department of Training and Employment, and VET training providers to ensure that courses of study and the level statements identified on the scales of achievement are recognised for the purpose of selection to post-school destinations.[23]

The implications for school teachers and tertiary educators in meeting the requirements of incoming students and the demands of the profession are manifold.

Undergraduate Study in Classical Music Performance

Although many conservatories around the world have changed in response to the demands of the profession, changes within the education sector have often been overwhelming. This has been seen in Australia over the past 25 years. In 1982 each Australian state was required by the federal government to combine smaller Colleges of Advanced Education (CAEs), reducing the total number from 79 to 47. Sixteen of the 47 remaining institutions (including conservatories) offered music or music education courses. Six years later, the Australian Higher Education Policy mandated institutions with less than 2000 students to merge with a university, as a result of which CAEs and universities were combined in 1991 to create a single sector known as the unified national system (UNS).[24] Over the course of these changes, Australia's three autonomous conservatories also amalgamated with universities. A small number of conservatories remain independent of their affiliate university, but the majority have become a university department, often devolving leadership to the non-discipline leader of a larger humanities faculty. Ironically, the devolution does not seem to have lessened the paperwork: one musician commented that 'the universities are so tied up in administration these days that they barely have enough time to put together the courses'.

Further cuts to higher education in the late 1990s led to additional amalgamation and far less budgetary control at the departmental level. The National Council of Heads of Tertiary Music Schools (NACHTMUS) has since raised with the Australian federal government many difficulties resulting from the UNS, the results of which have been much more complex than expected. Issues raised by NACHTMUS include funding for individual tuition and small group teaching,

---

22 Course of Study information, including proposed implementation dates, can be found at <http://www.curriculum.wa.edu.au/pages/pcreview/stagetwo/COS.html>.

23 Curriculum Council, *Post-Compulsory Education Review* (Perth, WA, 2000).

24 This period of change is often referred to as the Dawkins reform era. The policy statement: J. Dawkins, *Higher Education Policy. A Policy Statement* (Canberra, ACT, 1988).

artist residencies, recognition of creative research output and financial capital for physical resources. According to NACHTMUS, Australian conservatories are underfunded when compared to their overseas counterparts. This is due in part to university amalgamation, which has resulted in music schools having to vie for a share of already limited funding: 'many other resource-hungry fields such as science, medicine and engineering do not see why they should be subsidising a music school'.[25]

Australia Council data for the year 2000 illustrate that music was the most commonly offered arts discipline in Australia; a total of 26 institutions offered 312 courses incorporating 159 undergraduate degree courses and 121 postgraduate degree courses. The 5,528 people enrolled in music-related courses studied a total of 3,428 equivalent full-time units (EFTSU). An Australian survey conducted in 2004 reported a drop in the number of courses: a total of 246 courses included 106 undergraduate degree courses, 105 postgraduate courses, and 35 diploma and certificate courses from the pre-tertiary sector. Taking into account widespread implementation of the music industry training package (ITP), it is likely that the 35 pre-tertiary courses comprised multiple listings of the six ITP courses and approximately five non-ITP courses that are situated outside of the regular TAFE system.

The unmet potential for artists to make a substantial contribution to culture in a myriad of ways is obvious, and it would appear logical for musicians' training to include preparation for a range of educational and community roles. Listed in Table 4.1, in 2004 there were 24 Australian undergraduate degrees with a stream in classical music performance, three of which were delivered by private institutions and 21 of which were affiliated with a university. In order to determine the weighting given to subject areas within each degree, categories of study were derived from the curricula of the 24 bachelor degrees and a structural analysis was undertaken of the performance stream within each one. Analysis comprised the compulsory units within the performance stream of each degree. Categories of study are defined in Table 4.2, and the curricular weighting of each category is illustrated in Figure 4.1.

Training within a university context has led to inevitable conflict between academic and practical training requirements. Of concern within existing courses is the minimal emphasis given to teaching skills, research and self-directed study, experience in the workplace, career awareness, business skills, and music technologies.

Skills in both music technologies and information communications technology (ICT) are used extensively by musicians to run small businesses and for a variety of applications such as composition, recording, arrangement and the production of teaching resources. A survey of paid artists in the US, which included a subset of musicians, songwriters and music publishers, found that 83 per cent of artists use the Internet: 20 per cent more than the overall adult population.

---

25 Michael Hannan, 'The Future of Tertiary Music Training in Australia', *Australian Music Forum*, 7(3) (2001), available at <http://www.mca.org.au/index.php?id=147>.

Table 4.1   Australian Undergraduate Performance Degrees in Classical Music, 2003

Name of School	Affiliate University	Course Analysed
Australian Capital Territory		
School of Music	Australian National University	Bachelor of Music
New South Wales		
Australian Institute of Music	No affiliation (private)	Bachelor of Music
Australian International Conservatorium of Music	No affiliation (private)	Bachelor of Music
Department of Music	University of Sydney	Bachelor of Music
Faculty of Creative Arts	University of Wollongong	Bachelor of Creative Arts (Music and Theatre)
Newcastle Conservatorium	University of Newcastle	Bachelor of Music
School of Music	Wesley Institute (private)	Bachelor of Arts in Music Performance
School of Music and Music Education	University of New South Wales	Bachelor of Music
Sydney Conservatorium of Music	University of Sydney	Bachelor of Music
Northern Territory		
School of Creative Arts and Humanities	Charles Darwin University	Bachelor of Music
Queensland		
Central Queensland Conservatorium of Music	Central Queensland University	Bachelor of Music
College of Music, Visual Arts and Theatre	James Cook University	Bachelor of Music
Department of Music	University of Southern Queensland	Bachelor of Music
Queensland Conservatorium	Griffith University	Bachelor of Music
School of Music	University of Queensland	Bachelor of Music
South Australia		
Elder Conservatorium	University of Adelaide	Bachelor of Music
Tasmania		
Conservatorium of Music	University of Tasmania	Bachelor of Music
Victoria		
Faculty of Music	University of Melbourne	Bachelor of Music
Melba Memorial Conservatorium of Music	Victoria University of Technology	Bachelor of Music
School of Music	Australian Catholic University	Bachelor of Music
School of Music Conservatorium	Monash University	Bachelor of Arts Bachelor of Music
Victorian College of the Arts School of Music	University of Melbourne	Bachelor of Music Performance
Western Australia		
School of Music	University of Western Australia	Bachelor of Music
Western Australian Academy of Performing Arts	Edith Cowan University	Bachelor of Performing Arts (Music)

Table 4.2   Categories of Study within Australian Performance Degrees, 2003

Business Studies
•   Project management •   Small business skills •   Law (including copyright) •   Community cultural development •   Arts management •   Grant writing •   Information communications technology (ICT) skills
Communication Skills
•   Interpersonal skills •   Ensemble management
Core Studies
•   Musicianship •   History •   Composition and arrangement •   Musicology
Ensemble Training
Experience and Industry Awareness
•   Work placements in performance and non-performance roles •   Career planning •   Cultural industry studies •   Community music
Music Technologies
•   Music software and hardware •   Sound design •   Performance technology •   MIDI systems and application •   Broadcasting and recording
Practical Training
•   Individual tuition •   Performance seminars, workshops and master classes •   Performance psychology •   Performance wellness: physiology and injury prevention strategies •   Non-classical genres
Research and Self-directed Study
•   Research techniques •   Independent study units
Teaching Skills
•   Instrumental pedagogy •   Instructional design •   Curricular studies

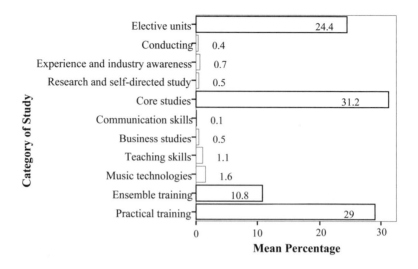

Figure 4.1   Category of Study Weighting within Australian BMus Courses

The project director summarizes that for 'independent musicians, in particular, this newfound ability to bypass traditional distribution outlets and geographic boundaries has been liberating'.[26] Andy Arthurs writes that 'the digital revolution has brought new opportunities for creative musicians, not only in the timbral music palettes that are now available at an affordable cost ... but also in the means and ease of distribution'.[27] It has also changed the face of the recording industry; music technologies have enabled musicians to become increasingly independent with respect to the production and promotion of their artistic product.

Nadel notes that an architect is not a designer of buildings but a business person whose product is architecture; similarly a musician is a business person whose 'product' results in music.[28] Business skills are a key component of musicians' practice. Combined as 'business practices', 73 per cent of musicians in the study use management skills (defined by musicians as the management of people); business skills (defined as the administrative skills used to run a small business); and marketing skills (defined as the promotion of skills or product). Musicians draw attention to the need for business skills to be included in music education and training, and lament that 'preparation for a career in classical music as a performer is often too focussed on the art and not enough on the business, social and cultural

---

26 Music Industry News Network, 'Artists and Musicians are Enthusiastic Internet Users' (12 July 2004), retrieved 21 December 2004, from <http://www.mi2n.com/print.php3>.

27 Andy Arthurs, 'Why Creative Industries?', *Australian Music Forum,* 10(5), (2004): 32–5.

28 See H. Nadel, *Exploring Ways to Strengthen a Practice for Long-Term Growth* (March 1998), retrieved 20 March 2002, from <http://www.isdesignet.com/Magazine/Mar'98sprep. html>.

conditions that performers must be a part of'; 'I needed to learn how to run a small business from scratch.'

The curricular emphasis on performance skills within classical music courses is to be expected considering the competitive nature and high standards of the classical music profession. However, performance will constitute the major or the only source of economic activity for a minuscule proportion of graduates: protean careers are 'entirely normal careers for music graduates'.[29] In the case of that small proportion, it is extremely unlikely that performance will remain the sole focus throughout an entire career. In any case, performance-oriented musicians require a vast range of non-performance skills and knowledge in order to achieve their performance objectives.

Philosophical Frameworks

How does the core content of the 24 Australian courses relate to the philosophical frameworks that underpin them? According to NASM, the prime objective of all music programmes is to 'provide the opportunity for every music student to develop individual potentialities to the utmost'.[30] NASM defines graduate attributes as follows: technical skills at a high enough standard for entry into the profession; possession of a logical group of artistic and intellectual objectives; and the skills to create and administer professional work. In common with the NASM guidelines cited earlier in this chapter, there has been no formal identification of the artistic and intellectual skills and objectives required by musicians to sustain professional practice. George Odam maintains that whereas 'in the earlier establishments the [conservatorium] students were to be conserved, that is, protected, reared, and trained, in the newer institutions, without any clearly defined change of mission, the focus began to shift from those who are taught to that which is taught'.[31] Michael Hannan agrees: 'a case may be made that the kinds of personal attributes being promoted in the graduate attributes policies are out of sync with the culture of the music industry'.[32]

Graham Bartle suggests that in Australia we train professional musicians 'because they are there to be trained'.[33] Describing the rationale as elitist, he continues by questioning the extent to which professional musicians are trained to communicate music to the communities in which they will work. The majority of performance degree placements are based on the aspirations and talents of students, whereas in

29 Marcellino and Cunningham, 'Australian Tertiary Music Education'.

30 National Association of Schools of Music, *Music Data Summaries* (2001), retrieved 22 February 2002, from <http://heads.arts-accredit.org/index.jsp>.

31 George Odam, 'Developing a Conservatoire: Research, Professional Development and Widening Participation', in O. Musumeci (ed.), *The ISME Commission for Education of the Professional Musician. Preparing Musicians: Making Sound Worlds* (Barcelona, 2004), pp. 175–83.

32 Michael Hannan, 'Preparing Musicians for the Commercial Music Industry', in O. Musumeci (ed.), *The ISME Commission for Education of the Professional Musician. Preparing Musicians: Making Sound Worlds* (Barcelona, 2004), pp. 69–80.

33 Graham Bartle, 'Feet on the Ground – Head in the Clouds', in G.M. Oliva (ed.), *The ISME Commission for the Education of the Professional Musician 1996 Seminar. The Musician's Role: New Challenges* (Lund, 1996), pp. 183–94.

Denmark 'enrolment in music higher education is based upon an evaluation of the needs of society, noting that the system will only produce what is seen as necessary ... What is necessary in Denmark is to educate the community as much as possible'.[34] Along the same lines, Ki-Beom Jang advocates the renovation of music curricula 'based upon the needs of the society and the student'.[35] Jang reports that Korean college music programmes do not meet the requirements of the profession, with the result that graduates are not qualified to apply for available non-performance positions when performance work is insufficient. Of 100,000 Korean graduate pianists, Jang estimates that only one will achieve the status of a top soloist.[36] Vetter reports a lack of documentation relating to the goals and purposes of university music programmes; his survey of faculty and students determined that students 'were not clear on what the goals were and faculty respondents claimed they had no goals'. Nielsen describes mission statements as often being 'a collection of platitudes and clichés';[37] however, the provision of clear programme goals or course objectives 'could be one step towards a better understanding of the nature of the degree and its effects on students' careers'.[38] The philosophy of each course should epitomize its *raison d'être*, its ethical position, its expectations, its value and its public image.

A broad approach was taken to determine the philosophy of Australia's 24 Bachelor of Music degrees. In cases where course objectives were not found in available course literature, course providers were asked to provide a rationale, mission statement, underpinning philosophy or objectives. Akin to Vetter's findings, only 14 (58 per cent) of the 24 institutions were able to provide the requested details. Several responded that there was no underpinning philosophy, and two institutions were unable to differentiate between course objectives and graduate attribute statements. Illustrated in Table 4.3 in decreasing order of frequency, the 14 existing philosophies were analysed in terms of the frequency with which categories of study are emphasized. In contrast to the weightings within categories of study, core studies do not feature strongly within the course philosophies, which focus almost entirely on practical training without addressing the diversity of roles in which future graduates are likely to work. This is often more of a marketing exercise than an informed judgement. It would appear that the objectives of the traditional, performance-based Bachelor of Music are unclear.

---

34 Larry Smith, 'Training the Performing Artist: More Than Music', in G.M. Oliva (ed.), *The ISME Commission for the Education of the Professional Musician 1996 Seminar. The Musician's Role: New Challenges* (Lund, 1996), pp. 117–21.

35 Ki-Beom Jang, 'Dear Friends! Let Us Start Over', in G.M. Oliva (ed.), *The ISME Commission for the Education of the Professional Musician 1996 Seminar. The Musician's Role: New Challenges* (Lund, 1996), pp. 125–36.

36 Ibid.

37 Ken Nielsen, 'Your Mission, Assuming You Choose to Ignore it ...', *Australian Music Forum*, 11/1 (2004): 42.

38 T. Vetter, 'The University Music Performance Program: Performance or Liberal Arts Degree? The Case of Voice Performance', unpublished Master's thesis, University of Toronto, Ontario, 1990.

Table 4.3   Categories of Study as Emphasized in Course Philosophies (f)

Categories of study	Frequency with which each theme arose	%
Practical training	26	37
Music technologies	10	14
Research and self-directed study	8	11
Teaching skills	8	11
Diversity of musical genre	6	9
Core studies	6	9
Experience and industry awareness	4	6
Ensemble training	2	3
Conducting	0	0
Communication skills	0	0
Business studies	0	0

The focus on performance is indicative not only of the philosophy but of the curricular structure of the courses, which negatively impacts the ability of graduates to build sustainable careers. The dilemma is an ethical one. In the year 2000, the British Musicians' Union was the second largest music union in the world. Of its 31,000 members, 85 per cent were freelance musicians running their own small businesses. It is hardly surprising that the Metier report commissioned by the union concludes that music education 'is focussed exclusively on music and performance skills, and not enough in ancillary skills such as business and freelance skills'.[39] Similarly, and reflecting Bartle's earlier comments, Rick Rogers is critical of the lack of generic skills such as communication within existing curricula. Having found that 72 per cent of musicians engage in teaching, he concludes that in 'their formation as artists, creative people are not commonly trained to communicate their process of "making" in a classroom. And they cannot be expected to work in the school setting intuitively'.[40] Artists are the foremost advocates of creating and performing, and yet few are trained to communicate the process to others. The need for student musicians to learn appropriate communication skills within an ensemble environment is evident in Henry Kingsbury's anthropological study of a conservatorium.[41] Observing the political turmoil of a college orchestra, he cites a student's claim that the orchestra is not about 'music', but rather about 'orchestra'. He situates the comment in 'the unpleasant social-institutional context of the tensions in the orchestra' as though the environment so described is something quite normal, and mirrors Crouch and Lovric's observation of the '"incestuousness" [sic] of social relationships within the profession'.[42] Communication skills were the single most important skill set for

---

39 Metier, *The Music Industry: Skills and Training Needs in the 21st Century* (London, 2000).

40 Rick Rogers, *Creating a Land with Music* (London, 2002).

41 Henry Kingsbury, *Music, Talent and Performance: A Conservatory Cultural System* (Philadelphia, 1988).

42 Mira Crouch and J. Lovric, *Paths to Performance: Gender as a Theme in Professional Music Careers. A Pilot Study of Players in Two Orchestras* (Sydney, NSW, 1990).

62 per cent of the UK musicians included in Rogers's study.[43] Although musicians are ideally placed to communicate their musical experience to a wider audience, they are at least initially ill-equipped to embrace such opportunities. Musicians emphasize that communication skills underpin their ability to create and sustain professional networks, and that they are essential to a musician's practice whether in an orchestral role, a teaching role, or in running a freelance business: 'learning to network effectively is a learned skill useful in virtually every field'.

Community cultural development (CCD) is a growing area that provides opportunities for musicians to communicate their work within diverse community settings. Although CCD involvement is increasingly a pre-requisite for funding, most musicians don't possess the requisite skills to make such applications. It is essential for musicians to be conversant with elements of community cultural development such as giving workshops, and this highlights the need for experiential learning and vocationally relevant skills to be incorporated into musicians' training. The lack of artist skills in this area was highlighted by a visual artist: 'the focus of funding has changed. Employment and funding are now related to community arts activities: CCD workshops etc. Money is often available, but artists don't know how to access it'. Musicians report limited opportunities for training and initial experience in community engagement, and yet feel the pressure to demonstrate prior experience. This could explain why musicians are less likely than other artists to apply for funding, and why practising musicians stress the need for skills in grant and submission writing.

Interviewed by Marcellino and Cunningham, one Australian tertiary music provider admitted that 'an inordinately large percentage [of graduates] are fully employed but in a combination of part-time and casual work'.[44] Despite the recognition of graduate destinations, the institution concerned includes no career planning or business units in its undergraduate curriculum. The representative of a second institution was quite clear about the fact that the 'majority of students have pursued teaching careers'. Again, despite a clear indication of graduate destinations, a look at the curriculum reveals that there is no compulsory pedagogy unit in the degree course. The likelihood of graduates undertaking at least some teaching activity ought to be reflected in conservatorium curricula, and not just for the development of teaching skills. As Janet Ritterman articulates, pedagogy training will assist students to understand the teaching process and as a consequence to become better learners; will encourage and empower graduates to train as teachers; will enable performing musicians to successfully assume community music roles; and will in turn facilitate high level performance training to music pedagogy students.[45]

Mathilda Joubert describes a 'double jeopardy' situation in that sustained arts study is no longer a requirement of primary school teacher training, nor does the

---

43 See Rick Rogers, *Creating a Land with Music* (London, 2002). The report can be downloaded via The Sound Station, at http://www.thesoundstation.org.uk/adult_site/Downloads/HEFCEreport1.pdf.

44 Marcellino and Cunningham, 'Australian Tertiary Music Education'.

45 Desmond Mark, 'The Music Teacher's Dilemma – Musician or Teacher?', *International Journal of Music Education*, 32 (1998): 3–23.

training of artists carry a requirement of teacher training.[46] These issues are strongly refected in Australia: in all Australian states other than Queensland the provision of music education in state-funded primary schools is the responsibility of generalist teachers who have an average of only 23 hours of music education within their teacher training.[47] The situation led to the Australian National Review of School Music Education, which resulted in the establishment of teaching awards, funding for resources and the development of a portal for networking, professional development and the sharing of expertise and resources. Critically, the Review recommended that every primary school should have access to a specialist music teacher.[48]

Contemporary and Digital Music Study

Globalization has had a profound influence on the level of interaction between the music sector and the wider cultural sphere. One result is that few musicians are involved only with classical music; rather, musicians are musically multi-lingual. The involvement of musicians in a plethora of musical genres and cultures leads to the conclusion that musicians need to be conversant in multiple musical genres. Working in multiple genres increases the opportunities for, and the enjoyment derived from, performance: 'trying new styles and genres has contributed greatly to my life as a musician'; 'in opening to other genres, my classical performances have increased'; 'I practise and perform classical music because I love the discipline; I practise and perform my own and contemporary music because I love the freedom of it'. Practising musicians strongly recommend the inclusion of multiple genres within formal education and training: 'A broader understanding of many types of music and styles should be incorporated into the course ... one should be a well-rounded musician.' Knowledge of multiple genres is also crucial to musicians' teaching: 'teachers need to know classical, jazz and contemporary musical styles'.

Musicians' involvement with both classical and non-classical music deems the structure and content of non-classical degrees to be of relevance to all musicians. Over three-quarters of the 292 classical musicians who responded to Rogers's survey of musicians performed in at least two other genres,[49] and the majority of classically trained musicians cannot realistically expect to pursue a career entirely in classical music: not even within the orchestral repertoire. Helen Lancaster, Chair of the aforementioned Australian survey of tertiary music education, suggests that

> the majority consensus—certainly it is so in Europe and creeping into Australia—is that the term 'classical musician' may not apply at all in future years, and we should be

---

46 Mathilda Joubert, All Our Futures: Creativity, Culture and Education (London, 1999).

47 See Thomas Canter, 'The Good, the Bad and the Ugly of Classroom Music', *available via the Music Council of Australia at <http://www.mca.org.au/index.php?id=401>*. See also the Australia Music Council website for their advocacy work on music education: <www.mca.org.au>.

48 The full review report is available at <http://www.dest.gov.au/sectors/school_ education/publications_resources/profiles/school_music_education.htm>.

49 Rick Rogers, *Response to the Working in Music Project* (2004), retrieved 28 May 2004, from <http://www.musiceducation.rcm.ac.uk/rogersresponse.htm>.

looking more to the 'composite' musician, or just 'musician'. Classicists will be even more specialised, marginal, than they have been before.[50]

There has been a marked and welcome increase in the availability of formal study in contemporary, world and digital music. In describing the establishment of the Institute for Popular Music (IPM) and the Liverpool Institute for Performing Arts (LIPA), Martin Featherstone-Witty describes a practical philosophy with seven key elements:

- versatility [in] … vocational studies (performance, business and collaboration);
- extensive practical performance training;
- preparation for the real world of work;
- the opportunity to work and study across age ranges and peer groups, (breaking down barriers between staff and students);
- an emphasis on the popular and contemporary;
- a socially and ethnically mixed pupil intake; and
- work in the local community.[51]

The institutions in Liverpool were established as an educational partnership between the public and private sectors and included professional artists, the European Commission, the British government and educators. Their philosophy alludes to careers in which performance, business and collaborative skills co-exist: also the case for classically trained musicians. According to the IPM web site, ideal vocational qualities for the musician include a passion for music; legal and contractual knowledge; practical involvement in multiple genres; technological knowledge; understanding of the cultural industries; artistic and intellectual rights; and business: all qualities that are needed by classically trained musicians. Strangely enough, teaching skills are not mentioned as either essential or desirable qualities. The philosophy of Berklee College of Music emphasizes the development of careers throughout the profession of music, and is reflected in an eclectic curriculum and enviable community programmes such as the City Music programme that provides free music education to inner-city Boston youth:

> Through a course of scholarly and practical learning experiences integrating performance and writing, our curriculum covers the variety of influential styles, relevant technologies, and career opportunities open to today's music professional … a Berklee student is likely to become friends with future producers, engineers, record company executives, composers, arrangers, performers, educators, and music therapists.[52]

It is unfortunate that the performance major does not include a compulsory unit in pedagogy, career development or business.

In Australia, an emphasis on broader graduate attributes and vocational skills in the 1990s led to increased opportunities for the study of contemporary and digital music as shown in Table 4.4. Contemporary music studies have contributed to the

---

50 Helen Lancaster, personal communication, 13 August 2003.

51 Martin Featherstone-Witty, *Optimistic, Even Then: The Creation of Two Performing Arts Institutes* (London, 2001).

52 Berklee College of Music (2007). See their website at <http://www.berklee.edu/about/>.

Table 4.4   Undergraduate Non-classical Music Degrees in Australia, 2003[53]

Year first delivered	Name of School	Affiliate University	Location	Course Analysed
Australian Capital Territory				
Not available	Australian Centre for the Arts and Technology, National Institute for the Arts		Australian National University	Bachelor of Arts (Digital Arts)
New South Wales				
1998	Centre for Contemporary Music		Southern Cross University	Bachelor of Contemporary Music
1999	Department of Contemporary Music Studies		Macquarie University	Bachelor of Arts (Contemporary Music)
1984	Faculty of Creative Arts		University of Wollongong	Bachelor of Creative Arts (Music Performance)
1988 (NSW) 2000 (VIC)	JMC Academy		University of New England	Bachelor of Arts (Music)
2004	School of Audio Engineering (private institution)		Affiliated with Middlesex & Southern Cross Universities	Bachelor of Digital Media
2000 1970	School of Contemporary Arts, Music/Electronic Arts		University of Western Sydney	Bachelor of Electronic Arts
1994	Sydney Conservatorium of Music		University of Sydney	Bachelor of Music Performance (Jazz)
2005	Sydney Conservatorium of Music		University of Sydney	Bachelor of Music Studies
1980	Victorian College of the Arts		University of Melbourne	Bachelor of Music Performance (Improvisation)
Queensland				
Not available	Faculty of Creative Industries		Queensland University of Technology	Bachelor of Music
1999	Queensland Conservatorium of Music		Griffith University	Bachelor of Popular Music, Bachelor of Music Technology
South Australia				
2002	Elder Conservatorium of Music		Adelaide University	Bachelor of Music Studies
Victoria				
1995	Faculty of Arts		Monash University	Bachelor of Performing Arts
1998	School of Education		RMIT	Bachelor of Arts (Music Industry)
Western Australia				
1993	Western Australian Academy of Performing Arts		Edith Cowan University	Bachelor of Music (Jazz)

53 Every effort was made to ensure the accuracy of the information contained within Tables 4.1 and 4.4, which were derived from online and other course information issued from each institution. In many cases, conflicting course information led to direct institutional inquiries and reliance on information from a single institutional representative. Each institution was invited to check the accuracy of the information.

increasing lack of distinction between TAFE and university programmes, evident in Australia where over four times as many graduates progress from university study to TAFE than from TAFE to university. In fact, TAFE institutions are an increasingly common destination for university graduates seeking vocational skills. Recognizing the availability of multiple study options, Richard Vella suggests that 'traditional music departments and conservatoriums are losing intellectual and creative status to other centres of inquiry and private industry'.[54]

To facilitate comparison with the skills and attributes utilized by musicians within their various roles, analysis was undertaken of the structure and content of five Australian contemporary performance degrees using categories consistent with those used for the classical music courses. Results for the non-classical degree courses are shown in Figure 4.2, and the two samples are shown together in Figure 4.3.

Comparison of the weighting between classical and contemporary music degrees demonstrates a distinct and somewhat logical difference in the emphasis given to skills in performance, core studies and music technologies.[55] Core (compulsory) studies within the classical programmes (31 per cent of compulsory unit weighting) encompass musicianship skills and the study of music history. In contrast, core studies within contemporary programmes (16 per cent) focus on developing the skills and knowledge necessary for a range of careers.

Sir Simon Rattle states that to 'be a performing artist in Britain in the next [twenty-first] century, you have to be an educator too'.[56] With the exception of six pedagogy units within Australia's 24 classical music performance degrees and a single communication unit within one of the contemporary degree programmes, neither sample included compulsory pedagogy or communication units, or more than a minimal focus on small business skills. As we will see in Chapter 6, classically trained musicians spend more time teaching than in any other activity, and teaching is also of critical importance to contemporary music graduates. Shown in Table 4.5, a Danish survey of alumni from contemporary music programmes found most graduates to be employed in a combination of teaching and performance roles.[57]

Surprisingly, research and scholarship including independent study receives more emphasis in contemporary programmes (4.2 per cent) than in the classical sample (0.5 per cent). Contemporary programmes also have a greater connection with the music sector, and work experience is often supported by the development of student portfolios including recordings, compositions and marketing materials. These aspects would be welcome additions to classical music study.

---

54 Richard Vella, 'Tertiary Music Education since 1988', in John Whiteoak and Aline Scott-Maxwell (eds), *Currency Companion to Music and Dance in Australia* (Sydney, NSW, 2003).

55 Determining the emphasis placed on music technologies is difficult because technology in particular is often used as a teaching tool, and is therefore often learned within the context of a specific subject area such as aural training, musicianship or composition.

56 Sir Simon Rattle, cited in Mathilda Joubert, *All Our Futures: Creativity, Culture and Education* (London, 1999).

57 Jan Ole Traasdahl, 'Rhythmic Music Education in Denmark', in G.M. Oliva (ed.), *The ISME Commission for the Education of the Professional Musician 1996 Seminar. The Musician's Role: New Challenges* (Lund, 1996), pp. 67–74.

Table 4.5   Danish Contemporary Music Graduate Destinations 1990–1993

Industry Roles	Engagement (%)
Performer	6
Music teacher	4
Performer and teacher	50
Performer and composer	11
Performer, teacher and composer	24
Performer, producer and arranger	5
Total	100

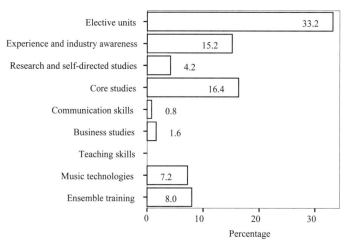

Figure 4.2   Category of Study Weighting within Contemporary Music Degrees (mean)

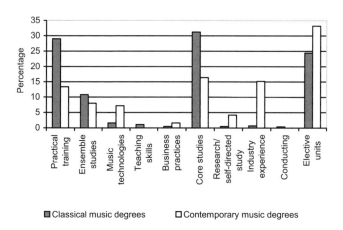

Figure 4.3   Comparison of Weighting between the Categories of Study within Classical and Contemporary Music Performance Degrees

Where do Graduates Go?

Before we look at the fate of performance graduates, I would like to state that this is not an exercise in 'conservatorium bashing'. There is a complex range of issues at play when determining performance curricula and the process is far from easy given that employment characteristics are so poorly understood and graduate destination surveys measure full-time employment with a single employer: a rare situation within music and the cultural sector as a whole.

Resembling national economic data collections, Australian graduate destination data collections were not designed to take into account sporadic employment or protean careers, and consequently they do not accurately record music graduate destinations. Formal tracking of graduates is vital to conservatories that wish to assess the career paths of graduates in line with course philosophy, curricular content and structure; and yet institutional graduate tracking rarely occurs. Given the poor employment rate for graduates, it is possible that low employment is a major factor in the absence of graduate tracking among music institutions. As long ago as 1969 concern was expressed at a UNESCO seminar about the lack of performance positions available to Australian performance graduates, and a demographic survey of employment trends and graduate numbers was proposed. Of the 26 Australian institutions surveyed by Marcellino and Cunningham 33 years later (in 2002), only eight formally track their graduates. In 2004 Helen Lancaster's survey of Australian conservatories posed an initial question relating to graduate tracking. There was a response rate of 73 per cent to the question, out of which 85 per cent of respondents claimed to track graduates. However, analysis of responses to a subsequent open question reveals that much of the graduate tracking takes the form of informal alumni contact and music networks.

In the US, the College Music Society (CMS) and NASM gather extensive annual graduate and student data. CMS reported in 2001 that just over half of music performance graduates were 'gainfully employed' in music making.[58] In that academic year there were 317,912 music students in the US: 2 per cent of the total student population.[59] CMS data confirm that 42 per cent of the music majors at that time were studying music performance. If you combine CMS data with NASM figures, it is apparent that of the 42 per cent of students majoring in music performance (133,523 students), 48 per cent ($N = 64,091$) of graduates were not employed in the performance field. The figures reflect Goodman's earlier suggestion (in 1970) that only 13 per cent of United States music school graduates would become professional performers.[60] The situation is replicated in the most prestigious schools: Barbara Sand describes Juilliard graduates as pouring 'out of Juilliard into a very small

58 College Music Society data cited in the review from the first Music Educational Professional Development Institute, held in Evanston, Illinois in 2001: *Music Teacher Education for this Century: a Working Institute for Change and Innovation in our Profession* (Montana, 2001).

59 National Association of Schools of Music, *Music Data Summaries* (2001), retrieved 22 February 2002, from <http://heads.arts-accredit.org/index.jsp>.

60 C. J. Goodman, 'Will the Next Mozart Please Step Forward: A Progress Report on the Singular, Expensive Business of Training America's Best Musicians' (California, 1970).

funnel en route to the classical music stream', and at least 27 per cent of the 1994 Juilliard graduates were found to have left music altogether.[61]

The scarcity of employment roles is reflected in other performance fields. When former British Prime Minister Margaret Thatcher was asked about arts training, she responded: 'Why train for unemployment?' At the time, 84 per cent of the actors registered with the performer's trade union, Equity, were unemployed. The figure is significant because Equity represents 37,000 performers and is the largest trade union of its kind. Recent research in the US and Australia has reiterated that performance graduates are unlikely to secure performance positions: Janis Weller posits that 'jobs, per se, are proportionally few in relationship to the vast numbers of highly qualified graduates in the field of music' and Michael Hannan proposes there to be 'an oversupply of graduates' in music performance.[62] Describing the established objective of the conservatorium as the production of high calibre performers for work in orchestras, opera houses and concert halls, Hannan suggests it to be 'difficult to make a case that even a small percentage of graduates are finding this kind of employment'.[63]

To make matters worse, the competitive nature and high demand for conservatorium places has changed. Conservatories traditionally received many more applicants than they had places available, and competition for places was reflected in a correspondingly high level of performance standard. As students make informed choices based upon a broad range of study options and career paths and as the number of private providers has increased, many conservatories have begun to actively recruit students in order to meet target student numbers. No longer can they set a benchmark and select only students who surpass it, resulting in the diminishing standards evident at many institutions. In view of the fact that standards vary each year according to applicants, it is more crucial now than perhaps ever before to consider the future of graduates. How many of the entrants to performance-based courses are likely to achieve a standard at which they can successfully attain one of the very few performance jobs available, and should there be a broader curriculum with realistic career planning in line with the strengths, interests and potential of all students?

An additional difficulty is the perception of conservatories as elitist institutions. This was highlighted in a British Government mandate issued to English conservatories, requiring the recruitment of at least 88 per cent of students from the state school sector. Principal of the Royal Academy of Music, Curtis Price, whose institution attracts just over 50 per cent of its entrants from the state school system, attributes the problem to a shortfall in instrumental music teaching in the state secondary school system. This places the financial burden of tuition with parents and inevitably increases the proportion of students from higher socio-economic

---

61 Barbara Sand, *Teaching Genius: Dorothy DeLay and the Making of a Musician* (Portland, OR, 2000).

62 Janis Weller, 'The Whole Musician: Journey to Authentic Vocation', in O. Musumeci (ed.), *The ISME Commission for Education of the Musician. Preparing Musicians: Making Sound Worlds* (Barcelona, 2004), pp. 245–56; Hannan, 'The Future of Tertiary Music Training in Australia'.

63 Hannan, 'The Future of Tertiary Music Training in Australia'.

backgrounds. Price suggests that the situation is improving, but the institution and others like it have already lost funding as a result.[64]

From a labour market perspective, Pierre-Michel Menger posits that 'full employment in the artistic labor market would require, on the one hand, a regulation on entry into the profession, and, on the other, either sufficient homogeneity on the supply-side or a high enough degree of insensitivity to differences in quality on the demand-side'.[65] Training for a wider range of careers, with the associated broad pre-requisite skills for entry into those specializations, would undoubtedly enhance the possibility of a wider socio-economic intake. Moreover, it would enable conservatories to set high entry standards for those wishing to specialize in performance. It would also provide opportunities for other specializations and would broaden the relevance of some courses to popular musicians. Perhaps it would also prompt governments to stop measuring the proportion of graduates 'gainfully employed in music making' and to measure instead the number of graduates creating sustainable careers.

Governmental pressure to produce performers epitomizes the lack of understanding about the roles in which musicians engage; when it was reported that less than half of performance graduates in the US are employed as performers, no data were collected about non-performance roles such as teaching, or about the casual and part-time performance work that form a protean career. Another striking example comes from the Higher Education Funding Council for England (HEFCE), which requested English conservatories to justify their funding by ensuring that 75 per cent of graduates are working principally in performance within five years of graduation. Firstly, it would be almost impossible to accurately measure the average proportion of performance roles over time given the tendency towards protean careers. More alarming, however, is the narrow definition of success suggested by such a statement. The situation raises many questions about education and training: is performance the only worthy profession for a conservatorium graduate, and do governments presume that graduates are equipped only for careers in performance? Are conservatories under pressure to train only for careers in performance? Certainly the philosophical frameworks suggests that performance careers are advocated above all else, and that doesn't help matters when arguing for funding.

Australia's Performance Graduates

Predictably there are no figures available on the number of full-time instrumental positions in Australia, and there is no collection of figures from which to extract the number of instrumental performance graduates from Australia's classical undergraduate degrees. However, 22 of the 24 institutions who delivered programmes in 2003 provided music graduate data for that year. Many of the music faculties found it difficult to secure such basic information from much larger university systems within which they have little administrative autonomy. Table 4.6 shows the

---

64 In Charlotte Higgins, 'Discordant Note over "Too Posh" Academy', *The Guardian* (4 October 2004).

65 Pierre-Michel Menger, 'Artistic Labor Markets and Careers', *Annual Review of Sociology*, 25/1 (1999): 541–74.

number of music performance graduates who completed undergraduate studies at the 22 represented institutions.

The majority of music performance graduates study orchestral instruments, and for them, full-time performance work equates to a position in an orchestra or chamber ensemble. What is the potential for such a position; how many full-time performance positions are there in Australia? The employment situation within Australia's eight full-time orchestras is shown in Table 4.7.

In 2006 there were 594 full-time orchestral positions in Australia, and approximately 838 orchestral musicians received contracts with the full-time orchestras for one or more concerts. To employ all of Australia's instrumental performance graduates each year in performance roles would require the annual creation of 113 new orchestral vacancies (or two medium-sized orchestras) and 75 new positions for guitarists and pianists. Put another way, the provision of full-time orchestral work for graduates of orchestral instruments requires one-quarter of Australia's full-time orchestral musicians to retire every year. It also requires that no existing musicians, previous graduates or overseas players apply for the positions. Even if this occurs, four years later it will be the graduates' turn to retire.[66]

Table 4.6   Undergraduate Degrees in Classical Instrumental Performance, Australia, 2003

Practical discipline	Number of graduates	%
Orchestral instrumentalists	113	60
Pianists/organists	59	31
Classical guitarists	16	9
Total	188	100

Table 4.7   Full-time Classical Instrumental Performance Positions in Australia

Orchestra	Permanent Positions	Casual Players*
Adelaide Symphony Orchestra	67	100
Australian Chamber Orchestra	13	Not available
Melbourne Symphony Orchestra	87	100
Queensland Orchestra	79	138
Sydney Symphony Orchestra	89	130
Tasmanian Symphony Orchestra	45	100
West Australian Symphony Orchestra	80	120
Australia Opera and Ballet Orchestra	65	
Orchestra Victoria	69 (full and part-time)	150
Total	594	838
*Average number of casual players engaged for one or more concerts each year		

66 Part-time/seasonal orchestras rate special mention. In Australia, most part-time orchestras were founded by musicians and some are specialist ensembles: for example, the Brandenburg and Antipodes orchestras (which utilize many of the same players) are Baroque orchestras. Part-time orchestras in Australia include the Academy of Melbourne, Australian Brandenburg Orchestra, and the Canberra and Darwin Symphony Orchestras. Most of the players come from academia and from the pool of quality freelance players who engage in a number of different roles both inside and outside of music.

To facilitate a broader perspective, orchestral vacancies in multiple countries were tracked for seven months from June until December 2004 using the e-bulletins of the Australian Music Council.[67] The results are shown in Table 4.8 and illustrate that there are approximately 405 orchestral vacancies each year in the represented countries. Only 12 of the 2004 vacancies were in Australia. In addition to these vacancies and in stark contrast with the demise of several orchestras during the past decade, a call was made in October 2004 for musicians to apply for positions in a new orchestra in Hyogo, Japan. Although these figures are from 2004, they are indicative of the employment situation for instrumental graduates. MyAuditions.com, which lists orchestral vacancies worldwide, listed only 94 full time vacancies in the three months to July 2007. A proportion of the advertised positions had been carried over from previous unsuccessful audition rounds.

Of course, competition for orchestral positions is international. I asked 33 full-time orchestral musicians from three Australian orchestras about their backgrounds. Responses confirm that Australian music performance graduates compete for positions with an international contingent of musicians: 33 per cent of the orchestral musicians had graduated from courses in other countries and a further 27 per cent had lived or studied outside of Australia. Results are consistent with Jang's findings that approximately one-third of Korea's orchestra members are from outside of Korea.[68]

Not surprisingly, many Australian performance graduates undertake further performance training. The most likely rationale for further study is the improvement of practical skills until such time as the student's performance ambitions are met, or until employment is secured. Keith Powers followed the progress of a graduate violist as she took auditions across the US in the hope of securing an orchestral position. Asked about her options if unsuccessful, the musician responded that she would go on to further study: it 'feels kind of silly to be auditioning to continue studying with the teacher I'm already studying with … [he] has told me that I don't need any more school. But it's my best option, if no job works out'.[69] Conversely, the most common reason for non-completion of study is an early transition to work, which is logical given that a performance degree is not required for performance positions.

Marcellino and Cunningham[70] reported in 2002 that 30 per cent of Australian graduate students go on to study overseas, and Lancaster found in 2004 that at least 48 per cent of post-graduate enrolment is from within an institution's own graduate ranks.[71] Johannes Johansson observes that contact with other faculties through a broad range of course options is crucial, as otherwise students' development is limited to the knowledge contained within one department. In consideration of the need for students to gain a variety of experience within the profession, limiting their experience to one institution (and especially one professor) over multiple courses is unwise.

---

67 These listings do not include positions for orchestras in the United States.

68 Jang, 'Dear Friends! Let Us Start Over'.

69 Keith Powers, 'Audition Mishaps Hit Sour Note but Offer Valuable Experience' (9 March 2004), retrieved 9 March 2004, from <http://theedge.bostonherald.com/artsNews/view.bg?articleid=812>.

70 Marcellino and Cunningham, 'Australian Tertiary Music Education'.

71 Lancaster, *Post-Secondary Music Education Guide*.

Table 4.8   Orchestral Vacancies from June until December 2004

Location	Instrument														
	vl	va	vc	d	fl	cl	o	b	fh	tr	tb	ta	ti	p	h
Australia	5	1	2		1		1	1	1						
Austria					1			1							
Belgium	4	2	3	1	3	2	1		1		1				
Brazil	1	1	1		1	1			1		1				
China	1		1					1	1						
Columbia	1						1		1						
Cyprus	1	1	1		1				1						
Denmark	1	3	1	1			1		2						
England	6				2			1					1		1
Finland		1			2	1				1			1		
France	2	4	3	1	2	4	2	2	1						
Germany	7	5	5	2	3	3	4	2	2	3		1		1	
Greece		1													
Ireland	1		1												
Italy	1									1	1		1		
Japan	2	1	1	1			1	1							
Mexico	1	1						1	1						
Netherlands	4	1	1	1	1		1	1						1	
Norway	3	1			1		1								
New Zealand	4		3	1			1		1	1					1
Portugal			1				1								
Scotland		1	1	1							1				
Spain	3	3	2	1	2	1	3	4	4	3		2			
South Africa	1					2			1						
South Korea	1							1							
Sweden			2	1		1	1	1			1				
Switzerland	1		1				1		1	1					
Wales	1														
Total	**52**	**27**	**30**	**11**	**20**	**15**	**20**	**17**	**19**	**10**	**5**	**3**	**3**	**2**	**2**

Legend for Table 4.8					
Violin	vl	Clarinet	cl	Trombone	tb
Viola	va	Oboe/cor anglais	o	Tuba	ta
Violincello	vc	Bassoon/contra	b	Timpani	ti
Double bass	d	French horn	fh	Percussion	p
Flute/piccolo	fl	Trumpet	tr	Harp	h

Perceptions of Success

Much of the research in the area of motivation and achievement relates to failure rather than to success. Martin Covington describes how the distress of failure increases in line with the amount of effort invested: 'trying hard in a failing cause leads to more shame, not less shame, in an apparent contradiction of work ethic morality ... high effort and failure implies low ability'.[72] This has particular relevance to classical performers, for whom the high level of motivation and commitment required to achieve and sustain performance standards has long been recognized. Musicians who hold predominantly non-performance roles report that the demands of maintaining performance standards at an appropriate level 'involve a level of stress ... that, if not a full-time performer, can be difficult to keep up with!' Martin Maehr describes two different goal situations that have converse effects on participants. The 'ego situation' is exemplified in competitive activities where one's performance is compared to that of others. Despite the obvious benefits for competition winners, the impact on those who do not win a competition is to de-motivate, and to introduce self-doubt. In contrast, task-goal situations encourage participants to attempt tasks for their intrinsic value, and to determine success based upon the realization or development of personal goals.[73] It could be argued that initial training in music at the pre-vocational level is much more task-oriented or intrinsic than that required at the tertiary level due to the competitive nature of the music profession. Shown in Table 4.9, intrinsic-extrinsic rewards are described in terms of possible goals or perceived outcomes, which in turn motivate continued personal investment in the activity.

Table 4.9   Progression from Intrinsic to Extrinsic Goals[74]

Intrinsic ◄───► Extrinsic			
Task	*Ego*	*Social solidarity*	*Extrinsic rewards*
Understanding something	Doing better than others	Pleasing others	Earning a prize
Experiencing adventure/novelty	Winning	Making others happy	Making money

We have seen the pressure on conservatories to produce performers: consequently, perceptions of success and failure are an important consideration for both educators and practitioners. Julliard Principal Joseph Polisi calls for success to be redefined for Julliard graduates: 'to see more of them accept that a full-time performing

72 Martin Covington, 'Musical chairs: who drops out of music instruction and why?', in K. Dean (ed.), documentary report of the Ann Arbor Symposium in the application of psychology to the teaching of and learning of music: Session III. Motivation and creativity, Reston, VA, 1983.

73 Martin Maehr, 'The Development of Continuing Interests in Music', paper presented at the Ann Arbor Symposium in the application of psychology to the teaching and learning of music: Session III. Motivation and creativity, Reston, VA, February 1983.

74 Figures were drawn from Maehr, ibid.

career is "just not very tenable any more"'.[75] In my own research, the perception of teaching as a fall-back career is commonly expressed by educators, in this case describing the situation for European conservatorium graduates of piano: 'there are musicians who are not successful and they begin to teach, and they are terrible'. One educator revealed that at least 50 per cent of her institution's graduates go on to further study in performance or teaching, adding to the notion that teaching is viewed as a backup career: students 'have an idea of their performance standard by the time they have finished the Diploma. Maybe they choose teaching at that point: a bit of a reality check'. Another institutional representative emphasized that many musicians 'are good enough to play as casuals, but most are compelled to teach as their main occupation'. Teaching was relegated to a less desirable – and less successful – option. Similar comments are made by practising musicians: 'I had tried to get into a professional orchestra but had not succeeded, so I have to look at other options. Teaching really was the only one.'

The characteristics of work as a musician appear not to reflect the career ambitions of those entering the field; thus it is interesting to consider the factors that influence musicians' perceptions of a successful career. Aspirations of greatness are frequently instilled before students commence university-level training, and often the intensity of commitment is dictated by parents when training commences. Barbara Sand hypothesizes that it is often early teachers and families 'who make these performers feel that they have failed if they do not make it as soloists. The unspoken threat of being a disappointment to these adults has loomed over them from the beginning and can remain a source of trouble throughout their lives'.[76] Kurt Loebel suggests that most music performance students 'are not made aware of the practical aspects involved in making a living as a classical instrumentalist'.[77] In contrast, Vetter speculates that students in general are realistic about the lack of performing opportunities and low financial rewards, but that the desire to perform overrides those concerns.[78] Cellist David Pereira agrees that

> most noticeable until very lately has been the assumption that if you do a B.Mus. in cello then the world is going to rush to offer you a playing job. The tertiary sector has sometimes encouraged this nonsense even as it enrolled more and more students. Today's freshmen seem to have wised up to this game.[79]

Music students often give the outward impression of having a very narrow view of success; most aspire to careers as soloists rather than as orchestral players,

---

75 Gregory Freed, 'President of Juilliard Sings Job-Market Blues', *Star Tribune* (23 October 2002), retrieved 30 October 2002, from <http://www.startribune.com/stories/462/3382950.html>.

76 Sand, *Teaching Genius: Dorothy DeLay and the Making of a Musician*.

77 Kurt Loebel, 'Classical Music Instrumentalist', *Music Educators Journal*, 69/2 (1982): 48–9.

78 T. Vetter, 'The University Music Performance Program: Performance or Liberal Arts Degree? The Case of Voice Performance', unpublished Master's thesis, University of Toronto, Ontario, 1990.

79 J. Dempster, feature interview with David Pereira, *Stringendo*, 25 (2003): 10–12.

teachers or other arts professionals. Perhaps students would not aspire so quickly to solo careers if they understood what life would be like at the top: according to Gerald McDonald, 'a career just as a soloist makes demands that few can meet artistically, temperamentally or financially'.[80] Top soloists admit that the stress can be overwhelming: Isaac Stern describes the profession of the solo performer as 'both simple and cruel'.[81]

The difficulty of measuring musicians' roles has been discussed in terms of ineffective data collection processes; however, it is also the result of self-report, on which most statistical collections rely. A typical example of the ambiguity of self-report is found in figures derived from an Australian Bureau of Statistics (ABS) 1998–99 national survey of work in the cultural industries: 345,700 people reported a vocational involvement in music, and yet only 28 per cent of those people received any income as a musician.[82] For many people, as in the case of an accountant, professional identity is the same as job title. For a musician who engages in a protean career, the situation is much more complicated; self-definition as a musician can in fact relate to a career as a performer, teacher, audio technician, administrator or researcher; and to a variety of employments in and outside of music. Many musicians hold skilled or unskilled roles outside of music and still identify as musicians. In fact, Janet Mills and Jan Smith suggest that conservatorium alumni often have a career identity that does not correspond with their income sources: alumni's subjective and objective careers are not the same.[83]

There is also a hierarchical inference in musicians' self-report as a soloist, instrumentalist or teacher: one musician commented that a soloist 'wouldn't say "look at me: I'm a musician", because that is lower than a soloist'. Another noted the perception that 'you are a lesser musician if you teach music, and you are an even lesser musician if you teach in schools or in other settings'. The hierarchy of self report is perpetuated in the separation of education and performance students during their university education. In fact, Brian Roberts suggests that music education students don't see positive identity constructs for the music educator, and often 'disidentify [sic] themselves with the music education world in favour of the more prestigious performer identity'.[84] A study at The University of Western Australia investigated the effects of providing a positive engagement with teaching by means of a unit of study delivered to a combined cohort of second year undergraduate music education, composition and performance students. Performance students tended towards a negative view of teaching at the start of the project; however, at the end they reported a positive change in their perception of teaching and its place in their careers. Likewise, the music education students signalled a growing awareness of the benefits of working in partnership with performers. The study demonstrates

---

80 Gerald McDonald, *Training and Careers for Professional Musicians* (Surrey, 1979).

81 Isaac W. Stern and Chaim Potok, *Isaac Stern: My First 79 Years* (Philadelphia, 1999).

82 Create Australia, *Creating a Position: Education, Training and the Cultural Industries* (Sydney, NSW, 2001).

83 Janet Mills and Jan Smith, 'Working in Music: Becoming Successful', paper presented at the Musikalische bebabung in der lebenzeitperspektive, University of Paderborn, 2002.

84 Brian Roberts, *Musician: a Process of Labelling* (Newfoundland, 1991).

that positive teaching experiences increase the likelihood that performance students will plan a positive engagement with teaching.[85]

Previous research with classical instrumental musicians highlights the intrinsic benefits of teaching in addition to the perhaps more obvious benefits of securing a regular income, and yet despite the presence of educational activities in the portfolio of most musicians it remains on the periphery of many music performance programmes. A study conducted at the Royal College of Music (RCM) brings to light that only 1 per cent of RCM graduates undertake formal teacher training leading to qualified teacher status (QTS) despite the majority of students expecting to include teaching in their careers, and a United Kingdom government evaluation of 500 instrumental lessons shows that teachers who have achieved QTS consistently provide instrumental teaching of a higher quality than otherwise observed. One of the strategies engaged for a selection of RCM students was the provision of a ten-day teaching associate position in a secondary school, after which students were found to be much more positive about considering teaching as a career option. Students who participated in the survey reported that prior to the teaching placement they had rarely considered secondary school music teaching to be 'doing music', which illustrates the narrow boundaries within which students perceive musicians' careers, and the hierarchical perception of success.[86]

Weller describes the education of musicians as having altered very little in that music students still tend to view performance and teaching as the two primary career options, with teaching viewed often 'as a "fall-back career" if they "fail" to make it big in the performing arena'.[87] Reflecting on her own transition from the pursuit of a soloist career to that of a piano teacher, Kaija Huhtanen writes that having been

> labelled as a member of a group of very privileged and gifted potential pianists … the fate of a young music student looks like being sealed for the rest of his or her life … How might a newly emerged pianist feel when finding himself or herself in a music school as a piano teacher? That surely was not the primary goal.[88]

Huhtanen draws on a theory of mourning as posited by Freud to explain that, following a failure, the restoration of self-image and orientation towards reality requires the individual to release the fulfilment obtained previously from that which has been lost. She categorizes the piano teachers in her research as either 'realists' who accept teaching as an integral part of their musical identities, or as 'dreamers' who engage in teaching to meet financial obligations, and who possess a traumatic relationship with their playing as a result of not having moved on from their performance dreams.

---

85 Dawn Bennett and Andrea Stanberg, 'Musicians as Teachers: Developing a Positive View through Collaborative Learning Partnerships', *International Journal of Music Education*, 24/3 (2006): 219–30.

86 Janet Mills, 'Addressing the Concerns of Conservatoire Students about School Music Teaching, *British Journal of Music Education*, 22/1 (2005): 63–75.

87 Weller, 'The Whole Musician: Journey to Authentic Vocation'.

88 Kaija Huhtanen, 'Once I Had a Promising Future (Facing Reality as an Ex-promising Pianist)', *Australian Music Forum*, 10/3 (2004): 21–7.

Teaching skills are used by over 80 per cent of the musicians who have contributed to my research, and Huhtanen's classification of teachers as dreamers or realists can be seen quite clearly; musicians hold a teaching role either because of a desire to teach and the acceptance of a teaching role (the realist), or the inclusion of teaching to supplement inadequate work in performance (the dreamer). Dreamers mull over the development of a teaching role due to a lack of performance income: 'I am a performer by nature and am still trying to obtain full-time performance work as a performer, so therefore I teach and accompany'; 'I have developed teaching skills in order to support my desire to become a full-time performer'; 'teaching is the only semipermanent income I can get'. Realists, however, talk about the enjoyment found in teaching: 'I teach for the satisfaction of passing on skills and knowledge to others, and to have a fairly regular income'; 'teaching is an integral part of most musicians' lives. I consider it my most important role and find it very satisfying.' The process of guiding a student or 'learning how to learn' enhances musicians' ability to analyse their own interpretation and technique, and many musicians highlight that teaching and performance are mutually beneficial: 'my work as a teacher helps me to identify good practice techniques which help me as a performer, and being a performer is a role-model to assist my students'; 'Teaching has been an adjunct to my income for most of the years I have played. Whilst it is important to pass on the craft of instrumental performance, I have also learnt in turn to analyse and consider some basic factors in playing.'

Career identity stems from musicians' aspirations and goals. If as in Huhtanen's research a musician is teaching as a means of financial support whilst aspiring to a performance career, the individual is likely to have a subjective career as a performer rather than as a teacher. Conversely, someone who takes on a teaching role as part of a protean career and who views teaching as a positive professional activity is more likely to have a subjective career identity that concurs with their objective one. Mills and Smith submit that musicians feel increasingly successful as the gap narrows between their objective work and their aspirations, and that success is achieved when there is concurrence between the two. Success is an individual concept and can vary for the same person at different times throughout their career. Modelling and advocating a broader definition of success will greatly enhance the potential for musicians to achieve it.

Concluding Comments

A musician is not just a performer: musicians adopt numerous roles including those of business people, educators, conductors, performers, writers, administrators and managers. The reality of a sustainable career as a musician is the demand for a diverse range of skills that most music graduates do not possess, and which are not reflected in current curricula. However, writing vocationally relevant curricula requires understanding of the working lives of musicians. It is necessary to determine how closely curricula and practice align and whether any differences impact the potential to build sustainable careers. Moving towards this objective, the next chapter considers the characteristics of work for musicians and other artists.

Chapter 5

Cultural Practice:
Visual and Performing Artists

'It isn't necessarily the best ones who make it: it's the ones with the know-how to keep going until they get what they want'

We have now looked at the formal education and training that prepares musicians for professional practice, and the environment in which that practice takes place. Given that musicians work alongside other performing and visual artists within the cultural industries, is it possible that the characteristics of cultural practice in a range of arts disciplines reflect the practice of musicians? If so, could musicians draw on opportunities within the wider cultural industries for employment, training, funding and networking?

To find out, a study of practitioners from a wide range of the visual and performing arts examined the rate, characteristics and impact of cultural industry change; attrition; industry related communication; education and training; and the skills and attributes considered by artists to be crucial to the achievement of a sustainable career. Both classical and non-classical musicians were included in the study. The classically trained musicians talked about gigs, business and sound systems in the same way as other musicians and artists. This chapter records the findings of that study. The methodology is included in Chapter 1.

Cultural Industry Change

We all know people who have reduced or ceased their arts work – their cultural practice – in favour of other occupations. Anecdotally, we also know that low and inconsistent income, long periods of travel and unsociable hours are significant factors in such decisions; however, to what extent has change within the cultural industries impacted the cultural workforce, and is the impact of change felt in the same way across different artforms?

Cultural practitioners were asked about the level of financial security within their profession. They were also asked about the occurrence and causes of attrition, which led to dialogue about cultural industry change and the impact of that change. Eighty-one per cent of artists reported significant change within the previous five years, and the most commonly cited impact of industry change was a much greater necessity to be multi-skilled. Shown below, participants' observations about industry change have been grouped into four emergent themes: cultural practice; artistic product; business administration; funding; and technology.

Cultural Practice

- 'The industry continues to get tougher. Everyone has to be everything.'
- 'There are too many people for the available jobs.'
- 'It is much harder, and there is a need to know more roles than before, and to run a practice properly.'
- 'People have to be multi-skilled: a band member who composes original material also sets up a sound system, runs a home studio and sub-contracts or forms partnerships with band members.'
- 'There is more pressure now.'
- 'Artists need knowledge of more than performance.'
- 'There are less [sic] gigs available for part-time bands.'
- 'Many cash jobs have ceased post-GST[1] and with insurance changes. This means fewer gigs, and so less opportunities for new and part-time bands. Many part-time bands have stopped performing.'

Artistic Product

- 'Less creative, more realistic-based work leads to the use of technology, providing the skills to produce perfect (but robotic) results.'[2]
- 'Increase in contemporary theory and practice.'
- 'More cover work is inevitable in order to earn "bread and butter" gigs.'
- 'You have to combine teaching and performing.'
- 'Business Administration'
- 'There is more paperwork and less cash work.'
- 'Artists have to be multi-skilled and understand management and business.'
- 'The amount of paperwork has increased due to the introduction of the GST.'
- 'More competitive, global markets.'
- 'There's a public perception that artists aren't professionals. Artists are business people. Artists have to be very multi-skilled.'
- 'Legal and financial issues are at the fore.'
- 'There is a lack of artist protection because they [artists] don't understand their rights.'
- 'Legal/contractual/insurance implications are more evident.'
- 'Artists need knowledge about funding initiatives, policy, and legal/financial matters such as GST, insurance and legal obligations.'

---

1   Comments reflect the introduction of an Australian tax on Goods and Services (GST) in the year 2000. See <www.gstaustralia.com.au> for information.

2   The sculptor who made this comment specializes in figurative work. He had recently discovered software with which perfect, three-dimensional sculptures could be made using multiple photographs. He bemoaned both the lack of practical skill involved and the accuracy of the computer model which, he believes, removes creativity from the process.

Funding

- 'There is less money to go around.'
- 'There's a decrease in funding for traditional styles.'
- 'Funding is available only for "new art."'
- 'The focus of funding has changed. Funding is now related to community arts activities; community cultural development (CCD) workshops etc. Money is often available, but artists don't know how to access it.'

Technology

- 'There is a loss of fundamental skills as students rely on electronic media to produce work.'
- 'Some artists get left behind, especially with technology.'
- 'There are more home studios, so bands are becoming much more self-sufficient.'
- 'The use of multimedia and technology is increasing.'

Sustainability and Attrition

Participants underline that cultural practitioners supplement their income with both arts and non-arts roles as available, and that the creative work of an artist does not provide a sufficient level of financial security to make it a full-time career. Work outside of the cultural industries was undertaken by one-third of the sample, and the only participants who considered there to be potential for secure employment were those who include arts education as a major component of their practice. Educational roles were often adopted as a 'temporary' means to secure a regular income.

Six key factors emerge as crucial to the achievement of sustainable careers. Definitions, drawn from participants' comments, provide a fascinating picture of the requirements for sustainable careers:

Entrepreneurship and Business Skills

- The use of entrepreneurial skills and attitudes for the development of innovative ideas, to harness available resources, and to realise career and personal goals.
- The ability to establish, maintain and market a business. Knowledge of rights and responsibilities in relation to legal issues, policy and taxation.

Industry Experience and Awareness

- Exposure to and experience within a wide range of cultural professions for the development of a portfolio of applicable skills and knowledge. Awareness of the components and inter-relationships of the cultural industries to increase the potential for a broad practice.

Ongoing Professional Development

- Ongoing access to professional development including formal study, informal courses and seminars.
- The ability to utilise current information communications technology (ICT) for business purposes, and the skills to use specialist technologies in order to be independent and competitive.

Professional Networks and Industry Mentors

- Ongoing communication with arts organisations and professional networks, which are the most effective and commonly used means of intra-industry communication.

Teaching Skills

- Skills for teaching, coaching and mentoring: 1) to be able to teach and communicate effectively; 2) to meet the requirements of funding schemes; 3) to meet changing employment requirements. [Increasing numbers of school teachers, including peripatetic music tutors and specialist art teachers, are required to hold a formal teaching qualification. There is also mounting debate about the need to accredit artists who run private teaching studios and workshops. This has led to a significant amount of concern among unqualified teachers.]

Community Cultural Development

- The ability to work alongside communities in cultural projects. Increasingly a pre-requisite for grants, training opportunities in CCD are perceived as very limited.

Comments made by musicians were separated from those made by other cultural industry practitioners, which for clarity are referred to as the non-musician sample. Shown in Figure 5.1, the two cohorts nominated exactly the same six factors as being essential to providing independence, choice and opportunity: broadening the potential for a diverse range of contracted and independent employment. Entrepreneurial and business skills were considered by both cohorts to be by far the most crucial skills to developing and sustaining a career. The term 'entrepreneurship' was used by multiple participants in both samples to mean creativity in business: constantly seeking new opportunities and finding ways to make them a reality. Skills for teaching, coaching and mentoring featured more strongly for musicians than for the non-musician sample.

Both samples attributed the majority of attrition to the same five key factors: insufficiency of regular employment; a lack of career mobility; irregular working hours; high rates of injury; and low financial rewards. Practitioners lamented the lack of opportunities for professional development that would enable them to maintain

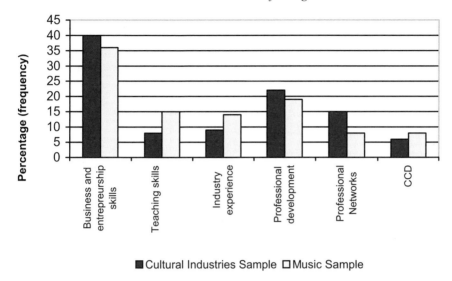

Figure 5.1   Factors Crucial to the Achievement of Sustainable Careers

skills and knowledge in line with cultural industry change. Musicians assigned insufficient regular employment to a lack of practitioner diversity. The attrition factors reflect previous cultural industries research such as that conducted by Pierre-Michel Menger, David Throsby and Virginia Hollister.[3]

Communication

Many artists work at least part of the time alone in their studio. Participants were asked the regularity of their contact with others within the industry, and the ways in which contact is made and maintained. Daily contact with colleagues was cited by 65 per cent of participants, and a further 22 per cent had weekly contact. The most common form of contact was through professional networks and associations, and only one participant reported no contact with peers. Most of the communication occurred within closely linked artforms. Performing artists commented that their interaction with colleagues is, for the most part, non-verbal. Conversation can be limited to rehearsal breaks and is often trivial at those times. Meaningful conversations most often occur away from the workplace: 'performing can be a solitary activity. You practise alone, and even when you're playing with others you spend most of your time absorbed in playing and not interacting socially'. Mentors and peers are particularly important for a wide variety of practising artists, including educators. Research indicates that many music teachers leave the profession early and new teachers, often finding themselves the only music teacher at their school, struggle

---

3   See, for example, Pierre-Michel Menger, 'Artistic Labor Markets and Careers', *Annual Review of Sociology*, 25/1 (1999): 541–74; and David Throsby and Virginia Hollister, *Don't Give Up Your Day Job: An Economic Study of Professional Artists in Australia* (No. 331.7617) (Sydney, NSW, 2003).

to cope. Similarly, lecturers in regional areas face small student numbers, and such programmes depend on the broad skills and knowledge of an individual lecturer rather than benefiting from a team approach. As arts associations and informal networks are the most common forms of intra-industry communication, they are the logical nucleus for mentoring programs.

What Does It Take? Personal Attributes of Artists

In addition to necessary skills and knowledge, artists were asked to identify personal attributes that are crucial to sustaining a career in the cultural workforce. Not surprisingly, *confidence and inner strength* was considered to be the most important attribute (33 per cent of responses) followed by *openness and adaptability to change* (20%); *motivation and drive* (17%), *resilience and determination* (17%) and a *passion for the field* (13%). Even though it is a given, it is ironic that talent didn't arise once. Definitions were again drawn from participants' comments. They constitute a valuable tool for self-reflection during the development and maintenance of a career in the cultural workforce.

Confidence and Inner Strength

- The ability to believe in oneself and one's talent, and the strength to sell one's talent to the artistic community and beyond.

Openness and Adaptability to Change

- The ability to maintain one's artistic vision whilst responding to the opportunities that arise.

Motivation and Drive

- Defining one's goals and remaining motivated to achieving them.

Resilience and Determination

- The determination to continue pursuing one's goals despite setbacks and disappointments.

Passion for the Field

- Unwavering commitment and passion for artistic practice.

The personal attributes underscore comments made by musicians for centuries. In 1752 Prussian musician Joachim Quantz published a treatise that began with a chapter about personal attributes. The three key qualities listed in the text were physical strength, a natural talent without vanity, and passion: a 'perpetual and untiring love for music, a willingness and eagerness to spare neither industry nor pains, and to bear steadfastly all the difficulties that present themselves in this mode of life'.[4]

The passion or enthusiasm that drives this determination has commonly been described as a *labour of love*,[5] a *calling*,[6] or an *inner drive*.[7] The personal attributes cited by participants align with advice given by the American Conservatory of Music (ACM) that those who succeed in the music profession are not necessarily the ones with the highest technical mastery, but rather those who have the determination and the self-confidence to implement creative and time-consuming strategies to promote career opportunities.[8] The advice reflects a comment made by one of the musicians: 'it isn't necessarily the best ones who make it: it's the ones with the know-how to keep going until they get what they want'. In Chapter 6 we will see that exactly the same attributes were nominated by musicians who answered the survey and attended interviews.

Contemplating Education and Training

Cultural practitioners regard new graduates as 'naïve' with little or no knowledge of, or experience within, the profession. This was particularly emphasized by the musician sample; whilst possessing high levels of performance skill, music graduates are largely considered to be unable to manage their own business or to effectively promote their product and skills, and practitioners recalled their own experiences as new graduates as a time of un-preparedness and confusion: 'Immediately after graduating I still lacked the confidence to go searching opportunities out, and the only thing that landed in my lap was teaching.' Asked to consider their careers retrospectively, practitioners note the initial absence of business and marketing skills as a particular disadvantage. They observe the number of additional opportunities that would have been available to them had they graduated with a broader base of skills on which to build more holistic practice or supplementary income.

As discussed, industry change is rapid: eighty-one per cent of artists cited substantial change in the past five years. Although all participants had completed formal education and training relating to their profession, almost two-thirds considered it necessary to access further education and training in order for their practice to remain viable. Areas of training need include business and management skills, arts law, career development in the broad cultural industries, and the development of a broad range of applicable skills including teaching and new technologies.

---

4   Joachim J. Quantz, *On Playing the Flute*, trans. E.R. Reilly (New York, 1966) (original work published 1752).

5   Eliot Freidson, 'Labors of Love: A Prospectus', in Kai Erikson and Steven Vallas (eds), *The Nature of Work: Sociological Perspectives* (New Haven, CT, 1990).

6   See Ernest Kris and Otto Kurz, 'Artistic Labor Markets and Careers', in P. Menger (ed.), *Annual Review of Sociology*, 25/1 (1999): 541–74.

7   Joan Jeffri and David Throsby, 'Professionalism and the Visual Artist', *European Journal of Cultural Policy*, 1 (1994): 99–108.

8   Janet L. Poklemba, 'Career Education: An Integral Part of the Education of the Undergraduate Music Performance Student?', unpublished Master's thesis, The American University, Washington, 1995.

The lack of regular employment arises as a crucial attrition factor, and the necessity for a diverse and fluid range of skills suggests a discrepancy between the purely creative skills of artists, and the skills required to pursue more varied opportunities for employment. A 2001 Metier study found that despite the evident deficiency of employment for British artists in general, artists' lack of appropriate combinations of skills results in the ironic situation of a skills shortage, which has led in turn to numerous positions that organizations are unable to fill.[9] Employers report particular difficulty finding administrators with performance experience and people who can communicate effectively across the business and arts sectors. The Metier study describes two trends relating to the skills of artists: (1) an increasing need for very specific specializations; and (2) an increasing need for practitioners with a combination of flexible and diverse skills and experience across artforms and genres. Skills combinations are essential to artists seeking to develop and sustain their careers. Not only do such combinations heighten the potential for work; they also offer opportunities to develop unique abilities and to create a stimulating and flexible blend of activities.

Artists stress the need for tertiary educators to maintain the relevance of arts curricula, and they recommend the inclusion of business skills, industry experience, career development, mentors, teaching skills and elementary law. There follows a summary of their comments.

- Students should be made aware of the industry and how hard it is.
- There is a need for ... both formal and informal ongoing professional development opportunities at various levels.
- There needs to be more information about jobs, careers, and what options there are in terms of employment.
- Arts managers need to be very multi-skilled, particularly in regional locations. This includes knowledge of sound and lighting systems so that one isn't totally dependent on others.
- Teaching skills should be included wherever possible. Courses should include talks by visiting industry workers. Courses ought to address industry change, and should address how to interpret or deal with rejections.
- Courses should involve practising artists, and ensure that graduates understand the industry and what will be required of them. Business skills are crucial. Course designers could network with practising artists to host students: a no-cost partnership.
- More industry experience is required within education and training.
- People need to become more self-sufficient: to understand emerging technologies, CCD and the leisure industries. Artists need to understand business and management concepts, and to be realistic in terms of employment.
- Artists need knowledge of business administration including business plans, small business administration, marketing, technology, web page design, business cards and self-promotion.

---

9   Metier, *AS2K: Arts Skills 2000* (London, 2001a).

- Artists need knowledge of other disciplines. They need to understand the moral rights of artists, contemporary theory and arts education. Students need to have work experience within the industry.
- There is a need for higher education courses relevant to the field, and for workshops: informal professional development opportunities.
- Curriculum writers should ensure that education and training is relevant to industry requirements. Most work is for post-production labourers, and for tool masters (tracking, sound engineers): the people who get the recording ready for the record company. Mentoring is badly needed.
- There is a need for formal qualifications. Even studio music teachers may need to have formal qualifications in the future. All primary school teachers should have enough knowledge to run an arts program, as schools increasingly cannot afford specialists. A professional network and mentoring system is crucial. There isn't so much a shortage of instrumental music teachers as a shortage of qualified ones. Australia needs an external studies graduate diploma in studio music teaching, incorporating a practicum.
- Teachers need more experience, and better knowledge of curricula and assessment management. Teachers also need greater awareness of multiple musical genres.
- Courses need to include legal basics. This could prevent many problems.
- Mentoring and networking are required to increase the level of communication and to assist new practitioners.
- There are fewer students now; hence less money. Artists need to have more industry experience.
- Education and training are not always relevant to professional practice.
- Teachers need to know classical, jazz and contemporary musical styles. Artists need to have teaching skills and some basic business and management skills. Universities should look towards collaborative programs.

Concluding Comments

This chapter presents a broad cross-section of cultural practice, and the commonalities of arts practice suggest that musicians could find opportunities within the wider cultural industries. The testimony of musicians and other artists is strikingly similar in terms of industry change; attrition; education and training; and professional development needs. Significantly, the personal attributes, generic skills and knowledge required for sustainable practice are also markedly similar. This clearly indicates the potential for vocationally relevant, interdisciplinary curricula for the initial and ongoing development of all cultural practitioners.

Conservatories and universities would benefit from the efficiencies of inter-arts delivery in many areas, and there are opportunities to provide collaborative professional development programmes with and for artists: drawing upon artists' experience and expertise, developing a long-term relationship with graduates as lifelong learners, and providing a much broader experience for intending and practising artists.

Chapter 6

Out in the Real World:
The Case for Change

Musician *n.* a person who practises in the profession of music within one or more specialist fields

Dictionary definitions of a musician describe *one who performs*, and a musician is to most people someone who spends his or her time performing music to others. Often there is the assumption that musicians hold an additional 'day job' in order to pay the bills: '*You're a musician? What do you play? How often do you do that?*' In previous chapters we have examined historical and contemporary employment characteristics of musicians, performance-based education and training, and the diversity of the cultural industries within which musicians work. We have also observed striking similarities in the careers of artists across multiple artforms, which suggests the logic of collaborative inter-arts based practice, education, funding and support.

These factors are all vital influences on the ability of musicians to create and sustain their careers, and already we can see a picture that contradicts the image of the musician as a performer; but what, exactly, is a musician? In this chapter we get down to the facts and figures. Starting with a longitudinal view of how instrumental musicians apportion their time and the skills and attributes utilized in the management of their careers, the chapter reveals that most musicians are wholly or partly self-employed. With an average of more than two different roles they work in a variety of often interdependent roles throughout their careers, tend not to be paid for all of their work, and over one-third of musicians hold employment outside of the music profession. Significantly, the most common role for musicians is teaching, and very few musicians practise solely in performance. As one musician advises, 'Learn how to teach! All musicians will have to teach at some time'. Musicians' roles change throughout their careers as they adapt their practice to reflect personal circumstances and professional goals, and significant influences in this respect are stability of employment, level of job satisfaction and family responsibilities.

Put together, the pieces of this complex puzzle demonstrate that musicians identify vocationally with the profession of music whether or not income is derived elsewhere: the term *musician* is in fact an umbrella term for the profession. This is critically important to the question of what constitutes a musician, and the chapter concludes that it is incomplete to describe a musician as a performer: musicians engage in multiple roles within and outside of the music profession, and should consider the success of their practice on the basis of personal career satisfaction rather than a pre-conceived hierarchy of roles. The dictionary definition ought to be revised to read quite differently:

> **Musician** *n.* a person who practises in the profession of music within one or more specialist fields.

Thus defined, the practice, education and support of musicians can be viewed with fresh and innovative eyes towards systems that will enable more musicians to sustain their careers and to take pride in their achievements.

Chapter 6 discusses the findings of a study designed to extend understanding of the performance and non-performance skills and attributes required by classical instrumental musicians to achieve sustainable practice. The study built on the artist study reported in the previous chapter, gathering in-depth longitudinal information about the careers of classical instrumental musicians in terms of career structure, skills, attrition, and education and training. In total, 159 musicians completed the survey or attended interviews. Chapter 6 includes lots of facts and figures, which are hopefully not too difficult to negotiate. A summary of the main points is provided as an Appendix.

The Survey

The survey of musicians asked questions about work, education and training. Longitudinal analysis of careers in classical, instrumental music necessitated the participation of a representative sample of musicians from age eighteen years to sixty-six years onwards, and a range of experience from new practitioner to highly experienced. A location variable was included to enable identification of potential differences in data gathered from different locations. Musicians from Australia, the United Kingdom, Europe, Asia and the United States participated in the study.

Information about the career structure of respondents was obtained through a series of questions that explored: (1) whether respondents worked solely within the music sector; (2) roles held and the proportion of time committed to each; and (3) the skills utilized by practitioners when undertaking those roles. Resulting data enabled further analysis of the relationship between the skills taught within a classical, performance-based music course and the skills utilized in professional practice.

The survey gathered information about the roles held by musicians outside of the music sector, and whether or not these roles are held in order to supplement deficient opportunities in performance. Information was also collected about the role changes that occur during a musician's career and the reasons for that interchange, including whether there is a relationship between gender and career structure. In addition, the survey aspired to find out whether the careers of musicians form a longitudinal pattern, and whether the attrition factors identified in Chapter 5 are identified by the musician cohort.

What Musicians Do

The survey asked musicians about their work and found that 82 per cent teach, 70 per cent perform and 27 per cent conduct ensembles. Musicians engage in an average of 2.2 different roles. As discussed in Chapter 3, research indicates that women artists earn less than their male counterparts.[1] This study identified a gendered difference in the amount of work for which payment is received: over three times more female than male musicians received payment for 0–25% of their work as musicians. Payment for 26–50% and 51–75% of work was received respectively by 2.3 times and 2.2 times more males than females. Correspondingly, males were more likely to receive payment for 76–99% of their work. This supports the notion that women more commonly adopt avocational roles. Of the musicians who received payment for 100 per cent of their work, there were clear differences between the primary roles held by male and female musicians; performance being the primary role of 35 per cent of females and 55 per cent of males, and teaching the primary role of 58 per cent of females and 41 per cent of males. Australian Government data on extra-systemic teachers in music, art, dance and drama show a similar gender breakdown of teachers, 69 per cent of whom are female and 32 per cent male.[2]

The longitudinal pattern of primary roles was analysed by gender, and reveals contrasting patterns in the performance and teaching patterns of male and female musicians. For clarity, longitudinal patterns were separated by gender for the two most common roles: performance and teaching. Illustrated in Figures 6.1 and 6.2, data indicate that female musicians increase the extent of their performance role until somewhere between their mid-thirties and mid-forties, at which point it is much less likely to be their primary role. In contrast, male musicians tend to continue their performance roles until their mid-fifties. Primary teaching roles become less common with age for women and more common for men. Administrative roles are common for both male and female musicians, although it is more common for women to have an administrative primary role. Administrative roles include ensemble management and the administration of a small business.

There is also a clear gendered difference in musicians' distribution of time. Illustrated in Figure 6.3, musicians spend a greater percentage of their working time engaged in teaching than in performance. Surprisingly, conducting featured strongly for female respondents; however, qualitative data indicate that the high occurrence of conducting is due to the number of female musicians who direct student ensembles as part of their teaching roles.

---

1   There is a growing body of research relating to gender studies and careers in music or the cultural industries, some of which was discussed in Chapter 3. Interrupted careers are those that are put on hold for reasons such as raising a family. Interruptions impact earning ability, superannuation and average income, in addition to the loss of proficiency where technical skills are involved.

2   Commonwealth of Australia. (2002). *Australian job search*. Retrieved February 14, 2002, from <http://jobsearch.gov.au/joboutlook/ASCODesc.asp?ASCOCode=249>.

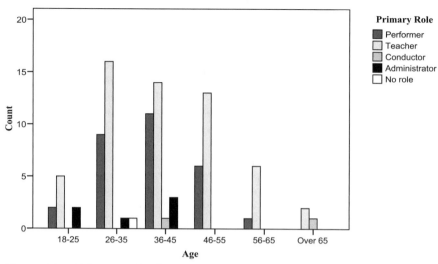

Figure 6.1　　Primary Role of Female Musicians by Age Group

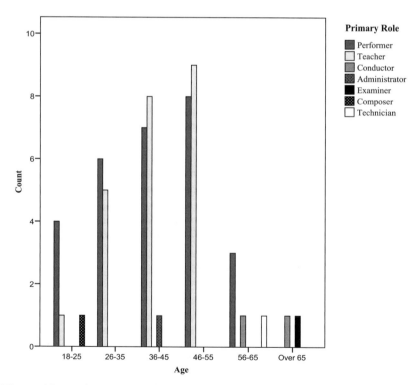

Figure 6.2　　Primary Role of Male Musicians by Age Group

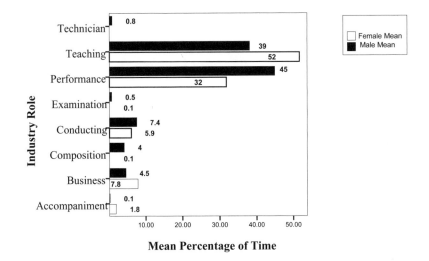

Figure 6.3   Average Percentage of Time Spent in Each Role

Non-industry roles were cited by 37 per cent of musicians and include unskilled roles (such as waiting tables at a restaurant), engagement in other professions such as medicine or law, and formal study.

Only 40 of the 103 musicians working full-time within music responded to the question: 'Is it your preference to work entirely within the music industry?' and 13 per cent of those stated that they would prefer not to be employed full-time within music. The remaining musicians worked part-time in music, and only one-third of those aspired to work full-time. This suggests that many musicians make an active choice to work outside of music rather than being forced to retain non-music roles because of insufficient opportunities within the profession. It could also – as we saw in Chapter 4 – signal musicians' acceptance of roles that were initially taken for financial reasons. Figures 6.4 and 6.5 illustrate the pattern of full-time and part-time employment held by male and female musicians, and highlight the prevalence of part-time work for female musicians.

Performance patterns   Seventy per cent of musicians included a performance role in their work. Given that orchestral musicians were included in the survey, it was surprising to learn that only 8 per cent worked solely in performance, and that less than half of those musicians had undertaken an undergraduate degree in performance.

Only 55 per cent of musicians answered the question: 'During your career, have you changed the extent of your performance role, or adjusted your career goals with respect to performance ambition?' Questions relating to performance patterns and employment preferences were the only ones to attract a low response rate, which suggests reluctance on the part of musicians to consider possibly enforced changes to their performance aspirations. The 76 musicians who reported a change in the extent of their performance role were asked to answer three more questions about those changes.

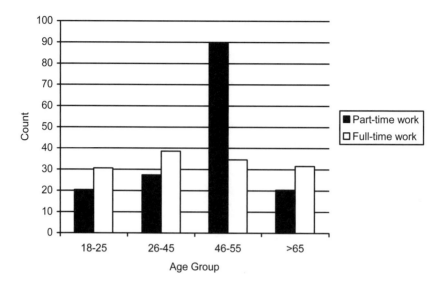

Figure 6.4   Pattern of Full-time and Part-time Work for Female Musicians

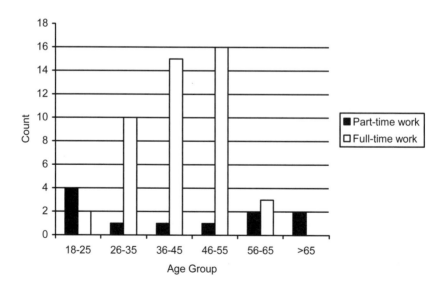

Figure 6.5   Pattern of Full-time and Part-time Work for Male Musicians

Q14 asked: 'For how many years did you work/have you worked as a performer? This may be in combination with other roles.' Q14b was an open question, and asked: 'At what stage(s) did you change the extent of your performance role or adjust your performance-related ambitions?' It was followed by a multiple response question that asked respondents to indicate factors that influenced their decision to move in part or wholly to non-performance roles.

Data were grouped into themes according to respondents' comments, and were then separated by gender. The results are illustrated in Figure 6.6.

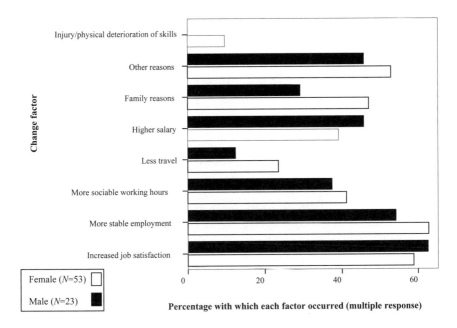

Figure 6.6   Factors Influencing a Change in Performance Roles

Musicians expanded on the factors that had influenced changes in their performance roles, and comments reflect the attrition factors identified in the artist study (Chapter 5): *insufficiency of regular employment, a lack of career mobility, irregular working hours, high rates of injury, and low financial rewards.* Comments relating to injury focused on excessive playing in an orchestral role (50%), repetitive strain injury (25%) and other injury or the deterioration of skills (25%). Musicians bemoaned the difficulty of maintaining a sufficiently high performance standard when not performing full time. The pressure of maintaining performance standards was felt in the same way by musicians who were seeking immediate performance work, and by those who had made the active decision to delay or to alter their career patterns for external reasons. It seems that changes to performance roles are often involuntary, despite the subsequent enjoyment found by many musicians within non-performance roles such as teaching. A summary of the most common themes follows:

More Stable Employment

- Limited opportunities for employment, leading to insufficient income (56%);
- A positive progression to other activities (16%);

Orchestral Work

Musicians who had ceased full-time orchestral work highlighted a lack of individual recognition, and opportunities for career progression, particularly among rank and file orchestral players.

- The lack of artistic input (32%);
- A difficult and political workplace culture (28%);
- A positive shift to freelance or academic work (20%).

Teaching

Respondents noted the attraction of teaching in providing regular income, regular hours and a level of artistic and administrative control.

- A quest for new challenges and the intrinsic rewards found in teaching (61%): 'After 25 years of practical performing experience, I found myself more and more drawn to teaching, having earlier always seen it as something to fall back on';
- The need to find a balance between performance and teaching (33%)

Social Factors

Comments relating to family and working hours were made by both male and female musicians, who referred to spending more time with family than is possible in a performance role, and to the unsociable and irregular nature of performance roles. Of the musicians who commented about family commitments, 82 per cent were trying to maintain their performance standard (mostly whilst they worked within teaching roles) so that performance-based employment could be resumed at a later date. This aligns with the concept of interrupted careers, where career ambitions are put on hold rather than abandoned:

- 'Now they [my children] are older I have every intention of expanding my performing career as well as continuing to teach.'

Musicians' Skills

Given that musicians engage in multiple and changing roles, it is reasonable to expect them to need multiple and changing skills to maintain their careers. In fact, musicians use an average of 3.9 different skills including performance (96%), teaching (88%), business administration (64%), human resource management (49%), marketing (45%) and technology (43%):

- 'I have tried to develop some business skills largely to survive materially in a very unstable industry.'
- 'Business is critical to being successful as a musician. I had to develop marketing as a way of getting my name out there, and for the "networking" to be able to start.' 'It's amazing, how musicians have to sell themselves to get gigs.'
- 'The marketing skills are necessary in order to survive as a musician, as is a good business sense to understand finances.'
- 'People like music, but they don't realise how much business sense is needed to maintain a career.'

Formal Education and Training

Ninety-four per cent of musicians had undertaken formal music education and training. The most common form of formal education and training was a Bachelor of Music (undergraduate performance) degree, which 88 per cent of musicians had studied in Australia, Europe or the United States. Forty per cent of musicians had also studied performance as a graduate student. A total of 293 undergraduate and 114 graduate courses had been undertaken by the musicians. Incomplete courses were reported by only nine musicians, three of whom left study because they had secured employment. Musicians were fairly satisfied with the effectives of their education and training, giving a mean effectiveness rating of seven out of ten for undergraduate and eight out of ten for graduate study. The relationship between course satisfaction and age was analysed, and musicians seem to become more satisfied with increasing age. Musicians who have remained in the profession for a long time are likely to have enjoyed a degree of success. Having sustained their practice, it is logical that they attribute their success in part to their education and training.

Musicians were asked what changes they would recommend to education and training, and their comments emphasize the following themes: *career planning and experience, conducting skills, core studies, curricular structure, ensemble experience, the inclusion of multiple genres, injury prevention, instrumental pedagogy, music technologies, practical studies, psychology of performance* and *small business skills*. We will look more closely at their responses in Chapter 7.

Informal Education and Training

Almost 70 per cent of musicians had engaged in informal education and training or professional development, the most common being performance tuition and teaching skills. Performance was the second most common activity for musicians, but it was the most common form of informal education and training. This reflects the finding that many musicians retain their performance aspirations whilst in other roles. The high incidence of professional development relating to teaching skills emphasizes the commonality of teaching in musicians' practice. The importance of professional networks in providing informal education and training highlights the earlier finding that professional networks and associations are a crucial form of industry communication and an obvious starting point for mentoring schemes.

The Interviews

Interviews were held with two representatives of Australian conservatories in the process of curricular change. Students were said to possess a narrow view of success and an unrealistic expectation of the music profession, and tended to view teaching as a backup career: 'an ongoing necessity'. The educators implied there to be inadequate career planning, one stating: 'we don't see that as our role' and yet stressing the competitive nature of the profession, and the other expressing the dilemma of telling students 'how difficult it is out there as a performer, without damping that passion'. A further set of in-depth interviews was conducted with five music practitioners based in Europe, Australia and the United States: practising musicians and music educators who could represent the experiences of multiple musicians. For example, one musician is a professor of music at a leading European conservatorium, maintaining a high-profile career as a soloist and undertaking an active mentoring role for new artists. A second musician, chief conductor of a European orchestra, works with orchestras around the world and mentors aspiring conductors. The interviews comprised questions on five key themes: (1) factors considered crucial for the achievement of sustainable careers; (2) personal attributes; (3) musicians' skills; (4) musicians' roles; and (5) recommendations for the education and training of musicians.

A recurring interview theme was that musicians need to be entrepreneurial in their outlook, and need to possess effective business skills in order to create and manage opportunities for employment and career development. Interviewees reiterated the recommendations made by survey respondents and artists for the inclusion of real and simulated experience within musicians' education and training. Experience within the profession was considered to be a vital engagement from which student musicians could learn the potential for engagement in a variety of roles, and the importance of non-performance skills in maximizing available opportunities. The increasing requirement for practitioners to be aware of community cultural development was iterated by three of the five interviewees. Comments relating to mentors and networks referred particularly to new practitioners, and interviewees concurred with the significant finding that teaching is the most common activity for musicians.

Also emphasized was the need for musicians to possess skills in pedagogy, and the psychological stress experienced by musicians when teaching is undertaken as a result of insufficient performance opportunities, or as 'bread and butter work'. Likewise, discussion concerning performance skills centred on the difficulty of achieving and sustaining a performance role. Comments relating to building sustainable careers in music were grouped thematically, and are summarized to follow:

Business Skills

- 'It's so important to train people with the attitude to be an entrepreneur right from the word go. Not, "Oh, my God, I didn't get this job, and now what am I going to do?" And at that point they are already out of school and they don't have the mindset, they don't have the skills.'
- 'It used to be that you would just perform, but then people stopped [performing] all the time. So you need different skills and that means also that most people are freelancers, and they are entrepreneurs.'
- 'Marketing is very important. You have to develop an image that attracts oneself to promoters: individuality.'
- 'Before you get anything off the ground … you have to write a submission and you have to have a board, and you have to know how a board works.'

Community Engagement

- '[Community engagement has become increasingly important for getting funding in a wide range of areas] with many government foundations and private foundations in the US.'
- '[Engagement with communities] dictates whether they get the job. In the cities they can ring up the teacher and perform: for example, in kindergartens, in schools. But some of them can't do that.'
- 'Community cultural development should be included in courses and is increasingly important.'

Teaching Skills

- 'Pianists who haven't the chance to be top, or don't reach the highest quality, cannot survive in concert life … So either they accompany … or (and this is a major problem) they begin to teach. I'm convinced that teaching is a very special power and needs motivation for teaching and for education … In Europe there are musicians who are not successful and they begin to teach, and they are terrible. They are disappointed, the students are disappointed.'
- 'Musicians at all levels teach. The notion that pedagogy is not an essential part of the curriculum I find very bizarre.'

Peer Networks and Mentors

- 'I think mentors and a network is really something very important, especially when beginning. You need somebody who has contacts.'
- 'Self-promotion relates to peer-networks in getting oneself known … Industry networks generally will get work.'
- 'From a composer's point of view, mentoring probably is the best way to develop.'

Performance Matters

- 'I think that competitions are an industry. And how do they win? ... It depends on what the jury likes ... To focus on competitions and winning competitions is a little like false economy. It can harm their creativity and individual style.'
- 'I really look at conservatories where students of piano are not obliged to accompany, and it's beyond reality. The reality is that beyond their diploma they try to get a job, and they will not get an invitation from 20 orchestras to play with them in a concert.'
- 'Conducting is an essential source of work for composers, particularly conducting for community groups. Most successful composers also are conductors.'
- 'Musicians need to have good physical stamina ... and be encouraged to develop it, be encouraged to play sport and be physically active and to lead active lifestyles, because whilst at 20 it doesn't seem very important, by the time you reach 50 it's essential.'

Personal Attributes

In line with Quantz's thesis that musicians need the three key qualities of passion, physical strength and a natural talent without vanity, musicians identified personal attributes that they perceive crucial to achieving a sustainable career. They placed passion at the core of personal attributes; passion drives motivation, confidence, resilience and determination, and openness or adaptability to change. The attributes are exactly the same as those defined by the cultural industries sample in Chapter 5.

Musicians suggest that there are innate elements in all of the personal attributes, but that all attributes can be developed through effective training programmes. Illustrated in the form of a matrix at Figure 6.7, the personal attributes are defined without hierarchical inference: focusing rather on interaction and process. The matrix is based on a conditional/consequential matrix model, described by Anselm Strauss and Juliet Corbin as representing 'constant interplay inter/action [process] with conditions/consequences [structure] and the dynamic evolving nature of events'.[3] In light of the consideration that personal attributes can be developed and, therefore, that they can diminish, the matrix includes both positive and negative influences.

Education and Training

The aspirations of students were a constant topic of discussion. Comments included a perceived hierarchy of courses from performance at an elite level to teaching at a less significant level, and the desire of many students to become a superstar: 'students generally aspire to be a 'big hit'; a superstar. The passion for students is the attainment of stardom and money'. Many musicians wrote or talked about an initial

---

3   Anselm Strauss and Juliet Corbin, *Basics of Qualitative Research* (Thousand Oaks, CA, 1998), 2nd edn.

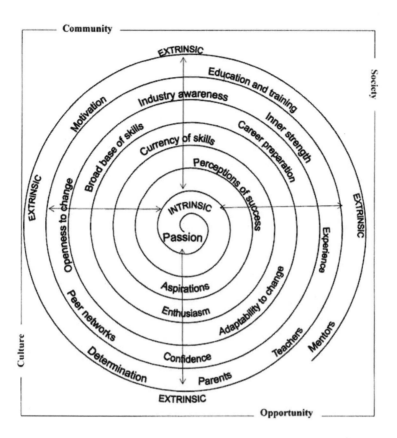

Figure 6.7　　Personal Attributes of Musicians

quest for stardom: 'I love performing, but the quest is no longer associated with fame … my ideal has become musical rather than self-centred.'

The conductor described a reduction in the level of injury caused by physical and emotional stress since the introduction of regular physical support for orchestral musicians in Europe, and recommended the inclusion of injury prevention programmes within education and training. The majority of comments relating to recommended changes to education and training concern industry experience and career awareness, the inclusion of which was described as an 'ethical issue' for educational institutions. Particularly noteworthy was the comment that performance courses are not long enough to provide students with the skills and knowledge that they require: 'Make courses longer, or don't expect to fit it all in'. A summary of comments follows, grouped thematically:

Teaching

- '[M]ost of the classical musicians who leave here [and] who don't become performers, are teachers. Some get out of music altogether.'

Planning Sustainable Careers

- 'One should at least tell people [students] the truth about the profession. If you can build broader skills into the [education and training] programs: take a lateral approach, in a sense, exiting graduates will have a much greater chance of staying in the profession in some capacity.'
- 'Students go into music because of passion. The trick for institutions is to help retain and encourage that passion whilst informing students of the profession.'
- 'The lack of career awareness is an ethical issue, and it becomes even more of an issue if they [conservatories] don't recognise it as one.'
- '[It is important] not only to heighten awareness at an institutional level, but also to heighten awareness at a student level, because students come in thinking "I'm training to be an orchestral player", and there may be one or two openings per year in the whole country [the US].'
- 'I think that professional work is very important to get them [students] experience and to meet people.'
- 'Access to the profession. I would like to see much more interaction between what happens in the professional performance area at the top level, and the students' access to it … there should be considerable cooperation between the musical educational institutes and the major performing organisations. Undergraduates could be more prepared for the realities of life as a musician.'
- 'Students should be aware that very few will make it. Students are probably not aware of that fact. A crucial element of any business course or unit would be to create an awareness of the industry and the realities of professional practice.'
- 'It seems to me that the main activities of classical instrumental musicians are driven by degrees of talent. Many have the desire/ambition to enter a high-class orchestra and pursue this as a career. Unfortunately, the number of positions available is relatively small compared to the number of applicants.'
- 'Pianists do not see the reality that for most of them it's impossible to survive as a pianist in concert.'
- '[Students] mostly want to be performers.'
- 'Preparation for auditions should be included as standard for all students because only a handful 'make it' as soloists.'
- 'Rehearsal skills are very important in order that musicians are able to work as a team player and as a leader.'
- 'I think there could afford to be more time devoted to pedagogy and psychology.'
- 'To achieve the [student] quota the criteria have to be lowered, which undervalues the value of the course.'
- 'Should the selection for performance degrees and performance courses be

much tougher? That would be my recommendation: that actual performance degrees should be much tougher on selection and tougher on promotion through the course, and that there should be perhaps a broader range of degrees that are combined.'

Skills Development

- 'There has also been the impact of large audiences/mass audiences upon the culture of performance, and the demands that this makes upon the musician. It's quite a different scene than that of an intimate chamber recital, and makes very different demands of the performer in terms of audience engagement and communication.'
- 'We know that musicians are employed in a number of different areas, and there are a growing number of musicians who realise the necessity to be multi-skilled and able to cross musical genres with expertise.'
- 'The psychology of performance could be a profession on its own, much the same as specialists attached to sports institutes who coach athletes to cope with issues such as stress prior to an important race. A trained musician would be ideally placed to take on this role, having experienced the psychological stresses of musicians.'
- 'I know that languages are being cut across the board in music programs and it's a crime. It's like cutting mathematics out of a medical degree … [It is] the same with music: if you don't speak German, how do you instinctively phrase a piece of German music? … If you want to be a really top level artist, you need to have at least two or three languages.'

Graduate Tracking

The issue of graduate tracking was raised by both educators and practising musicians, with the point made that graduate data collections do not measure employment outcomes for those in protean careers. However, musicians are not overly sympathetic to the plight of conservatories, suggesting that reluctance on the part of institutions to release available statistics relates to poor graduate employment:

- 'I suspect that there hasn't been graduate tracking of music performance courses because the results would be too unwelcome. There is much information now through more sophisticated data on alumni in institutions, but probably not widely publicised as many musicians trained mainly as performers move into the teaching area.'
- 'That [graduates go on to further study] is not something that we track. I can only give you an anecdotal figure of maybe about 50 per cent I guess. Maybe even more. Especially those who want teaching as a backup. They want to be earning some professional salary.'
- 'NASM [National Association of Schools of Music] in the United States publishes statistics on music graduates. Three or four years ago there was

something like 15,000 – 20,000 graduating with degrees in music. And that's just one year! You know, so there are no jobs for those people.'

- 'Yes, but the institutions won't admit that stuff [graduate employment statistics] individually. NASM will do it generically, say in music education these are the figures, and so on and so on.'
- 'I met a woman from [name of institution] and she offered to get it [graduate destination data]. Later, she wrote back and said "they won't release it." No way, because it's too scary. Some schools in engineering can say that they have a 90% placement, something like this. In music it would be zero point nothing.'
- 'If you define placement as getting "a job", there's no way.'

The next section of this chapter presents musicians' feedback on: (1) the definition of a musician; (2) intrinsic and extrinsic factors impacting on the development and sustainability of careers in music; and (3) changes to education and training.

What is a Musician?

The findings were shared with two groups of musicians, who discussed their practice and the profession. The springboard for discussion was a proposal to redefine the term *musician* to read: 'A musician is someone who practises in the profession of music in one or more specialist fields.' The first group of musicians discussed at length changes in the role of the musician over time and across different cultures according to the societal uses of music. Practising solely in performance was recognized as very rare and the group cited examples of musicians such as Bach, who pursued multiple roles.

Musicians agree that the diversity of music to which musicians are exposed is greater now than perhaps ever before. Resembling comments made by survey respondents, exposure to non-classical genres is considered beneficial to personal development, to the acquisition of a greater range of work, and to classical music performance.

The terms 'vocational' and 'professional' were discussed at length, and although the group initially considered vocational activity to be essential to the definition of a musician, the notion was eventually rejected on the basis of notable exceptions such as Borodin, who was a chemist, and Kreisler, who was a doctor. Likewise, the completion of formal training was rejected as a criterion. The group then considered the term 'practising', and one group member stated that being a musician is 'as fundamental as being involved'.

The conversation progressed to the question of whether the inclusion of performance is integral to being a musician. It was noted that less than 70 per cent of the musicians who participated in the musicians' survey had reported performance roles, and this led to discussion on the status of composers and musicologists who may not perform. Can they be considered musicians? The consensus of the group was that, given the new definition, both composers and musicologists can be categorized as musicians in their own specialities; therefore, the inclusion of performance is not essential to being a musician, but rather to being a performer.

The group next considered background as a criterion: I was considered to be a musician because of my performance background. I didn't 'lose' my musician identity as a result of my later research activities. One group member, who ran an instrumental ensemble, was asked whether she would remain a musician if she ceased performing with her ensemble and focused exclusively on the administrative role, to which she replied 'of course I would. It's as fundamental as being what I have always looked at myself as doing'. The same participant noted that when she had commenced undergraduate performance training, she was aiming to become a violinist and not a musician. Everyone agreed that self-definition as a musician comes later, when other roles have been added. One musician claimed that she was no longer a musician as she had ceased to perform for medical reasons. The group insisted that she was still a musician; she was simply no longer a violinist: 'being a musician does not [necessarily] mean performing, but if you say you are a performer, paid or unpaid, then that is your sole occupation'. A week later the musician called me to say that the loss of her performance role had led to the loss of her identity as a musician, to which she had no longer felt eligible. This had caused a significant amount of psychological stress. Having listened to the other musicians' comments, she had regained her musician identity. Rather than being a performer, she now identified as a musician focusing on non-performance activities. The group concluded that the term musician refers to engagement within the wider profession rather than to the specialization of the individual. Self-definition is crucial.

Involvement had been earlier described as fundamental to being a musician, and the group debated direct and indirect involvement with performance: one group member suggested that an 'instrumentalist may not now be a performer. It's just what they have done to become a musician'. This again implies that a musician is someone practising within the field of music rather than specifically within performance. The group also emphasized that musicians engage in multiple roles: 'how often is it that a musician only plays? That is very unrealistic in our society'. The inclusion of indirect involvement underpins the acceptance of self-identity as a musician regardless of the regularity with which performances are secured.

Akin to the first focus group, musicians in the second group spent a considerable amount of time discussing the issue of definition. The societal role of musicians was considered with respect to Merriam's functions of music: namely emotional involvement, communication, societal contribution, and entertainment.[4] Following the suggestion that a criterion for being considered a musician is society's support for the musician's activities, the historical civic and community involvement of musicians was discussed. One group member suggested that both the dictionary definitions and the suggested definition are 'correct but incomplete', in that a performer is someone who performs and a musician includes 'whatever else we do that is attached to being a musician'. Thus the identification of specialist fields within the profession of music arose as a vital issue. It was noted that the new definition could classify a concert

---

4   Alan P. Merriam, *The Anthropology of Music* (Evanston, IL, 1964).

hall usher as a musician, reflecting Small's concept of 'musicking'.[5] The group concluded that it is crucial to identify specialist fields, all of which require specific musical skills and knowledge. The group suggested that specialist fields ought to include, but should not be limited to, the performer, composer, conductor, teacher and artistic director. Another point of reference raised by the group was Elliott's term 'musicing', which refers to music as an activity.[6] The musician who cited Elliott's work suggested that musicians perform active work within fields of music, echoing the first focus group's inclusion of the term *practising*.

The inclusion of performance in one's practice was rejected as a criterion for being a musician on the basis that musicians such as composers may not perform, and it was agreed that a composer's intimacy with the music is most often with the musical product rather than with the expression, or performance, of that product. The group agreed that a performer is a specialist within the profession of music: 'All musicians can be performers, but performers can have the exclusivity of being a performer.' Echoing the first focus group, musicians noted that they trained initially to be instrumental specialists such as pianists or saxophonists. Self-definition as a musician arose with the addition of roles other than performance, and the group reflected that very few musicians work solely in performance (Illustration 6.1).

Illustration 6.1   Evolution of the Musician

A mention of Yehudi Menuhin as one of the world's most revered performers prompted the observation that many top performers include a teaching role in their practice. One group member observed a difference in the role of the elite jazz musician, who is often not a teacher. The point was made that the process of teaching and learning in jazz is evolving; whereas jazz was once learned informally, it is increasingly studied formally. As a consequence, the traditional roles of jazz performers as teachers rather than mentors may also be changing. The participant described himself as a commercial performer on the basis that his performance activities are driven by the need to earn an income.

---

5   Christopher Small, *Musicking: The Meanings of Performance and Listening* (Hanover, NH, 1998).

6   David J. Elliott, *Music Matters* (New York, 1994).

A recurring theme was that of the hierarchy or status of the various roles within the music profession. Musical hierarchy is a societal view and the dictionary definition of a musician as a performer echoes the general perception of a musician's role. The consensus of the group was that musicians' roles evolve according to political, industrial, social and personal circumstances. It is not feasible to define someone as a musician based on a set of criteria such as performance, income or formal training: 'You can't lock one person into a narrow definition because that's the way music is – always evolving'. The group concluded that the term musician is 'an umbrella term under which all these other activities happen', and that the inclusion of specialist fields within the suggested definition would provide clarity and specificity.

Musicians in the first group concurred with the recommendations for educational change, and reiterated the importance of industry experience and career preparation: 'I do feel that musicians in whatever field need to be equipped a little better or to have the specific resources available to them to help them become effective.' Requisite skills included those in teaching and business. Grant writing was emphasized by one group member, and it was acknowledged that many musicians do not possess the skills to access available funding.

Psychological and physiological injury prevention was a key focus, and musicians highlighted the importance of prevention at the earliest stages of development, and for safe working practices to be modelled within orchestral, educational and community settings. Communication skills were raised in connection with leadership roles, particularly within orchestral settings. The group acknowledged that, in general, university-level performance degrees have increased their vocational focus; however, they concluded that an extra year (or a drastic change in curriculum) is needed to provide music graduates with the requisite skills and knowledge for professional practice in music.

The second group of musicians discussed the necessity of training in generic skills such as those used in teaching and business. A particular focus was the need for musicians to be taught effective communication skills, which are vital to a musician's practice in every musical field and particularly in teaching and ensemble roles. Musicians in both groups concurred with the recommended changes to education and training given by participants in the artist and musician studies. Musicians emphasize the importance of experiential learning, communication skills and both psychological and physiological injury prevention.

Asked about personal attributes, musicians wholeheartedly placed passion at the core of their practice. Passion, they said, drives their determination to succeed.

Concluding Comments

The term *musician* is, in fact, an umbrella term for the profession. Musicians work within protean careers – undertaking multiple roles – and tend not to be paid for all of their work. The most common role for musicians is teaching. Very few musicians practice solely in performance, and those who do are most likely to self-define according to their specialty: as a violist or clarinettist. Likewise, composers are most likely to describe themselves as composers rather than as musicians.

Musicians' roles change throughout their careers as they adapt their practice to reflect personal circumstances, and significant influences in this respect are stability of employment, level of job satisfaction and family responsibilities. Factors influencing attrition from creative or performance roles or from the profession altogether are the same for artists and musicians, and further highlight the similarities in the practice of artists across multiple artforms. Musicians use a variety of skills to sustain their practice and these skills are strongly reflected in their recommendations for education and training, which emphasize the need for musicians to graduate with foundation skills in teaching and business, and advocate for education and training to incorporate career planning and industry experience.

Chapter 7

Dilemmas and Opportunities

'Far from making a living by making music, the majority of musicians finance music making by making a living'

In the preceding chapters we have looked at the realities of life as a musician and the dilemmas faced by practitioners, educators, funding bodies and policy-makers in meeting those realities. In this chapter we bring each element into focus and move from dilemmas to opportunities: exploring ways to fundamentally change the development and sustainability of careers. The conceptual framework shown at Figure 7.1 highlights important elements in that it: (1) is situated within the context of the communities in which musicians practice; (2) recognizes the similarities between professional practice for all cultural practitioners; (3) acknowledges the value and relevance of both performance and non performance-based study in the training of musicians; and (4) positions practitioners and the cultural industries within a Cultural Practice Framework.

Dilemmas

Dilemmas in the Environment

The existing milieu of weak cultural intelligence and ineffective communication contribute to a less than satisfactory environment that inhibits the potential for cultural practitioners such as musicians to create sustainable careers. We have identified that artist attrition across multiple artforms is influenced by insufficient financial security, unsociable hours, injury and a lack of practitioner diversity. The desire for increased job satisfaction, stable employment and a higher salary have also transpired as the three most common factors influencing musicians to change the extent of their performance role. Abandonment of creative roles is often the consequence of insufficient opportunities and a resulting sense of failure: 'securing a mortgage ... required a steady income. Performance engagements [were] never assured or regular: little financial security'. In fact, the only artists who consider there to be potential for secure employment tend to be those working within education.

Andy Arthurs reports that musicians make a living by making music,[1] but I have to disagree: far from making a living by making music, the majority of musicians finance music making by making a living. The profession of geology includes geologists who specialize in areas such as exploration, mining or resource definition.

---

1   Andy Arthurs, 'Why Creative Industries?', *Australian Music Forum*, 10(5), (2004): 32–5.

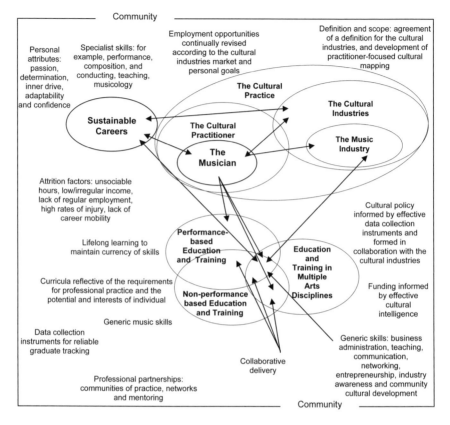

Figure 7.1   Conceptual Framework

No one would suggest that the sole role of a geologist is to look at rocks. Neither is the sole role of musicians to perform music. Most musicians are wholly or partly self-employed and work in a variety of different and often interdependent roles throughout their careers. Holding an average of more than two different music industry roles, approximately one-third of musicians undertake work outside of the sector. Protean careers are normal practice not only for freelance musicians but for musicians employed in full-time performance roles; the majority of full-time orchestral musicians include teaching, freelance performance and other roles in their practice.

Musicians spend more time teaching than performing. On average, male musicians spent a greater percentage of their working time in performance, composition, examining and technical roles; and female musicians spent more time in teaching, ensemble direction and business roles. Performance is the second most common activity for musicians, few of whom work exclusively in performance. Metier writes that 77 per cent of UK musicians earn over half of their income from teaching, and that almost 90 per cent hold a secondary occupation.[2] Performance as a secondary

---

2   Metier, *Orchestral Research Final Report* (London, 2002).

role for over half of the UK respondents indicates that many musicians combine teaching and performance activities within their careers. Likewise, a Danish study of contemporary musicians reports only 6 per cent of music graduates working solely in performance and 50 per cent of graduates working in a combination of teaching and performance roles.[3]

The Dilemma of Success

It is highly unlikely that a musician will achieve a career solely in performance, despite this being the primary aim of most music students; therefore, it is incomplete to describe a musician as a performer. Musicians in the twenty-first century engage in multiple roles within and outside of the music profession, and success is marked by the achievement of sustainable practice. This requires musicians (and everyone else) to break down attitudinal and hierarchical barriers; musicians should consider the success of their practice on the basis of personal career satisfaction rather than a pre-conceived hierarchy of roles.

During their initial training and practice, musicians are inclined to self-define according to their instrumental speciality: as a pianist or an oboist. Self-definition as a musician arises once musicians add non-performance roles to their professional practice, and signals a change in identity that is not always welcome. The only way for musicians to be at ease with their professional identity is to adopt the wider definition of what it is to be a musician, which one musician described as: 'based on the activities that you do rather than on the status you have achieved'. The Cultural Practice Framework presented in this chapter provides a tool with which to explore the diverse range of activities that represent holistic cultural practice, all of which activities should be considered equally successful if they meet an individual's personal and professional needs. Later in this chapter we will discuss how these opportunities can be developed, understood and positively communicated.

Dilemmas in Education and Training

The most common reason given by musicians for the non-completion of study is an early transition to work, which is logical given that a performance degree is not a pre-requisite for the workplace; however, formal education and training is critical to the development of classical musicians, almost all of whom study formally. The undergraduate performance degree is the single most important form of initial training, thus it is crucial to consider the relationship between the practice of musicians and the content of performance degree courses.

Given that musicians typically hold protean careers, in common with other business people they sustain their practice by recognizing and meeting the needs of the market: 'it's so important to train people with the attitude of entrepreneurs right from the

---

3   Jan Ole Traasdahl, 'Rhythmic Music Education in Denmark', in G.M. Oliva (ed.), *The ISME Commission for the Education of the Professional Musician 1996 Seminar. The Musician's Role: New Challenges* (Lund, 1996), pp. 67–74.

word go'. In addition to performance skills, musicians require the skills to run a small business, the confidence to create new opportunities, pedagogical and communication skills for use in educational, ensemble and community settings, industry knowledge, and strong professional networks. These should form core elements of education and training, but education providers are faced with the dilemma of insufficient funding, inflexible curricula (which influence insufficient funding), and incomplete graduate destination data (which result in insufficient funding).

The effectiveness of training and education for any profession is determined by the extent to which the profession is perceived and understood. The four roles in which musicians spend the highest average proportion of time are (in order) teaching, performance, business administration and ensemble direction. Shown at Figure 7.2, a comparison of the proportion of time that musicians spend in each of the four most common roles, and the extent to which each role is incorporated into musicians' training as described in Chapter 4, strongly suggests that existing training does not adequately prepare musicians for the profession. In fact, most Bachelor of Music degrees ought to be renamed Bachelor of Performance degrees.

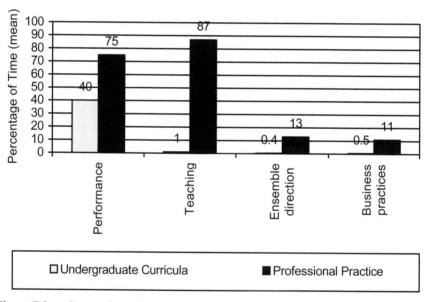

Figure 7.2   Comparison of Focus within Professional Practice and Undergraduate Training

In describing their use of different skills, musicians note a wide variety of arts-related roles such as orchestral, freelance and chamber work, retail and hire businesses, teaching practices, artist management and positions on boards and committees. The skills that musicians describe are indicative of the dominance of protean careers. Given that musicians spend more time teaching than in any other activity, there is a clear need for performance degrees to incorporate an accredited teaching qualification that is recognized by the professional bodies with which graduates will work: 'there isn't so much a shortage of instrumental music teachers, as a shortage of qualified ones'.

At the very least, musicians should graduate with foundation-level teaching skills and with some credit towards a teaching qualification. Practising musicians identify inadequate career preparation relating to insufficient industry experience, a lack of skills in business and poor awareness of the music profession: 'when I sub-contract a 23-year-old musician for a gig who has just graduated from a music degree and doesn't even know what an invoice is let alone how to write one I know there is something definitely wrong'.

Another dilemma is that of motivating student interest in non-performance studies, given that students often select their school for the quality and reputation of performance staff and aim – for the most part – for performance careers. Self-identity is crucial to career satisfaction, and it is imperative for students and artists to identify success as being the establishment of a sustainable career that meets personal and professional needs, rather than aspiring to purely creative careers that are few and far between. One of the issues is that students often don't see the relevance of learning non-performance skills, and are not aware of the exciting possibilities to do a wide variety of things in their lives as musicians; again, marking the need to move away from the perception that a musician is a performer, and that performance is top of the 'success ladder'. However, artists are not simply performers and creators. Success as an artist is the achievement of a sustainable career, regardless of whether it includes the performance or the creation of art.

Opportunities

The Cultural Practice Framework

The cultural industries are significant, and they continue to grow in size and scope as leisure time increases and the population ages. Together, the cultural industries have the potential to effectively communicate the tangible and intangible values of culture, and to help practitioners to meet their economic and creative needs. Whatever definition one gives to the cultural industries, they form an important part of society and contain a wealth of inter-disciplinary opportunities for cultural practice. Practitioners and educators would do well to keep their fingers on the pulse of the cultural industries, and to explore the potential for holistic practice.

The Cultural Practice Framework illustrates the application of the generic and specific attributes of artists beyond more obvious vocations and towards holistic employment throughout the cultural industries. It highlights the diversity of roles available to cultural practitioners not only as a means to make ends meet, but to build intrinsically satisfying artistic careers. Practitioner-focused mapping of the cultural industries looked beyond existing barriers and focused instead on elements that constitute cultural activity, regardless of artform, genre, perceived hierarchy or statistical 'label'. The resulting Framework consists of four practitioner-focused, non-hierarchical groups that were determined through analysis of the major foci characterizing roles within the cultural industries. These foci are informed by Hans Hoegh-Guldberg's observation that a statistical framework should distinguish between primary creation and creative expression.[4] Accordingly, the four Framework groups are titled *primary creation, expression of creative activity, essential services* and *related activities*. Australian statistical category numbers have been included to illustrate the alarming number of cultural activities currently reported in data collections as 'not elsewhere classified' (miscellaneous). Reducing the number of miscellaneous occupations is particularly important to the development of improved cultural intelligence. The Framework was informed by:

- Interview and survey data from a wide range of practising artists;
- A review of the Australian Bureau of Statistics (ABS) data, Australian Standard Classification of Occupations (ASCO),[5] and Australia and New Zealand Standard Industry Classifications (ANZSIC);
- A review of UK, US and Canadian statistical categories and data collections;
- A review of literature relating to the cultural industries; and
- Consultation with economists, social researchers, and representatives from the government departments, arts support and advisory organisations and unions.

Figures 7.3 to 7.6 illustrate the Framework and are described below.

Figure 7.3: Primary creation   The primary creation group stems from roles such as composition, painting and sculpture; namely the process of creating something that displays qualities such as sensibility and imagination.

Figure 7.4: Expression of creative activity   Deborah Barker and Larry Gaut suggest communication to be 'a process in which two or more elements of a system interact in order to achieve a desired outcome or goal'.[6] This category represents the communication of artistic work and includes performers of music, dance and drama in addition to performing artists such as street performers and acrobats.

Figure 7.5: Essential services   The communication of artistic product most often requires the involvement of people beyond those who create or perform it: artistic works are commonly exhibited in a gallery, performed in a concert hall or broadcast over the radio. Sound and lighting, design, ticketing and production are just some of the roles on which the vast majority of artistic communication depends. Occupations providing these and other services form the essential services group.

---

4   Hans Hoegh-Guldberg, 'The Arts Economy 1968–98: Three Decades of Growth in Australia' (Sydney, NSW, 2000).

5   Australian Culture and Leisure Classification (ACLC) coding includes sub-categories that are indicated with two additional numbers: 2537.<u>79</u>.

6   Larry L. Barker and Deborah A. Gaut, *Communication* (Massachusetts, 2001), 8th edn.

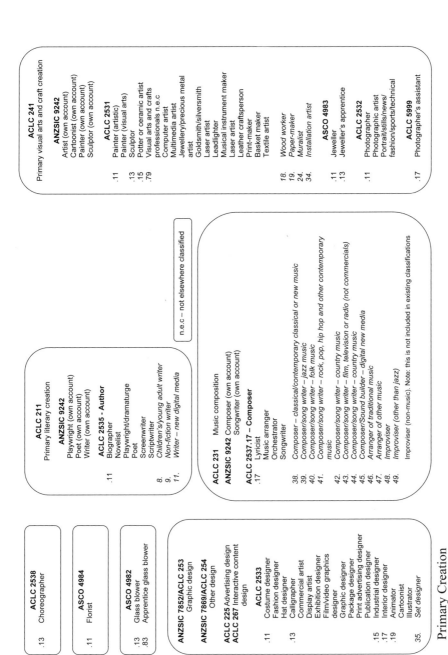

ACLC 241
Primary visual arts and craft creation

ANZSIC 9242
Artist (own account)
Cartoonist (own account)
Painter (own account)
Sculptor (own account)

ACLC 2531
.11 Painter (artistic)
  Painter (visual arts)
.13 Sculptor
.15 Potter or ceramic artist
.79 Visual arts and crafts professionals n.e.c
  Computer artist
  Multimedia artist
  Jewellery/precious metal artist
  Goldsmith/silversmith
  Laser artist
  Leadlighter
  Musical instrument maker
  Laser artist
  Leather craftsperson
  Print-maker
  Basket maker
  Textile artist

ASCO 4983
.18 *Wood worker*
.19 *Paper-maker*
.24 *Muralist*
.34 *Installation artist*

ACLC 2532
.11 Jeweller
.13 Jeweller's apprentice

ACLC 2532
.11 Photographer
  Photographic artist
  Portrait/stills/news/fashion/sports/technical

ACLC 5999
.17 Photographer's assistant

---

n.e.c – not elsewhere classified

ACLC 211
Primary literary creation

ANZSIC 9242
Playwright (own account)
Poet (own account)
Writer (own account)

ACLC 2535 - Author
.11 Biographer
  Novelist
  Playwright/dramaturge
  Poet
  Screenwriter
  Scriptwriter
8. *Children's/young adult writer*
9. *Non-fiction writer*
11. *Writer – new digital media*

ACLC 231 Music composition

ANZSIC 9242 Composer (own account)
  Songwriter (own account)

ACLC 2537.17 – Composer
.17 Lyricist
  Music arranger
  Orchestrator
  Songwriter
38. *Composer – classical/contemporary classical or new music*
39. *Composer/song writer – jazz music*
40. *Composer/song writer – folk music*
41. *Composer/song writer – rock, pop, hip hop and other contemporary music*
42. *Composer/song writer – country music*
43. *Composer/song writer – film, television or radio (not commercials)*
44. *Composer/song writer – country music*
45. *Composer/Sound builder – digital new media*
46. *Arranger of traditional music*
47. *Arranger of other music*
48. *Improviser*
49. *Improviser (other than jazz)*
  Improviser (non-music). Note: this is not not included in existing classifications

---

ACLC 2538
.13 Choreographer

ASCO 4984
.11 Florist

ASCO 4982
.13 Glass blower
.83 Apprentice glass blower

ANZSIC 7852/ACLC 253 Graphic design
ANZSIC 7869/ACLC 254 Other design
ACLC 225 Advertising design
ACLC 267 Interactive content design

ACLC 2533
.11 Costume designer
  Fashion designer
  Hat designer
.13 Calligrapher
  Commercial artist
  Display artist
  Exhibition designer
  Film/video graphics designer
  Graphic designer
  Package designer
  Print advertising designer
  Publication designer
.15 Industrial designer
.17 Interior designer
.19 Animator
  Cartoonist
  Illustrator
35. *Set designer*

Figure 7.3   Primary Creation

ANZSIC 9241 – Music and Theatre Productions

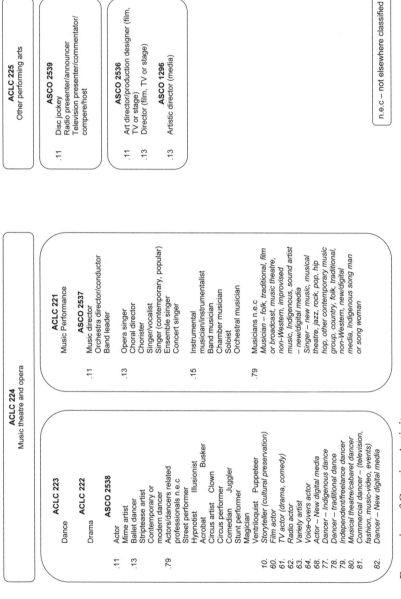

ACLC 224
Music theatre and opera

ACLC 221
Music Performance

.11 **ASCO 2537**
Music director
Orchestra director/conductor
Band leader

.13 Opera singer
Choral director
Chorister
Singer/vocalist
Singer (contemporary, popular)
Ensemble singer
Concert singer

.15 Instrumental
musician/instrumentalist
Band musician
Chamber musician
Soloist
Orchestral musician

.79 Musicians n.e.c
Musician – folk, traditional, film
or broadcast, music theatre,
non-Western, improvised
music, Indigenous, sound artist
– new/digital media
Singer – new music, musical
theatre, jazz, rock, pop, hip
hop, other contemporary music
group, country, folk, traditional,
non-Western, new/digital
media, Indigenous song man
or song woman

ACLC 223
Dance

ACLC 222
Drama

ASCO 2538

.11 Actor
Mime artist

.13 Ballet dancer
Striptease artist
Contemporary or
modern dancer

.79 Actors/dancers related
professionals n.e.c
Street performer
Hypnotist   Illusionist
Acrobat   Busker
Circus artist Clown
Circus performer
Comedian   Juggler
Stunt performer
Magician
Ventriloquist Puppeteer

.10 Storyteller (cultural preservation)
.60 Film actor
.61 TV actor (drama, comedy)
.62 Radio actor
.63 Variety artist
.64 Voice-overs actor
.68 Actor – New digital media
.77 Dancer – Indigenous dance
.78 Dancer – traditional dance
.79 Independent/freelance dancer
.80 Musical theatre/cabaret dancer
.81 Commercial dancer – (television,
fashion, music-video, events)
.82 Dancer – New digital media

ACLC 225
Other performing arts

.11 **ASCO 2539**
Disc jockey
Radio presenter/announcer
Television presenter/commentator/
compere/host

ASCO 2536
.11 Art director/production designer (film,
TV or stage)
.13 Director (film, TV or stage)

ASCO 1296
.13 Artistic director (media)

n.e.c – not elsewhere classified

Figure 7.4   Expression of Creative Activity

ACLC 469 Other culture and leisure services n.e.c
ACLC 2537 .79 Musicians/related professionals n.e.c
Music copyist
ACLC 4999 .17 Ethnomusicologist
ACLC 2535 .13 Piano tuner
Script editor
Book editor
ACLC 2533 .11 Costume designer

ACLC 252 Advertising production
ACLC 461 Booking and ticketing agencies
ACLC 8312 .11 Entertainment usher
Ticket collector/usher/venue attendant
ACLC 8292 .11 Ticket seller

ANZSIC 9259 Services to the arts n.e.c
Casting agency operation
Costume design service
Set designing service
Theatre lighting service
Theatre ticket agency operation
ACLC 1231 .11 Supply and distribution manager
ACLC 462 Music group management or agent services

ANZSIC 9241 Music and Theatre Productions
Ballet company operation
Band operation
Choral group operation
Music group operation
Musical comedy company operation
Opera company operation
Orchestra operation
Performing artist operation
Puppet show operation
Theatrical company operation
ACLC 1299 .79 Specialist managers n.e.c
Personal manager
Performing arts road manager

ACLC 263 Film and video production
ANZSIC 9111 Film and video production
Motion picture editing
Motion picture film or tape production
Newsreel tape production
Television film or tape production
ACLC 2536 .11 Art director (film, TV or stage)
.13 Production designer (film, TV or stage)
Director (film, TV or stage)
Radio producer
.15 Director (film, TV or stage)
Director of photography (cinematographer)
.17 Film and video editor
.19 Stage manager
.21 Programme director (radio or TV)
Broadcaster (radio)
.23 Technical director
.79 Casting director
Video producer
ACLC 1296 .11 Executive producer
Stage producer
Media producer
.13 Artistic director (media)
ACLC 4992 .11 Audio operator
Camera operator (film, TV/ video)
Dubbing machine operator
Dubbing projectionist (sound mixing)
Focus puller
Pre-recording mixer
Sound/audio technician
Sound editor
Sound effects editor/person
Sound effects recordist
Sound effects technical
Sound mixer
Video and sound recorder
TV equipment operator
.15 Vision mixer
Broadcast transmitter operator
.17 Motion picture projectionist
.19 Light technician/assistant/electrician
.21 Production assistant (film, TV or radio)
Make-up artist
.27 Lighting director
.79 Boom operator

ACLC 226 Performing arts venues
ANZSIC 9251 Sound recording studios
Sound recording studio operation (excludes radio services – class 9121)
ANZSIC 9252 Performing arts venues
Concert hall operation
Entertainment centre
Music bowl operation
Music hall operation (excludes theatre restaurant)
Opera house operation
Playhouse operation
Theatre operation (except motion picture theatre)
ANZSIC 9330 Other recreation services
Circus operation
Dance hall or studio operation
Merry-go-round operation
Railway operation (historical/tourist)
ANZSIC 9113 Motion picture exhibition
ACLC 265 Cinema operation
Drive-in theatre operation
Film or video festival operation
Motion picture screening
Motion picture theatre operation
Newsreel theatre operation
ACLC 463 Event management
ACLC 2549 .19 Activities officer
Recreation advisor
Recreation officer
ACLC 3391 .21 Museum/gallery curator
.15 Entertainment centre manager
.79 Sport and recreation managers n.e.c
ACLC 3399 .27 Theatre/cinema manager
ACLC 3324 .11 Club manager (licensed premises)
ACLC 1299 .79 Arts Centre manager
Studio manager
ACLC 4992 .79 Performing arts support workers n.e.c
Theatrical dresser

n.e.c: not elsewhere classified

Figure 7.5   Essential Services

ANZSIC 9220 Museums
- Art museum operation
- Historic house operation
- Museum operation
- War memorial operation

ANZSIC 2942 Toy and sporting goods manufacturing n.e.c (ACLC 481 alignment)
ANZSIC 2949 Musical instrument manufacturing
ANZSIC 2849 Electronic equipment manufacturing n.e.c
ANZSIC 2430 Recorded media manufacturing and publishing
ACLC 481 Other culture and leisure goods manufacturing n.e.c
ACLC 233 Record companies and distributors
ASCO 2531 .79 Musical instrument maker/repairer
ASCO 4999 .79 Tradespersons and related workers n.e.c

ANZSIC 4113 Non-residential building
ACLC 471 Culture and leisure facilities construction
ASCO 2121 .11 Architect
ASCO 2523 .11 Town planner
ASCO 3121 .13 Architectural associate / Building drafting officer / Architectural draftsperson
ANZSIC 7821 Architect (own account) / Architectural consultancy service

---

ACLC 234 Recording music retailing
ANZSIC 5235 Recorded music retailing
ANZSIC 5235 Audiocassette retailing
ANZSIC 5249 Retailing n.e.c

ACLC 271 Music instrument retailing
ANZSIC 5259 Musical instruments retailing / Musical instruments wholesaling

ANZSIC 4795 Art gallery operation (retail)
ANZSIC 5243 Artists' supplies wholesaling
ANZSIC 9423 Artists' supplies retailing
ACLC 212 Books and other publishing
ACLC 217 Newspaper printing and publishing

ACLC 215 Literature retailing including newspapers
ACLC 232 Other printing / Music publishing/printing

ASCO 2222 .79 Technical sales representatives
ACLC 5999 .15 Visual merchandiser

ANZSIC 9112 Motion picture distribution / Motion picture leasing / Video leasing (excludes hire to the public via video outlets)

ACLC 2534 .11 Editor/associate editor / Features/news/pictures editor / Sub-editor
- .13 Print journalist / Columnist/feature/leader/special
- .15 TV journalist/reporter
- .17 Radio journalist/reporter
- .19 Copywriter
- .79 Critic / Arts journalist

ANZSIC 2413 Artwork preparation service
ACLC 242 Commercial photography services
ACLC 5999 .17 Photographer's assistant
ASCO 7298 .11 Photographic developer and printer

ACLC 2529 .11 Cultural historian
ACLC 2537 .79 Musicologist/Ethnomusicologist
ACLC 2292 .11 Special librarian
ACLC 2299 .15 Manuscripts archivists / Film archivist

ANZSIC 9621 Business and Professional Services n.e.c
ASCO 2299 .79 Business/information professionals n.e.c
ACLC 464 Culture/leisure business professionals and labour associations / Art union operations n.e.c
ANZSIC 9321 Accountant
ASCO 2211 .11 Accountant
- .13 Marketing specialist
- .15 Market research analyst
- .17 Advertising specialist
ASCO 3292 Project or programme manager
ANZSIC 9629 Associations operation (for the promotion of community or sectional interests)
ACLC 2605 .99 Legal professionals n.e.c
ASCO 2521 .79 Arts lawyer
ASCO 2221 .11 Public relations officer
- .13 Marketing specialist
- .15 Market research analyst
- .17 Advertising specialist
ANZSIC 8622 Medical service specialist (music therapist)
ACLC 273 Copyright collection services

ANZSIC 8440 Other education
- Music school operation n.e.c
- Art school operation n.e.c
ACLC 272 Arts education
ASCO 2491 .11 Art teacher (private)
- .13 Music teacher (private)
- .15 Singing teacher (private) / Ballet teacher (private)
- .17 Dance teacher (private) / Drama teacher (private) / Elocution teacher (private)
- .79 Extra-systemic teachers n.e.c
ASCO 2411 .11 Pre-primary school teacher
ASCO 2412 .11 Primary school teacher
ASCO 2413 .11 Secondary school teacher
ASCO 2414 .79 Special education teachers n.e.c
ASCO 2421 .11 Special education teacher
ASCO 2422 .13 University lecturer / University tutor
ASCO 2493 .11 Vocational education teacher
ASCO 2549 .11 Education officer / Recreation officer
- .19 Recreation advisor
ASCO 3901 .11 Community worker (CCD) *Primarily – writer, visual art/craft practitioner, theatre/physical performance, musician/singer, dancer, film/video/sound, new/digital media*

---

n.e.c – not elsewhere classified

Figure 7.6   Related Activities

Figure 7.6: Related activities   The fourth group concerns activities that are associated with the creation and/or the communication of an artistic product. Activities selected for inclusion form an important part of the roles often performed by practising artists. Related activities include the manufacture and distribution of equipment, business and professional services, arts journalism, publishing, editing and education.

Key to the Cultural Practice Framework

ACLC: Australian Culture and Leisure Classifications Industry Classification
ACLC: Australian Culture and Leisure Classifications Occupation Classification
ANZSIC: Australia and New Zealand Standard Industry Classifications
ASCO: Australian Standard Classification of Occupations
---   Occupations/activities included in Throsby and Hollister[7], and not elsewhere classified or defined

Community of Practice

Effective advocacy for the cultural industries requires a united voice, and increased competition for limited funding is counter-productive and divisive in that regard. As Geoffrey Bolton suggests, we 'are more likely to be given patronage by both the private and public sector if we show ourselves willing to maximise our existing resources through intelligent and voluntary cooperation'.[8] The importance of partnerships is highlighted by Donald Horne, past Chair of the Australia Council, who urged a National Ideas Summit meeting in Canberra to support a manifesto that reads: 'we urge that the various [cultural] organisations ... establish some form of consultation to further their common interests and to build bridges with the rest of the community'.

One of the ways in which contact is maintained within the cultural sector is through networks, which are the most common form of intra-industry communication. Such networks have existed for centuries in forms such as early European guilds, professional meeting groups or peer networks. However, the term *Community of Practice* (CoP) was first used by Jean Lave and Etienne Wenger to describe situated or active learning, and refers to a group of people who communicate upon a topic of common interest.[9] A valuable organizational resource that improves performance and contributes to successful knowledge management, the CoP has been described as having the potential 'to be an organisation's most versatile and dynamic knowledge resource'.[10] Networks result in what Pierre Bourdieu and Jean-Claude Passeron term 'cultural capital'. Acquired through opportunities provided by socio-economic

---

7   See David Throsby and Virginia Hollister, *Don't Give Up Your Day Job: An Economic Study of Professional Artists in Australia* (Sydney, NSW, 2003).

8   Geoffrey Bolton, *The Muses in a Quest for Patronage* (Perth, WA, 1996).

9   Jean Lave and Etienne Wenger, *Situated Learning: Legitimate Peripheral Participation* (New York, 1991).

10 John Mitchell, Sarah Wood and Susan Young, 'Communities of Practice: Reshaping Professional Practice and Improving Organisational Productivity in the Vocational Education and Training (VET) Sector' (Melbourne, VIC, 2001).

circumstances, supportive peers or parents, and exposure to music programmes and other cultural activities, capital plays an important part in securing work.[11] Practitioners stress that involvement in networks is vital to sustainable practice: 'the only way you will ever make it as a professional musician is to get up and personally promote yourself'; 'industry networks generally will get work'. Henry Mancini summarizes the importance of networks for the freelance musician: 'one of the best ways for an instrumentalist to crack through is to find the people who do the same thing he [sic] does. A trumpet player should know every trumpet player in town if he can, because that's the only way he is going to break in'.[12] The importance of networks has been heightened by the emergence of technology that enables artists, including musicians, to become established with self-produced recordings, books and printed music. Hoegh-Guldberg describes the trend as the DIY revolution, and cites the Creative Industries Research and Application Centre (CIRAC) definition of '"a value web" of grass roots people, artists, producers and other small and micro businesses who create value through networking and what CIRAC calls "creative entrepreneurism"'.[13]

Musicians describe the music profession as a 'tough business' and 'a very unstable industry'. Communication within the cultural industries is diffuse, and practitioners comment that communication is particularly poor between the government and non-government sectors. Mentorship and networking is very important for practitioners such as freelance musicians, who struggle to locate advice on issues such as arts law, business and career development. Likewise, many music educators operate in isolation from peers and would benefit from a network of mentors. There is also the potential for online communities of practice to assist increasing numbers of educators to participate in national and global debate, in cross-campus organizational planning and in the collaborative delivery of curriculum. Although online delivery was traditionally based on the use of pre-developed text and had limited use in practical activities, synchronous and asynchronous delivery tools are increasingly useful. According to Brad Beach, 'the power of this medium is so strong that it actually changes the traditional social hierarchy of the classroom'.[14]

Previous research has shown communities of practice to be effective catalysts for much-needed partnerships across the cultural industries, and external partners from the education and music sectors have proven to be valuable drivers with the researcher a facilitator of the change process.[15] The drive towards constant renewal of curricula benefits from effective organizational strategies, organizational knowledge, effective strategic alliances, and strategic alliances for flexible learning.[16] A CoP for

---

11   Pierre Bourdieu and Jean-Claude Passeron, *Reproduction in Education, Society and Culture*, trans. R. Nice (London, 1990) (original work published 1977).

12   Betty Stearns and Clara Degen (eds), *Careers in Music* (Washington, 1976).

13   Hoegh-Guldberg, 'Statistical Light Dawns on the Music Sector', *Australian Music Forum*, 11(2) (2005). Available at <http://www.mca.org.au/index.php?id=38>.

14   Brad Beach, 'Flexible Learning Leaders' Final Report' (Melbourne, VIC, 2001).

15   Dawn Bennett, 'Watch this space! Developing a music/education partnership', *The Knowledge Tree*, 4(1) (2003). Available from <http://flexiblelearning.net.au/knowledgetree/edition04/html/dawn_intro.htm>.

16   Anthony Bates and Peter Smith, *Critical Issues in Flexible Learning for VET Managers* (3 vols, Melbourne, 2001), vol.3.

the music sector is most likely to be effective when organized around the categories of issue evolution as defined by Norman Denzin and Yvonne Lincoln: 'topical issue; foreshadowed problem, issue under development, and assertion'.[17] The potential for a CoP to be developed using issue evolution can be simply illustrated using the question of how music practitioners and educators can establish and maintain curricula relevant to the skills and attributes required to sustain professional practice:

Foreshadowed Problem

- There are radical changes occurring at all levels of education and within the cultural industries, and musicians have to maintain the currency of their skills in order to sustain their professional practice.

Issues under Development

- Could a CoP provide an effective tool in a process of continuous curriculum renewal designed to establish and to maintain course relevance?
- In what ways could a CoP assist practitioners and educators to work in partnership on the development and delivery of collaborative units, courses and research?

Assertion

- Practitioners, educators and students would benefit from an interactive community of practice situated within and operating across the cultural industries.

Communities of practice often traverse existing boundaries as participation draws together people interested in a common topic rather than working towards a pre-defined organizational goal. Shaping a new CoP requires discussion about the current needs of the members in order to motivate interest and participation, illustrated in Figure 7.7 as an algebraic formula for a sustainable online community.[18]

If $P = (I \times F)$ then $C = (P \infty)$	
P = Participation	(people actively engaged)
I = Individual	(the individual person)
F = Feelings	(positive feelings)
C = Community	(the online place)

Figure 7.7   Formula for Sustainable Online Communities

---

17 Anselm Denzin and Juliet Lincoln, *Handbook of Qualitative Research* (Thousand Oaks, 2000), 2nd edn.

18 The formula was developed by Marlene Manto. See: Marlene Manto, 'On the Road to Community', retrieved August 16, 2003 from <http://members.ozemail.com.au/~marleman/index.html>.

The six key points for consideration are identity, ownership, need, whole person, sense of place, and value. To sustain involvement, all six are crucial for each individual involved in their community. The management challenge of these communities is to ensure that people have the time and technology to participate, that there is common interest, and that participation builds on core values. Dispersed leadership is one of the keys to a successful CoP, which succeeds or fails according to the needs and motivation of a shifting member base.

The cultural sector is unlikely to respond to an entirely online forum as observed in the lack of activity in existing online initiatives; thus a blended approach of online and offline communication would be much more effective. Although an advanced forum is preferable, people are more likely to participate in a community with mediocre infrastructure and stimulating debate than in one with a superb website and little to say. Cultural industry communication will be enhanced with the establishment of a CoP operating across artforms, and across the publicly funded and privately funded sectors. A CoP will assist with particular reference to the following issues:

- meeting the need for peer mentoring, and mentoring from experienced practitioners;
- a tool for ongoing communication and collaboration between cultural practitioners, educators, organisations and policy makers to maximise the effectiveness of existing funding, knowledge and support;
- an information point from which to access resources including existing websites and organisations;
- the identification of potential employment and continued professional development for practitioners, which is lacking in important areas such as community cultural development, teaching and technology;
- the communication and dissemination of valuable existing data.

Opportunities for Policy makers

The angst and attrition experienced by cultural practitioners can be somewhat relieved by taking heed of the critical issues; however, it is not sufficient for practitioners and educators to make these changes alone. Unnecessary barriers have so far prevented the development of informed and effective cultural intelligence, which inevitably impedes creative output. Significantly, if the fluid working lives of artists are a sign of things to come in the workforce as a whole, the inclusion of data on multiple job-holding is essential to statistical collections. In the same way, graduate destination surveys measure success in terms of full-time employment in a single position, and many systems favour performance positions above all else. It is imperative for the measurement of graduate destinations to recognize the protean careers in which most musicians and other cultural practitioners engage. Removing these hierarchical and systemic barriers will focus cultural intelligence on the real needs of practitioners, contributing towards an intelligent and informed cultural environment within which practitioners can maximize their creative energies and sustain their careers.

With a reliance on economic studies, there is much work to do to achieve a collective cultural industries voice that can proclaim effective advocacy, and to ensure that data collections are sufficiently informed and accurate to create effective policy change. Increased understanding of the cultural labour market should be used to facilitate industry-education partnerships: meeting the needs of artists throughout their careers. The following points bid further exploration:

- Design effective data collection instruments to reflect the contractual and diverse nature of artists' careers, and in particular the frequency of multiple job holding.
- Further develop the Cultural Practice Framework to reflect anticipated trends in the occupational roles pursued by artists, and incorporate emerging roles in data collection instruments.
- Establish mentoring schemes, and through them address vital issues such as gender inequity and attrition.
- Recognise the tangible and intangible value of the cultural industries and their vital importance to society. Central to recognising the values of culture is to avoid the uniform inclusion of culture in free trade agreements.
- Assist conservatories with the development of effective data collection instruments to measure graduate destinations in protean careers. Encourage conservatories to use the resulting data to inform the process of continued curricular development. Redefine the criteria of graduate success to reflect multiple roles. It is nonsensical to ask conservatories to produce only performers.
- Fund research into the establishment of systemised accreditation, paying specific attention to the areas of instrumental teaching and community engagement. Subsequent research would benefit from working with arts associations and informal networks, as these are the most common forms of intra-industry communication.
- Collaborate with educators to devise accredited courses and continuing professional development activities in teaching and community development.
- Investigate initiatives to encourage and support partnerships between creative and teaching artists.
- Practising artists bemoan the number of arts initiatives that operate in relative isolation, with multiple groups working alone on the same or similar projects. Inter-arts collaboration will curtail the number of duplicate projects, and will maximise the effectiveness of existing resources through the development of shared initiatives.

Opportunities in Orchestral Work

Orchestral work is an important source of employment for classical instrumental musicians, and it warrants specific discussion. The use of casual players is increasingly common in orchestras, and yet despite the apparent lack of performance work for graduates, orchestras struggle to secure casual players of a high enough standard. The question arises as to how there can be a shortage of players at the same time as there is a shortage of work. The difficulty is situated in the inflexible and inconsistent nature of orchestral rosters, which render it impossible for many musicians to be available for freelance orchestral work at the same time as meeting the obligations of other more regular work. The impact of unsociable and irregular hours contributes considerably to changes in career structure for all musicians, but the impact is felt most keenly by women, who are strongly influenced by family circumstances. The majority of female musicians who indicate a change of role due to their family situation emphasize their intention to return to or to increase the extent of their performance work once family circumstances permit such a move. Characteristic of interrupted careers, performance ambitions have been deferred rather than forgotten: 'I have chosen to focus on teaching at present, as I am able to set my own working hours ... In the future I can see myself changing [the extent of my] performance roles if the opportunity arises at a time I feel it will be mutually beneficial for both me and my family.' Orchestral work could provide valuable opportunities for women to maintain a professional performance role, and orchestral employers are advised to re-think existing rostering to ascertain whether more regular hours can be scheduled. Ironically, many orchestras treat casual players as being inferior to their full-time counterparts on the assumption that the players have yet to gain full-time positions; whereas lots of proficient and experienced players have made an active choice to do other things. More consistent rostering enables both permanent and casual players to be involved in other vocational and avocational activities, lessening the stress of uncertain work hours and increasing personal career satisfaction. Moreover, it will make available many more freelance musicians.

Orchestral musicians have skills and knowledge far beyond those utilized in their orchestral roles. The skills and knowledge contained within an orchestra of musicians is a vastly under-utilized and under-recognized organizational resource, and the potential for orchestral players to play a greater role within their organizations has yet to be widely embraced. Recognition of this valuable resource will enable a far more productive relationship between players and management than is usually the case. An added benefit of non-playing roles for orchestral musicians lies in the potential reduction and management of overuse injuries: 'physical injury is common among over-worked upper string players and is the major cause of distress in the workplace. Unreplaced [sic] injured colleagues add to the strain of others in the section'. There is reluctance on the part of many musicians (particularly male musicians) to discuss injury; only female study participants reported injury, and the report of injury was significantly lower than the rate suggested by the literature. Non-playing roles could offer an alternative or amended workload without loss of income or identity.

Secondary roles outside of the orchestra are generally condoned rather than supported. In fact, many orchestras retain a contractual clause that requires musicians to get the permission of orchestral management before they undertake outside work, (although most orchestras turn a blind eye to outside work in the knowledge that musicians' orchestral income is relatively low). However, it is time to recognize the positive contribution that musicians' secondary roles make to orchestral musicians, to the community within which the orchestra operates, and to the orchestra itself. Orchestral musicians are active within the social and musical fabric of their communities and are ideally placed to contribute to orchestral planning and programming. Orchestras so often strive to make connections with their communities, forgetting that the players already have these links. Although for many orchestral musicians the presence of a secondary role is essential for financial reasons, secondary roles in education, business and performance provide a creative outlet that is essential to sustaining musicians' interest in the profession, and to maintaining high personal standards of performance. An audit of musicians' skills is a logical first step towards recognizing the potential for systemic change involving musicians as key partners.

A final point to consider is the selection of orchestral leaders based almost exclusively upon performance reputation. As early as 1752, Joachim Quantz described as problematic the recruitment of orchestral leaders on purely soloistic and political grounds, and criticized the selection of orchestral leaders without investigation of the potential leadership and communication qualities of applicants:

> the old men often think it mortifying to submit to a leader not so rich in years as they, and the young imagine that they have all the skill required of a good leader, notwithstanding the multitude of duties incumbent upon him. But how can an orchestra subsist or prosper if only obstinacy, envy, hatred, and disobedience prevail among its members, instead of a sympathetic and docile spirit?[19]

Orchestral managers need to consider some important points:

- Increase the involvement of musicians in artistic programming to reduce unnecessary physical and psychological stress.
- The skills and knowledge contained within a whole orchestra of musicians is a vastly under-recognized and under-utilized resource. Conduct a skills audit of musicians to understand the wealth of knowledge and skills contained therein, and review orchestral structures accordingly.
- Review the criteria for the selection of orchestral players, and particularly of section leaders, to take into account the non-performance requirements of each role.
- Review existing injury prevention programmes and ensure that injury prevention strategies are established.
- Make orchestral rosters as regular as possible to give existing players more regular hours and to attract more casual players.
- Establish a job-share programme. Job sharing is an obvious solution to many issues, and will make it possible for many more musicians to retain performance roles whilst they meet other commitments. It will also assist musicians who need to reduce their performance time due to playing-related injuries. Players are more than happy to negotiate terms.
- Value players' secondary roles and recognize their community involvement and knowledge.

---

19 Quantz published the treatise titled *On playing the flute* in 1752. See the translation by Edward Reilly in 1966, published in New York by The Free Press.

Injury Prevention

Key inhibitors to satisfactory injury prevention are manifold, and can impact a performer from the earliest level of training. Particular issues in need of immediate attention include the availability and consistency of instrument-specific information, an appreciation of basic issues such as the importance of correct posture and effective practice, and teacher education. Aligned with these themes, musicians require an awareness of healthy and sustainable practices including care of the body, self-esteem and self-identity, social and relational wellbeing, and strategies for dealing with conflict and rejection.

In line with any field of medicine, the effectiveness of interventions can be expected to differ according to each individual. Many injuries arise from poor awareness of the physical processes involved in playing an instrument, and musicians need an understanding of ergonomics, anatomy and physiology relating to their instrument. More efficient practice techniques including 'hands-off' practice minimizes the amount of time that musicians spend actually playing their instrument. The responsibility to teach students injury prevention is a shared one, and it is unrealistic to place the responsibility solely on instrumental teachers.

Within orchestras and conservatories, carefully considered programming of repertoire and scheduling of rehearsals would reduce the amount of physical and psychological stress placed upon the performer. Similarly, technical syllabi require careful design. It is not wise, for example, to transpose violin technical work down a fifth for the viola (as happens all too often) and mandate its study without considering different technique and instrument size. Nor is it wise to require students to learn the same technical skill in 17 different positions without regard for the technical needs of each individual. Carefully designed technical syllabi not only reduce students' physical stress: they model a focused, transferable approach to skill development.

Opportunities in Education and Training

Existing performance-based education and training in classical music does not provide graduates with the requisite skills to achieve a sustainable career, and there are two solutions to the problem. The first is to have fewer graduates, and consequently fewer conservatories. The second and by far the preferred solution is for conservatories to accept and to advocate a broader definition of the term *musician* reflective of the profession, and to instigate a process of curricular change reflective of those realities. Of the utmost importance, adoption of the new definition provides the rationale for the design of education and training that will meet the needs of musicians practising in the twenty-first century and beyond. Given the financial plight of conservatories, recognition of the generic nature of skills across multiple artforms also provides the basis for the collaborative – and cost-effective – delivery of generic skills during initial and ongoing education and training.

There is clearly justification for education and training that considers the sustainability of music graduates' careers as cultural practitioners, and which develops individual strengths and talents according to the intrinsic and extrinsic influences driving the passion for music. There is no doubt that the inclusion of a wide range of skills in conservatorium curricula will enhance the potential for graduates to find sufficient performance and non-performance work; and practice throughout the cultural industries will enable musicians to diversify their roles in line with family and other commitments. In addition, the inclusion of skills relevant to a range of cultural industries practice will facilitate increased opportunities for the acquisition of skilled secondary or alternative positions with higher financial reward and intrinsic satisfaction than that gained from unskilled work.

Curricular Reform

A pivotal aim of this book has been to define opportunities in education and training, and the generic skills of cultural practice provide the basis for a curricular model that turns traditional curricular structures inside out. To sustain their careers and to feel secure in their abilities, artists have to continuously develop their abilities, personal strengths and attributes. This requires an evolving suite of skills that develops as a positive result of both successes and failures. Overcrowded curricula and the financial pressure under which many conservatories operate illustrate that conservatories cannot do it all. My favourite word in this regard is anupholsteraphobia, which is a fear of not being able to cover the material! To add more is not the answer: curricular reform, instructional change and collaborative delivery are essential. Musicians could not possibly graduate with all of the skills required for their future careers. However, an informed understanding of the cultural industries will enable graduates to select professional development based on the knowledge and skills required for wide-ranging professional practice. Resembling other artists, it is in the early stages of their careers that musicians are most likely to abandon their goals or to leave the profession altogether, and so it is logical to recognize as early as possible the potential for success in a broad variety of roles. This brings to the fore the notion that career preparation and industry awareness should be contained within the performance degree: adding vocational considerations to artistic ones. It also indicates that conservatories need to be both an integral part of the communities in which they operate and informed about the environment in which future graduates will live and work.

It is to be expected that there will be a degree of reluctance among undergraduate performance majors to expend valuable time learning the broader skills required to sustain their careers, especially when the intended career is entirely in performance. The development of positive attitudes towards non-performance study requires students to recognize their individual attributes and interests, and to develop them into realistic and achievable goals. Recognition of those strengths is most effectively realized through experiential learning and through contact with the profession. David Myers strongly encourages training facilitators to avoid prescriptive activities, the value of which may not be recognized by participants, and to base activities around self-discovery: 'self-recognition of the kinds of knowledge and skills necessary for effective educational practice provides a basis for self-initiated learning and openness to direction from other professionals'.[20] The musicians in Myers's study were more relaxed in community roles once they understood the overall objectives of the programmes with which they were involved, and when they identified as facilitators rather than taking on a teaching role.

Of particular importance is the effectiveness of learning transfer through investigative and reflective practices, cooperative learning, partnerships and the establishment of effective learning environments. Strategies used in popular music learning would be of enormous benefit to students of classical music, particularly in the emphasis given to self-directed study, peer-directed and group learning, imitation, experimentation, and the reassessment of student and teacher roles: 'orchestrated immersion of the learner in experience ... embraces both direct instruction and presentations and engagement by the student in long-term, open-ended projects and events'.[21]

Community involvement and work experience is essential to musicians, and education will to a large extent determine whether this exposure provides a wealth of new possibilities, or feelings of isolation and uncertainty. The use of physical, collaborative and virtual learning spaces enhances the teaching and learning process and provides opportunities for the application of learning from an early stage: 'more learning will take place when learners are situated in complex experiences where they are free to process, analyze, and examine experience for meaning and understanding and where they can relate what they have learned to their own purpose'.[22] Rather than expecting graduates to make social and cultural connections after graduation, the support of peers, mentors and teachers within a music performance degree provides the ideal environment for the inclusion of real and simulated situational learning as core delivery strategies. Judith Kogan stresses the importance of exploring life outside the conservatorium: 'Experience awakens the artist. One need not leave a room to experience life, but one must somehow connect with and respond to the world.'[23] Likewise, Lev Vygotsky maintains that social environment is the source of individual cognitive development. Collaborative work results in discussion and debate, leading to higher order thinking; situated activities where cognitive

---

20 David Myers, 'Preparing Professional Musicians for Effective Educational Work with Children', in O. Musumeci (ed.), *Preparing Musicians: Making Sound Worlds* (Barcelona, 2004), pp. 91–102.

21 Renate Caine and Geoffrey Caine, *The Brain, Education and the Competitive Edge* (Manham, MD, 2001).

22 Eunice Boardman, 'The Relationship of Musical Thinking and Learning to Classroom Instruction', in Eunice Boardman (ed.), *Dimensions of Musical Learning and Teaching: a Different Kind of Classroom* (Reston, VA, 2001), pp. 1–20. Individual learning accounts and action learning strategies were piloted in the United Kingdom by Metier. Initiatives included flexibly delivered professional development programmes, the extensive use of industry mentors, and both online and offline support networks incorporating technological and small business assistance. See Metier, *AS2K: Arts Skills 2000* (London, 2001).

23 Judith Kogan, *Nothing but the Best* (New York, 1987).

development takes place through problem solving may contextualize knowledge in ways that facilitate cognitive apprenticeship and the transfer of tacit knowledge.[24]

It is ludicrous that conservatories are the place at which aspiring musicians acquire their initial training, and are the last place to which most musicians return to further their skills and knowledge throughout their careers. Opportunities for music educators include the design of programmes that effectively equip musicians for sustainable careers, and making those programmes available to practising musicians. Continuing professional development (CPD) is vital to all musicians who strive to maintain their skills and to stay abreast of industry trends; however, professional development is lacking in multiple areas. The unmet demand for CPD places conservatories in an ideal position to offer lifelong training in addition to initial training. In addition to the obvious financial benefits of commercial delivery, ongoing links with the profession will provide opportunities to draw upon the expertise and networks of practising musicians. Professional development requirements include career development and planning, and a range of applicable skills such as business, conducting, pedagogy, teaching accreditation and new technologies. A further indication of the professional development needs of musicians can be found in the form of existing initiatives such as those offered by the Gateway Arts Industry Network (GAIN) in Scotland, which offers professional development for the cultural sector. The courses most in demand are those in fundraising; management of events, people, projects and time; business acumen; and presentation skills. The Association of British Orchestras (ABO) describes the popularity and importance of the programmes: 'the widening roles of musicians involved in education and outreach work continues to make such development programs essential'.[25]

The ABO raises the issue of cost as a barrier to continuing development for musicians, many of whom are unable to meet the cost of further training. In fact, time and money are the two most commonly cited barriers to CPD, which has to be flexible, and mindful of the hours in which musicians are most likely to be engaged in work: evening classes are unlikely to attract studio music teachers who teach the majority of their students out of school hours. Attendance at regular classes is also extremely difficult for musicians whose work involves travel, and for orchestral players who have inflexible rosters and different working hours every week. Flexible and self-paced programmes are popular, and musicians often request short courses, seminars and conferences, workshops and meetings. Many musicians prefer professional development to be delivered face-to-face rather than online, possibly because of the social isolation in which countless musicians work. For the majority of orchestral musicians, the design and delivery of CPD in consultation directly with orchestras would be of enormous benefit. In addition to time and money, barriers to CPD include

---

24 See, for example, Lev Vygotsky, *Mind in Society: The Development of Higher Psychological Processes* (Cambridge, MA, 1978) (original material published in 1930, 1933 and 1935); Alan Collins, John Brown and Susan Newman, 'Cognitive Apprenticeship: Teaching the Crafts of Reading, Writing, and Mathematics', in Lauren B. Resnick (ed.), *Knowing Learning and Instruction: Essays in Honor of Robert Glaser* (Hillsdale, 1989), pp. 453–94.

25 See Metier, *The Music Industry: Skills and Training Needs in the 21st Century* (London, 2000).

a lack of clear course information, availability of required training, uncertainty about what kind of training would be appropriate and geographical issues.

If the entry requirements for conservatories considered the potential for a candidate to achieve success as a musician rather than as a performer, the selection criteria would include skills and attributes demonstrable by a wide range of students and would enable conservatories to recruit students from a broad socio-economic group. Logically it would follow that the rate of employment would improve, and the potential for success (being the achievement of a sustainable career) would be much enhanced. Intending performers should be apprised of their skills and talents on entry to a course and then regularly thereafter. Of course, in order to offer appropriate guidance to students, school of music staff must themselves be current in their knowledge of the outside world. Governments have a crucial role to play in recognizing the success of graduates in a myriad of different roles and should fund conservatories accordingly.

The need for accreditation within music degree programmes is obvious, and the fields of engineering, medicine and law provide good examples of professions that accredit degree programs through a professional body. Many highly systematized music grading systems exist for students from an elementary level. Along with pre-tertiary study, they provide an ideal base for an accredited, seamless pathway. Accreditation will strengthen the role of professional associations and will help to meet some of the current skills shortages. Aside from the obvious benefits for practitioners is the potential for the sector to attract additional government support. There is vast potential for commercial and research activities that will increase the liaison between community and conservatorium in addition to making conservatories more financially independent. Research provides an additional and important source of funding, and lack of recognition for creative research output remains a crucial problem for many conservatories; however, the output of academic research would be improved by appropriately skilling staff. As Helen Stowasser points out, 'the only way to make change is to start with ourselves'.[26] There exists a vicious circle in training musicians without the necessary broad base of skills to direct research and commercial ventures when musicians are the most likely candidates to take future positions as conservatorium staff.

A report published in 1995 found that Australia's managers have good technical skills, but that they lack strategic, functional and cross-functional skills: they 'have depth but lack breadth'.[27] The report notes that the culture within education, in companies and amongst managers affords 'little attention to the personal and integrative skills that are critical to fulfil human resource management today and in the future', and calls for the development of an enterprise culture within formal and community education, and for Australia to more effectively utilize the talents of its diverse workforce. Similar leadership problems are found within conservatories and

---

26 Helen Stowasser is cited in the review from the first Music Educational Professional Development Institute, held in Evanston, Illinois in 2001. College Music Society, Montana.

27 Local Government Managers Australia, (Created 2001, July 17th). *Research Extract: Findings of the Karpin Task Force Report*. Retrieved April 5 2004, from <http://www.parklane.com.au/austext/karpin.htm>. The Karpin Report was published in 1995.

orchestras, which recruit their leaders based principally on performance reputation rather than on a broad base of skills. Tertiary music institutions most often seek their leaders from among the ranks of performing musicians, yet expect those artists to bring to their positions artistic, academic and administrative expertise. Such selection criteria have been likened to 'searching for Jesus Christ'. Not surprisingly, Helen Lancaster's research into leadership in music institutions identified that current leaders feel the need for professional development in financial skills (75%), management training (60%) and people skills (25%).[28]

The evidence overwhelmingly points to two strategies for the management of effective curricular change: the adoption of a learning organization model, and a curricular structure based around the collaborative delivery of generic skills. The instructional design of appropriate curricula will differ from the traditional system of prescribed, standardized programmes that hold the possibility of success for only a small minority, towards programmes that seek to educate for the profession according to individual strengths.

Adoption of a Learning Organization Model

Analysis of Australian performance-based undergraduate degree programmes highlights a critical lack of the clearly stated and understood goals that form the philosophical underpinnings of a course of study. The development of course objectives is an essential base on which to build and maintain relevant and effective curricula, but where do these objectives come from and can they be presented in such a way that they are attractive to potential students? Opportunities in this respect are underpinned by the adoption of a learning organization model that requires ongoing, in-depth communication with communities and practitioners. This can be achieved using a community of practice model and drawing on the knowledge and experience of staff and students, most of whom will be active in the community. Success depends upon acceptance that a music degree has to prepare musicians and not simply performers. Improved communication between the stakeholders will maximize the use of available funding, and offers the potential to attract new funding as a result of more united cultural advocacy. Improved communication will also benefit institutional collaboration, which is often influenced by empirical and political considerations rather than the pursuance of common goals.

Michael Armstrong advocates twelve factors that contribute to organizational effectiveness, the ninth of which is 'the operation of the organization as a "learning organization", i.e., one which facilitates the learning of all its members and one which continually transforms itself'.[29] The learning organization has three components: 'a well-developed capacity for double-loop learning, ongoing attention to learning how to learn, and key areas of organisational functioning'. Accepting that continual change is certain within any workplace, Laurie Field and Bill Ford

---

28 Helen Lancaster, 'Leading Musicians: Succession', *Australian Music Forum*, 10(3) (2004): 41–4.

29 Michael Armstrong, *A Handbook of Management Techniques* (New Jersey, 1993), 2nd edn.

stress the need to continually review workplace learning goals and objectives.[30] This has vital significance to the sustainability of relevant music curricula through continual curricular development and the involvement of staff in that process. The learning continuum defined by Field and Ford begins with 'haphazard learning', where learning takes place with insufficient goals and/or feedback, and data suggest that the majority of performance degree programmes currently operate at this end of the continuum. Analysis of Australian performance-based degree courses identifies a critical lack of clearly stated and understood goals that should form the philosophical underpinnings of any course.

One of the difficulties in sustaining the relevance of music curricula is the rapidity of change within the cultural industries and the educational sector; consequently, literature on organizational change should be considered in the development of a viable framework for change. The collaborative development of relevant goals and objectives will lead to goal-based learning, inclusive of strategic quality objectives. Double-loop learning combines goal-based learning with critical questioning of the objectives or goals themselves, creating the continuum from which constant curricular renewal is derived. Critical questioning ensures that the programme goals remain relevant and, as a result, that learning remains relevant. Without critical questioning, the cycle reverts back to haphazard learning.[31] A predictable factor in the need for change is a reluctance to alter institutional practices; hence successful change also requires motivational leadership. Empathy is crucial to lasting and effective change, and it is imperative that stakeholders understand the rationale for change and are conversant with the potential benefits. Acting in isolation wastes social and intellectual resources; effective change is not realized through unilateral effort, but rather through collaborative partnerships requiring the transfer of responsibilities from hierarchically structured systems to shared leadership with frontline workers.[32]

Mission statements are the outward manifestations of philosophical frameworks and course objectives, and form part of the change that has to be directed from within. By far the majority of the mission statements analysed in Chapter 4 were directed at external clients and did not include reference to human capital, which is an organization's most valuable resource. Mission statements and philosophies should be statements reflecting the organization's intent. They should clearly state where the organization is headed and the values it fosters to get there, which are fundamental aspects of operation and structure. Discussions with staff, students, graduates, practitioners and other stakeholders are an integral part of the development process.

---

30 Laurie Field and Bill Ford, *Managing Organisational Learning* (Sydney, NSW, 1995).

31 See also Nigel Benjamin, *Provide Leadership in the Workplace* (Sydney, NSW, 2000); Daniel Goleman, Richard E. Boyatzis and Annie McKee, *The New Leaders: Transforming the Art of Leadership into the Science of Results* (London, 2002); James P. Gee, Glynda Hull and Colin Lankshear, *Fast Capitalism: Theory and Practice, the New Work Order: Behind the Language of New Capitalism* (Sydney, 1996).

32 Sue Seavers, *Facilitate and Capitalise on Change and Innovation* (Sydney, 2000).

The revision of statements and underlying philosophies is about knowing the market – the profession – and continuously engaging with stakeholders to revise not only the words but also the intent. Based on a model posited by Chun Wei Choo,[33] the framework at Figure 7.8 illustrates a strategy for the development of continual collaborative curricular renewal, beginning with the establishment of course objectives and mission statements.

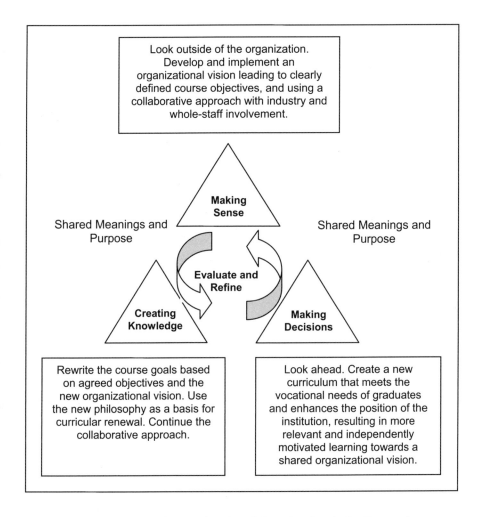

Figure 7.8   Framework for Continual Collaborative Curricular Renewal

33 Chun Wei Choo, 'The Knowing Organisation as Learning Organisation', *Education and Training*, 43, 4/5 (2001): 197–205.

The Cultural Practice Model

Conservatories need to recognize that musicians are cultural practitioners who undertake multiple roles. Performance-based music degrees tend to be designed around highly specialized skills in much the same way that most creative arts degrees are structured; however, musicians note numerous skills that are 'common to all aspects' of the profession. The inclusion of generic skills training in music education and training has the potential to maximize graduates' chances of generating, sustaining and managing their careers by providing a broad base of skills, ideas and industry information for career planning and development in response to the complex nature of the cultural industries: 'you can't afford to do university degrees and come out after three years with a degree to play the violin only'. To achieve sustainable practice, students need to develop a portfolio of materials on which to build their careers, and sufficient awareness of the cultural industries to be able to locate further training and advice as required. Many of the processes and skills mentioned by cultural practitioners are common to more than one facet of the cultural industries: the generic skills required by classically trained musicians resemble very closely the skills required by a range of visual and performing artists, and those of musicians practising in a variety of genres.

The Cultural Practice model does not detract from the concept of an elite standard of professional practice or lead to a degradation of the ability to produce such performers; in fact it enhances the effectiveness of conservatorium training. In essence, the model turns existing degree structures inside out: placing a core of generic skills at the centre of a collaborative delivery model, and freeing resources for specialist streams appropriate to the needs of individual students (Figures 7.9 and 7.10). A collaborative approach to delivery will enable conservatories to design programmes around the strengths of each individual by distributing the cost of human and physical resources required for such an undertaking.

Collaborative delivery across the arts can be facilitated by addressing the generic skills identified as common to artists in many visual and performing arts disciplines. Preparing students for work within multiple specializations according to individual strengths will inevitably lead to improved rates of sustainable careers, which will in turn strengthen the position of conservatories. Leaving aside for a moment the ethical need to offer a broad range of vocational skills, there is nothing to say that even the most virtuosic students will necessarily want to pursue performance careers. Many brilliant performers turn their creativity to other things, and yet there is an expectation that those who are proficient enough to follow the performance path should want nothing else. One happy musician recalled the moment when her aspirations changed: 'Oh my God, what a stupid idea that was: wanting to be a soloist, when there are in fact much more interesting things that I could be doing.' The Cultural Practice approach maximizes the potential, strengths and interests of each student, and directs students towards appropriate specialist study. An element of institutional specialization will enable multiple institutions to exist within the same geographic areas – as occurs increasingly in Europe – and will focus resources on manageable goals. Advantages of specialization include added media attention, the development of niche markets, and attracting students from farther afield.

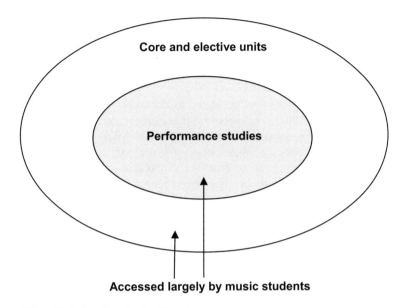

Figure 7.9   Existing Curricular Structure

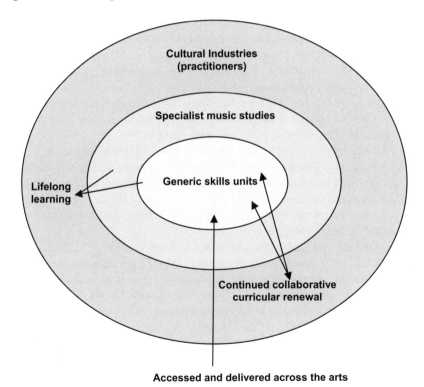

Figure 7.10   Cultural Practice Model

The Cultural Practice model is logically placed to meet the needs of cultural practitioners, placing the conservatorium in an ideal position to begin the transition towards becoming a lifelong learning institution. For curricular change to be truly effective, educators need to transcend existing barriers and consider several key points:

- Accept and demonstrate the suggested definition of a musician, and make it the basis for the development of appropriate curricula. Educate and train musicians rather than performers, composers or conductors.
- Entry into degree programmes based almost solely on performance skill is not reasonable given the destinations of graduates. Meet required quotas by adjusting the requirements for entry to reflect the protean nature of music careers.
- Make students aware of the realities of the music profession at the start of their studies. This should be done with the inclusion of a compulsory unit introducing students to the profession. Provide a representative range of specialities, and guide students through a continual process of goal setting and career preparation.
- Develop and sustain industry relevant curricula with (rather than on behalf of) industry partners, staff, and other educational institutions. Design and implement curricula based on generic skills for collaborative delivery across artforms. Establish cross-institutional management teams and facilitate cross-institutional enrolments. Extensive specialization within the first year of study is very rarely the best option.
- Incorporate accreditation into performance degree courses, starting with a basic teaching qualification.
- Adopt the position of a lifelong learning partner, and embrace opportunities to work with artists (including musicians) on a commercial basis. Where there is a demand, develop accredited programmes for artists.
- Establish specialized activities and programmes for niche markets.
- Articulation pathways to and from pre-tertiary, undergraduate, postgraduate and professional qualifications have not been adequately addressed. Organize qualifications as transferable skills packages across the different educational sectors. The use of dual-coded units for delivery within multiple sectors should be considered.
- Incorporate real and simulated workplace experience and industry-based mentors into musicians' training so that students are able to understand the need for the non-performance elements within their programmes and can apply their learning from an early stage. Ensure that students graduate with a portfolio of materials, and with the business savvy required to use them effectively.
- Incorporate vocational studies in healthy and sustainable practices, and educate staff to proactively model skills in this area. The responsibility for injury prevention rests with the whole profession: musicians, classroom and instrumental teachers, orchestras, music directors, youth orchestras and conservatories.

- Although the research supports the inclusion of additional curricular content, there remains a vital need for students to retain the time necessary for personal practice. Further research should include the use of task-oriented goals and effective delivery strategies within a more integrated curriculum. The inclusion of additional material will be possible only as part of a comprehensive review of curriculum, and may entail an additional year of study.
- Collaborate with existing and recently completed research initiatives such as the 'Polifonia' project conducted by the Association Européenne des Conservatoires (AEC) and the Royal College of Music in Stockholm.
- Many of these initiatives have the potential to attract external funding for further research, development and implementation.

Concluding Comments

It is evident that passion is at the centre of a musician's motivation to pursue music, and maintaining passion is very difficult in the face of unlikely success within the narrow parameters of musicians as 'performers'. However, there is an exciting future for the musician when defined as 'someone who practises within the profession of music in one or more specialist fields'. The new definition reflects the reality of professional practice. Broad acceptance will prompt a revision of the term as defined in general dictionaries, and will encourage its inclusion in music dictionaries. It will also stimulate a gradual change in public perception.

Success as a musician is the achievement of sustainable practice, and it is to be expected that the parameters of success will change for musicians throughout their careers. Responsibility for conveying the reality of musicians' practice rests not only with the tertiary sector: it rests with everyone whose involvement at the earliest stages of musical development provides the catalyst from which musical aspirations grow. Perhaps the flier illustrated at the end of this chapter (Illustration 7.1) will stimulate discussion about the numerous activities in which musicians engage.[34] The message for musicians is simple; accept the broader definition of a musician and reconsider your success in light of personal career satisfaction rather than a preconceived hierarchy of roles. If you are dissatisfied with your current roles, explore potential roles within and outside of the cultural industries. Recognize and value your unique skills and knowledge. Continually review and develop career goals and the skills and knowledge required to achieve them. Take control. Let no-one else define what your practice should be.

---

34 This flier is copyright free, so please feel free to use it. I will provide an e-copy on request.

Illustration 7.1   What Kinds of Musician Would You Like to Be?

Bibliography

A New Era – Orchestras Review Report 2005 (Canberra, ACT, Commonwealth of Australia, 2005).

Adams, Donald and Goldbard, Arlene, 'Cultural Policy and Cultural Democracy', *Crossroads: Reflections on the Politics of Culture* (Talmage, CA, 1990), pp. 107–9.

Aguilar, Maria, 'Education of the Professional Musician' (1998), retrieved 2 July 2002, from <http://www.mca.org.au/r18300.htm>.

Allen, James Sloan, 'The Morality and Immorality of Art', *Arts Education Policy Review*, 104/2 (2002): 19–24.

Allmendinger, Jutta and Hackman, 'Richard J., The More, the Better? A Four-Nation Study of the Inclusion of Women in Symphony Orchestras', *Social Forces*, 74/2 (1995): 423–60.

Archdall, Susan, 'Strains of Music That No Musician Wants', *Adelaide Advertiser* (2 July 2002), retrieved 2 July 2002, from <http://www.andante.com/article/article.cfm?id=17526>.

Armstrong, Michael, *A Handbook of Management Techniques* (East Brunswick, NJ, Nichols Publishing, 1993), 2nd edn.

Arthurs, Andy, 'Why Creative Industries?', *Australian Music Forum,* 10(5), (2004): 32–5.

Australian Committee on Technical and Further Education, *TAFE in Australia* (No. ACOTAFE 1974) (Canberra, ACT, 1974).

Australian Labor Party, *Federal Labor Arts Policy Discussion Paper* (2007), retrieved 12 December 2007, from <http://www.alp.org.au/media/0706/ms310.php>.

Bach, Carl Philipp Emanuel, *Essay on the True Art of Playing Keyboard Instruments*, trans. W.J. Mitchell (London, Eulenburg Books, 1974) (original work published 1753).

Barker, Larry L. and Gaut, Deborah A., *Communication* (Needham Heights, MA, Allyn & Bacon 2001), 8th edn.

Barrowcliffe, Kelly, 'The Knowledge of Playing-Related Injuries among University Music Teachers', unpublished Master's thesis, University of Western Ontario, London, Ontario, 1999.

Bartle, Graham, 'Feet on the Ground – Head in the Clouds', in G.M. Oliva (ed.), *The ISME Commission for the Education of the Professional Musician 1996 Seminar. The Musician's Role: New Challenges* (Lund, Universitetstryckeriet, 1996), pp. 183–94.

Bates, Anthony and Smith, Peter, *Critical Issues in Flexible Learning for VET Managers* (3 vols, Melbourne, Australian National Training Authority, 2001), vol. 3.

Beach, Brad, 'Flexible Learning Leaders' Final Report' (Melbourne, Australian National Training Authority, 2001).

Benjamin, Nigel, *Provide Leadership in the Workplace* (Sydney, NSW, Pearson Education Australia, 2000).

Bennett, Dawn, 'Peas in a Cultural Pod? A Comparison of the Skills and Personal Attributes of Artists and Musicians', *Australian Journal of Music Education*, 1 (2004): 22–5.

Bennett, Dawn, 'The Classical Music Profession: Educating for Sustainable Professional Practice', unpublished PhD thesis, The University of Western Australia, Perth, 2005.

Bennett, Dawn, 'Watch this space! Developing a music/education partnership', *The Knowledge Tree*, 4(1) (2003).

Bennett, Dawn and Stanberg, Andrea, 'Musicians as Teachers: Developing a Positive View through Collaborative Learning Partnerships', *International Journal of Music Education*, 24/3 (2006): 219–30.

Bennett, Tony, Emmison, Michael and Frow, John, *Accounting for Tastes: Australian Everyday Cultures* (Cambridge, Cambridge University Press, 1999).

Boardman, Eunice, 'The Relationship of Musical Thinking and Learning to Classroom Instruction', in Eunice Boardman (ed.), *Dimensions of Musical Learning and Teaching: a Different Kind of Classroom* (Reston, VA, MENC, 2001), pp. 1–20.

Bolton, Geoffrey, *The Muses in a Quest for Patronage* (Perth, WA, The University of Western Australia, 1996).

Bonavia, Ferruccio (ed.), *Musicians on Music* (London, Routledge and Kegan Paul, 1956).

Bourdieu, Pierre and Passeron, Jean-Claude, *Reproduction in Education, Society and Culture*, trans. R. Nice (London, 1990), (original work published 1977).

Braun, Werner, 'The "Hautboist": An Outline of Evolving Careers and Functions', Herbert Kaufman and Barbara Reisner (trans.), in Walter Salmen (ed.), *The Social Status of the Professional Musician from the Middle Ages to the 19th Century* (New York, Pendragon, 1983), pp. 123–59 (original work published 1971).

Bukofzer, Manfred, *Music in the Baroque Era* (London, JM Dent & Sons, 1978), 4th edn.

Caine, Renate and Caine, Geoffrey, *The Brain, Education and the Competitive Edge* (Manham, MD, Scarecrow Press Inc., 2001).

Canter, Thomas 'The Good, the Bad and the Ugly of Classroom Music', available via the Music Council of Australia at <http://www.mca.org.au/index.php?id=401>.

Chartrand, Henry, 'International Cultural Affairs: A Fourteen-Country Survey', *Journal of Arts Management, Law and Society*, 22/2 (1992).

Chesky, Kris, Kondraske, George, Henoch, Miriam, Hipple, John and Rubin, Bernard, 'Musicians' Health', in R. Colwell and C. Richardson (eds), *The New Handbook of Research on Music Teaching and Learning* (New York, Oxford University Press, 2002), pp. 1023–39.

Choo, Chun Wei, 'The Knowing Organisation as Learning Organisation', *Education and Training*, 43, 4/5 (2001): 197–205.

Cohen, Louis, Manion, Lawrence and Morrison, Keith, *Research Methods in Education* (London, Routledge Falmer, 2001), 5th edn.

Collins, Alan, Brown, John and Newman, Susan, 'Cognitive Apprenticeship: Teaching the Crafts of Reading, Writing, and Mathematics', in Lauren B. Resnick (ed.), *Knowing Learning and Instruction: Essays in Honor of Robert Glaser* (Hillsdale, NJ, Lawrence Erlbaum Associates, 1989), pp. 453–94.

Costantoura, Paul, *Australians and the Arts* (Sydney, NSW, Australia Council, 2000).

Covington, Martin 'Musical chairs: who drops out of music instruction and why?, In K. Dean (ed.), documentary report of the Ann Arbor Symposium in the application of psychology to the teaching of and learning of music: Session III. Motivation and creativity, Reston, VA, 1983.

Create Australia, *Creating a Position: Education, Training and the Cultural Industries* (Sydney, NSW, 2001).

Creative Nation: Commonwealth Cultural Policy (Canberra, ACT, Commonwealth of Australia, 1994).

Crouch, Mira and Lovric, Jenny, *Paths to Performance: Gender as a Theme in Professional Music Careers. A Pilot Study of Players in Two Orchestras* (Sydney, NSW, Australia Council, 1990).

Cunningham, Harriet, 'Let Me Entertain You', *State of the Arts* (January–March 2004): 30–40.

Curriculum Council, *Post-Compulsory Education Review* (Perth, WA, Curriculum Council, 2000).

Dempster, J., feature interview with David Pereira, *Stringendo*, 25 (2003): 10–12.

Denzin, Norman K. and Lincoln, Yvonna S, *Handbook of Qualitative Research* (Thousand Oaks, CA, Sage Publications Inc., 2000), 2nd edn.

Eakin, Hugh, 'Women Are as Scarce as Change at Vienna Orchestra', *New York Times* (4 June 2003).

Elliott, David J., *Music Matters* (New York, 1994).

Faulkner, Robert, 'Career Concerns and Mobility Motivations of Orchestral Musicians', *Sociological Quarterly*, 14 (1973): 334–49.

Featherstone-Witty, Martin, *Optimistic, Even Then: The Creation of Two Performing Arts Institutes* (London, The Schools for Performing Arts (SPA) Press, 2001).

Field, Laurie and Ford, Bill, *Managing Organisational Learning* (Sydney, NSW, Longman Australia, 1995).

Fishbein, Martin, Middlestadt, Susan, Ottai, Victor, Straus, Susan and Ellis, Alan, 'Medical Problems among ICSOM Musicians: Overview of a National Survey', *Medical Problems of Performing Artists Journal*, 3/3 (1988): 1–8.

Florida, Richard, *The Rise of the Creative Class* (New York, Basic Books, 2002).

Freed, Gregory, 'President of Juilliard Sings Job-Market Blues', *Star Tribune* (23 October 2002), retrieved 30 October 2002, from <http://www.startribune.com/stories/462/3382950.html>.

Freidson, Eliot, 'Labors of Love: A Prospectus', in Kai Erikson and Steven Vallas (eds), *The Nature of Work: Sociological Perspectives* (New Haven, CT, Yale University Press, 1990).

Fuller, Sophie, 'Dead White Men in Wigs', in Sarah Cooper (ed.), *Girls! Girls! Girls!* (London, Cassell, 1995).

Gall, Meredith D., Borg, Walter and Gall, Joyce P, *Educational Research: An Introduction* (New York, Longman, 1996), 6th edn.

Gaunt, Helena, 'One-to-One Relationships: A Case Study of Teachers' Perspectives on Instrumental/Vocal Lessons in a Conservatoire', in O. Musumeci (ed.), *The ISME Commission for Education of the Professional Musician. Preparing Musicians: Making Sound Worlds* (Barcelona, Generalitat de Catalunya Department d'Ensenyament, 2004), pp. 55–69.

Gee, James P., Hull, Glynda and Lankshear, Colin, *Fast Capitalism: Theory and Practice, the New Work Order: Behind the Language of New Capitalism* (Sydney, Allen & Unwin, 1996).

Gessele, Cynthia M., 'Conservatories III(2) up to 1790: Other Countries', in *The New Grove Dictionary of Music and Musicians* (London: Macmillan Publishers Ltd., 2001), pp. 314–15, 2nd edn.

Goleman, Daniel, Boyatzis, Richard E. and McKee, Annie, *The New Leaders: Transforming the Art of Leadership into the Science of Results* (London, Little, Brown, 2002).

Goodman, C.J., 'Will the Next Mozart Please Step Forward: A Progress Report on the Singular, Expensive Business of Training America's Best Musicians' (California, published by the author, 1970).

Gray, Clive, *The Politics of the Arts in Britain* (London, Macmillan, 2000).

Gregory, Sean, 'Collaborative Approaches: Putting Colour in a Grey Area', paper presented at the CONNECTing With conference, Queensland Conservatorium, Brisbane, April 2002.

Gumport, Patricia J., Cappelli, Peter, Massy, William F., Nettles, Michael T., Peterson, Marvin W., Shavelson, Richard J. and Zemsky, Robert, *Beyond Dead Reckoning: Research Priorities for Redirecting American Higher Education* (Stanford, CA, National Center for Postsecondary Improvement, Stanford Institute for Higher Education Research, 2002). Reprinted 2003 in *International Higher Education*, 30 (Winter): 19–21. Reprinted 2003 in *Higher Education Digest*, 46 (Summer): 1–11.

Hannan, Michael, 'Preparing Musicians for the Commercial Music Industry', in O. Musumeci (ed.), *The ISME Commission for Education of the Professional Musician. Preparing Musicians: Making Sound Worlds* (Barcelona, Generalitat de Catalunya Department d'Ensenyament, 2004), pp. 69–80.

Hannan, Michael, 'The Future of Tertiary Music Training in Australia', *Australian Music Forum,* 7(3) (2001), available at <http://www.mca.org.au/index.php?id=147>.

Harman, Susan, 'Odyssey: The History of Performing Arts Medicine', *Maryland Medical Journal*, 42/3 (1993): 251–3.

Hawkes, Jon, 'Community Cultural Development According to Adams and Goldbard', *Artwork* (August 2003).

Headington, Christopher, *The Bodley Head History of Western Music* (London, Bodley Head, 1980), 2nd edn.

Higgins, Charlotte, 'Discordant Note over "Too Posh" Academy', *The Guardian* (4 October 2004).

Hoegh-Guldberg, Hans, 'Statistical Light Dawns on the Music Sector', *Australian Music Forum,* 11/2 (2005), available at <http//www.mca.org.au/index.php?id=38>.

Hoegh-Guldberg, Hans, *The Arts Economy 1968–98: Three Decades of Growth in Australia* (Sydney, NSW, Australia Council, 2000).

Hoegh-Guldberg, Hans and Letts, Richard, *Statistical Framework Report* (Canberra, ACT, Commonwealth of Australia, 2005).

Hortschansky, Klaus, 'The Musician as Music Dealer in the Second Half of the 18th Century, H. Kaufman and B. Reisner (trans.), in W. Salmen (ed.), *The Social Status of the Professional Musician from the Middle Ages to the 19th Century* (New York, Pendragon, 1983), pp. 191–218 (original work published 1971).

Huhtanen, Kaija, 'Once I Had a Promising Future (Facing Reality as an Ex-promising Pianist)', *Australian Music Forum*, 10/3 (2004): 21–7.

Hultberg, Cecelia, 'Instrumental Students' Strategies of Learning in Making Music', in O. Musumeci (ed.), *Preparing Musicians: Making Sound Worlds* (Barcelona, Generalitat de Catalunya Department d'Ensenyament, 2004), pp. 91–102.

James, Ian M., 'Survey of Orchestras', in Raoul Tubiana and Peter Amadio (eds), *Medical Problems of the Instrumental Musician* (London, Martin Duntz, 2000), pp. 195–201.

Jang, Ki-Beom, 'Dear Friends! Let Us Start Over', in G.M. Oliva (ed.), *The ISME Commission for the Education of the Professional Musician 1996 Seminar. The Musician's Role: New Challenges* (Lund, Universitetstryckeriet,1996), pp. 125–36.

Jeffri, Joan and Throsby, David, 'Professionalism and the Visual Artist', *European Journal of Cultural Policy*, 1 (1994): 99–108.

Jezic, Diane, *Women Composers: The Lost Tradition Found* (New York, Feminist Press, 1994), 2nd edn.

Joubert, Mathilda, All Our Futures: Creativity, Culture and Education (London, National Advisory Committee on Creative and Cultural Education, 1999).

Kingsbury, Henry, *Music, Talent and Performance: A Conservatory Cultural System* (Philadelphia, Temple University Press, 1988).

Kogan, Judith, *Nothing but the Best* (New York, Random House Inc., 1987).

Kris, Ernest and Kurz, Otto, 'Artistic Labor Markets and Careers', in P. Menger (ed.), *Annual Review of Sociology*, 25/1 (1999): 541–74.

Lancaster, Helen, 'Leading Musicians: Succession', *Australian Music Forum*, 10/3 (2004): 41–4.

Lancaster, Helen, *Post-Secondary Music Education Guide* (August, 2004), retrieved 22 October 2004, from <http://www.amcoz.com.au/education.htm>.

Lave, Jean and Wenger, Etienne, *Situated Learning: Legitimate Peripheral Participation* (New York, Cambridge University Press, 1991).

Letts, Richard, '(More than) 100 Ways Globalisation Affects Music', *Australian Music Forum*, 6/5 (2000): 1–16.

Letts, Richard, 'The Nugent Rescue', *Australian Music Forum*, 6/3 (2000): 3–5.

Llobet, Jaume Rosset I, 'Musicians' Health Problems and Their Relation to Musical Education', in O. Musumeci (ed.), *The ISME Commission for Education of the Professional Musician. Preparing Musicians: Making Sound Worlds* (Barcelona, Generalitat de Catalunya Department d'Ensenyament, 2004), pp. 195–209.

Loebel, Kurt, 'Classical Music Instrumentalist', *Music Educators Journal*, 69/2 (1982): 48–9.

McCarthy, Kevin, *Change of Scene: Traditional Arts Organizations Need To Update the Plot* (Santa Monica, CA, RAND, 2001).

McCarthy, Kevin, Brooks, Arthur, Lowell, Julia and Zakaras, Laura, *The Performing Arts in a New Era* (Santa Monica, CA, RAND, 2001).

McCarthy, Kevin and Jinnett, Kimberly, *A New Framework for Building Participation in the Arts* (New York, RAND, 2001).

McCarthy, Marie, *Toward a Global Community: The International Society for Music Education 1953–2003* (Perth, WA, International Society for Music Education, 2004).

McDonald, Gerald, *Training and Careers for Professional Musicians* (Surrey, Unwin Brothers, 1979).

Macquarie, *The Budget Macquarie Dictionary* (Sydney, NSW, 2000), 3rd edn.

Maehr, Martin, 'The Development of Continuing Interests in Music', paper presented at the Ann Arbor Symposium in the application of psychology to the teaching of and learning of music: Session III. Motivation and creativity, Reston, VA, February 1983.

Major Performing Arts Inquiry Final Report: Securing the Future (Government No. DOCITA 44/99) (Canberra, ACT, Commonwealth of Australia, 1999).

Maraire, Dumisani, 'The Task of Preparing Future Musicians in a Once Colonized Developing Country, in G.M. Oliva (ed.), *The ISME Commission for the Education of the Professional Musician 1996 Seminar. The Musician's Role: New Challenges* (Lund, Universitetstryckeriet, 1996), pp. 35–51.

Marcellino, Raffaele and Cunningham, Harriet, 'Australian Tertiary Music Education', *Sounds Australian*, 60 (2002): 3–34.

Mark, Desmond, 'The Music Teacher's Dilemma – Musician or Teacher?', *International Journal of Music Education*, 32 (1998): 3–23.

Menger, Pierre-Michel, 'Artistic Labor Markets and Careers', *Annual Review of Sociology*, 25/1 (1999): 541–74.

Merriam, Alan P., *The Anthropology of Music* (Evanston, IL, Northwestern University Press, 1964).

Metier, *AS2K: Arts Skills 2000* (London, Department of Culture, Media and Sport, 2001).

Metier, *The Music Industry: Skills and Training Needs in the 21st Century* (London, Department of Culture, Media and Sport, 2000).

Miles, Matthew B. and Huberman, A. Michael, *Qualitative Data Analysis* (Beverley Hills, CA, Sage Publications Inc., 1994), 2nd edn.

Mills, Janet, 'Addressing the Concerns of Conservatoire Students about School Music Teaching, *British Journal of Music Education*, 22/1 (2005): 63–75.

Mills, Janet and Smith, Jan, 'Working in Music: Becoming Successful', paper presented at the Musikalische Bebabung in der Lebenzeitperspektive, University of Paderborn, 2000.

Mitchell, John, Wood, Sarah and Young, Susan, 'Communities of Practice: Reshaping Professional Practice and Improving Organisational Productivity in the Vocational Education and Training (VET) Sector' (Melbourne, Australian National Training Authority, 2001).

Mozart, Leopold, *A Treatise on the Fundamental Principles of Violin Playing*, trans. E. Knocker (Oxford, Oxford University Press, 1971), 2nd edn (original work published 1756).

Myers, David, 'Preparing Professional Musicians for Effective Educational Work with Children', in Orlando Musumeci (ed.), *The ISME Commission for Education of the Professional Musician. Preparing Musicians: Making Sound Worlds* (Barcelona, 2004), pp. 149–63.

Nadel, H., *Exploring Ways to Strengthen a Practice for Long-Term Growth* (March 1998), retrieved 20 March 2002, from <http://www.isdesignet.com/Magazine/Mar'98sprep.html>.

Nielsen, Ken, 'Your Mission, Assuming You Choose to Ignore it ...', *Australian Music Forum*, 11/1 (2004): 42.

O'Brien, Jane and Feist, Andy, *Employment in the Arts and Cultural Industries: An Analysis of the Labour Force Survey and Other Sources* (London, Arts Council, 1997).

Odam, George, 'Developing a Conservatoire: Research, Professional Development and Widening Participation', in O. Musumeci (ed.), *The ISME Commission for Education of the Professional Musician. Preparing Musicians: Making Sound Worlds* (Barcelona, Generalitat de Catalunya Department d'Ensenyament, 2004), pp. 175–83.

Oliva, Giacomo M. (ed.), *The ISME Commission for the Education of the Professional Musician. The Musician's Role: New Challenges* (Lund, Universitetstryckeriet, 1996), pp. 5–8.

Pearsall, Judy and Trumble, Bill (eds), *The Oxford English Reference Dictionary* (Oxford, Oxford University Press, 1996), 2nd edn.

Persson, Roland, 'Brilliant Performers as Teachers: A Case Study of Commonsense Teaching in a Conservatoire Setting', *International Journal of Music Education*, 28 (1996): 25–36.

Petzoldt, Richard, *Georg Philipp Telemann*, trans. H. Fitzpatrick (London, University Press, 1974) (original work published 1967).

Petzoldt, Richard, 'The Economic Conditions of the 18th Century Musician', H. Kaufman and B. Reisner (trans.), in W. Salmen (ed.), *The Social Status of the Professional Musician from the Middle Ages to the 19th Century* (New York, Pendragon, 1983), pp. 161–88.

Pincherle, Marc, *The World of the Virtuoso*, trans. L.H. Brockway (Toronto, Ontario, W.W. Norton and Company, Inc., 1963) (original work published 1961).

Poklemba, Janet, 'Career Education: An Integral Part of the Education of the Undergraduate Music Performance Student?', unpublished Master's thesis, The American University, Washington.

Powers, Keith, 'Audition Mishaps Hit Sour Note but Offer Valuable Experience' (9 March 2004), retrieved 9 March 2004, from <http://theedge.bostonherald.com/artsNews/view.bg?articleid=812>.

Quantz, Joachim J., *On Playing the Flute*, trans. E.R. Reilly (New York, The Free Press, 1966) (original work published 1752).

Raynor, Henry, *A Social History of Music from the Middle Ages to Beethoven* (London, Barrie & Jenkins Ltd., 1972).

Raynor, Henry, *Music and Society since 1815* (London, Barrie & Jenkins Ltd., 1976).

Renshaw, Peter, 'Remaking the Conservatorium Agenda', *Music Forum*, 8/5 (2002), retrieved 18 March 2004, from <http://www.mca.org.au/mf2008renshaw.hml>.

Rieger, Eva, '*Dolce Semplice?* On the Changing Role of Women in Music', H. Anderson (trans.), in G. Ecker (ed.), *Feminist Aesthetics* (London, The Women's Press Limited, 1985) (original work published 1976).

Roberts, Brian, *Musician: a Process of Labelling* (Newfoundland, St. John's: Memorial University of Newfoundland, 1991).

Rogers, Rick, *Creating a Land with Music* (London, Youth Music, 2002).

Rossman, Gretchen and Wilson, Bruce, 'Numbers and Words: Combining Quantitative and Qualitative Methods in a Single Large-Scale Study', *Evaluation Review*, 9/5 (1984): 627–43.

Sadie, Stanley and Tyrrell, John (eds), *The New Grove Dictionary of Music and Musicians* (London, Macmillan, 2003), 2nd edn.

Salmen, Walter, 'Social Obligations of the Emancipated Musician in the 19th Century', H. Kaufman and B. Reisner (trans.), in W. Salmen (ed.), *The Social Status of the Professional Musician from the Middle Ages to the 19th Century* (New York, Pendragon, 1983), pp. 265–81.

Salter, Lionel, *The Musician and His World* (London, The Garden City Press Ltd., 1963).

Sand, Barbara, *Teaching Genius: Dorothy DeLay and the Making of a Musician* (Portland, OR, Amadeus Press, 2000).

Schmidt, Elaine, 'MSO Trombonist Didn't Just Slide into Her Spot', *Milwaukee Journal Sentinel* (15 June 2003): 1E, 6E.

Seaton, Douglass, *Music and American Higher Education* (1997), retrieved 14 July 2003, from <http://www.music.org/InfoEdMusic/HigherEd/SumSeaton.html>.

Seavers, Sue, *Facilitate and Capitalise on Change and Innovation* (Sydney, NSW, Education Australia, 2000).

Small, Christopher, *Musicking: The Meanings of Performance and Listening* (Hanover, NH, University Press of New England, 1998).

Smith, Larry, 'Training the Performing Artist: More Than Music', in G.M. Oliva (ed.), *The ISME Commission for the Education of the Professional Musician 1996 Seminar. The Musician's Role: New Challenges* (Lund, Universitetstryckeriet, 1996), pp. 117–21.

Smith, Ralph, 'Reflections about Policy during Troubled Times', *Arts Education Policy Review*, 103/3 (2002): 29–34.

Smith, Stephen and Robinson, John, *Working Musicians* (Fremantle, WA, Fremantle Arts Centre Press, 1990).

Stearns, Betty and Degen, Clara (eds), *Careers in Music* (Washington, American Music Conference, 1976).

Stern, Isaac W. and Potok, Chaim, *Isaac Stern: My First 79 Years* (Philadelphia, Da Capo Press, 1999).

Stevenson, Deborah, *Art and Organisation* (Brisbane, QLD, University of Queensland Press, 2000).

Strauss, Anselm and Corbin, Juliet, *Basics of Qualitative Research* (Thousand Oaks, CA, Sage Publications Inc., 1998), 2nd edn.

Throsby, David, 'Centenary Article – Public Funding of the Arts in Australia, 1900–2000', *Year Book Australia, 2001* (Canberra, ACT, Australian Bureau of Statistics, 2001).

Throsby, David, *Does Australia Need a Cultural Policy?* Platform Papers issue 07 (Sydney, NSW, Currency House, 2006).

Throsby, David, *Economics and Culture* (Cambridge, Cambridge University Press, 2001).

Throsby, David, *The Artist in Australia Today: Report of the Committee for the Individual Artists Inquiry* (Sydney, NSW, Australia Council, 1984).

Throsby, David and Hollister, Virginia, *Don't Give Up Your Day Job: An Economic Study of Professional Artists in Australia* (No. 331.7617) (Sydney, NSW, Australia Council, 2003).

Throsby, David and Thompson, Beverley, *But What Do You Do for a Living? A New Economic Study of Australian Artists* (Sydney, NSW, Australia Council, 1994).

Ticehurst, G. William and Veal, Anthony J., *Business Research Methods: A Managerial Approach* (Sydney, NSW, Longman, 2000).

Traasdahl, Jan Ole, 'Rhythmic Music Education in Denmark', in G.M. Oliva (ed.), *The ISME Commission for the Education of the Professional Musician 1996 Seminar. The Musician's Role: New Challenges* (Lund, Universitetstryckeriet, 1996), pp. 67–74.

Trotter, Robin, 'Cultural Policy', *The Year's Work in Critical and Cultural Theory,* 10/1 (2002): 202–25.

Vella, Richard, 'Tertiary Music Education since 1988', in John Whiteoak and Aline Scott-Maxwell (eds), *Currency Companion to Music and Dance in Australia* (Sydney, NSW, Currency Press, 2003).

Vetter, T., 'The University Music Performance Program: Performance or Liberal Arts Degree? The Case of Voice Performance', unpublished Master's thesis, University of Toronto, Ontario, 1990.

Vitale, Sidra, 'The 3rd WWWave: What's All This, Then?' (1999), retrieved 23 April 2003, from <http://www.3rdwwwave.com/display_article.cgi?144>.

Vygotsky, Lev, *Mind in Society: The Development of Higher Psychological Processes* (Cambridge, MA, Harvard University Press, 1978) (original material published in 1930, 1933 and 1935).

Weller, Janis, 'The Whole Musician: Journey to Authentic Vocation', in O. Musumeci (ed.), *The ISME Commission for Education of the Musician. Preparing Musicians: Making Sound Worlds* (Barcelona, Generalitat de Catalunya Department d'Ensenyament, 2004), pp. 245–56.

Wichterman, Catherine, *The Orchestra Forum: A Discussion of Symphony Orchestras in the US* (New York, The Andrew W. Mellon Foundation, 1999).

Williamon, Aaron, 'Healthy Body, Healthy Mind, Healthy Music: Practice-Based Research Leading to Research-Based Learning', in O. Musemici (ed.), *The ISME Commission for Education of the Professional Musician. Preparing Musicians: Making Sound Worlds* (Barcelona, Generalitat de Catalunya Department d'Ensenyament , 2004), pp. 257–70.

Yffer, Louis, 'The Investigation Proceeds', in *Music Is the Victim* (Melbourne, Vic., published by the author, 1995), pp. 1–40.

Appendix

Summary of Survey Findings

Chapter 6 included lots of facts and figures, which were hopefully not too difficult to negotiate. The following summary is intended as useful reading for those planning or re-evaluating their careers in music and for those involved with curricular design.

Employment

- Thirty per cent of musicians work outside of music for at least some of the time. Musicians engage in non-performance and non-music roles for their intrinsic value as well as for more obvious extrinsic benefits such as regular income.
- Survey respondents included musicians working full-time (68%) and part-time (32%). Eighty-one percent of males and 60 per cent of females worked full-time.
- Of the 68 per cent of musicians who worked full time in music, one-third indicated that they would prefer to be part-time.
- Only one-third of the musicians working part-time in music aspired to become full-time.
- Musicians tend to have at least two different music industry roles, reflecting the multi-faceted nature of careers in music.
- The most common role for musicians is teaching, where over 80 per cent of musicians spend over half of their time. This does not include classroom music teaching, which falls within a separate occupational group. Despite the commonality of instrumental teaching, only 1 per cent of core course time is devoted to pedagogy within Australia's undergraduate performance degrees. Many degrees include no pedagogical training whatsoever.
- Performance is the second most common role for musicians, and involves 70 per cent of musicians, who spend on average just over half of their time in performance.
- Of the 40 per cent of musicians who were paid for all of their work, 42 per cent cited performance as their primary role, 52 per cent were primarily instrumental teachers and the remaining 6 per cent were primarily administrators. Female musicians are more likely to work primarily in teaching, and male musicians are more likely to work primarily in performance.
- On average, male musicians spend a greater percentage of their time in performance, composition, examining and technical roles. Female musicians spend proportionately more time in teaching, ensemble direction and administration.

- Women increase the extent of their performance role until somewhere between their mid-thirties and mid-forties, at which point performance becomes less likely to be their primary role. Male musicians appear to maintain their performance role until their mid-fifties.
- Primary teaching roles tend to become less common with age for women and more common for men.
- Only 8 per cent of respondents worked solely in performance, and less than 4% had completed an undergraduate performance degree such as a Bachelor of Music.
- The most common factors influencing musicians to change the extent of their performance role are: (1) increased job satisfaction (30%); (2) stable employment (30%); (3) a higher salary (20%); and (4) family reasons (20%). Responses were similar for male and female respondents in most factors; however, there were three exceptions: (1) responses relating to family reasons came predominantly from female musicians (47% compared to 29% male responses); (2) a reduction in the amount of travel was a factor for 24 per cent of female and 13 per cent of male respondents; and (3) injury was cited only by female respondents (10%). Injury is often not spoken about, even with colleagues. Self-report may, therefore, have been a factor in deciding whether or not to report injury, particularly for male respondents.

Musicians' Skills

- Musicians use an average of 3.9 different skills in the maintenance of their careers. The two most common are performance skills, which were used by 96% of respondents, and teaching skills, which were used by 88 per cent of respondents. The need for teaching skills was emphasized at every stage of the research, and by both educators and practising musicians.
- Taking into account survey and interview data, skills in business, marketing and management were grouped under the term 'business practices'. Skills in business practices were used by 72 per cent of respondents.
- Visual and performing artists need to be entrepreneurial, and to utilize effective business skills. Corresponding data from the musician study further strengthens the hypothesis that the work patterns and associated generic skills of musicians and other artists are closely aligned. Musicians advocate the need to be entrepreneurial in order to manage opportunities for employment and career development.
- It is increasingly important for all cultural practitioners to be aware of community cultural development, or cultural engagement.
- It is difficult and rare for a musician to achieve and sustain a career entirely in performance, and musicians emphasize that a performance career will not suit everyone.

Sustainability and Attrition

- Five key factors influence attrition from the cultural industries, and attrition factors between musicians and other creative artists are almost identical. The five key factors are: (1) insufficiency of regular employment due to a lack of practitioner diversity; (2) a lack of career mobility; (3) irregular working hours; (4) high rates of injury; and (5) low financial rewards.
- Importantly, the same five key factors influence musicians' decisions to change the extent of their performance role – often moving away from or reducing performance work to find a solution.

Personal Attributes

- The key component to sustaining a career in music is passion, which drives motivation, confidence, resilience and openness/adaptability. The personal attributes are illustrated in the matrix (Figure 6.7, p. 113).

Education and Training

- Formal education and training is extremely important to classical instrumental musicians and was undertaken by 94 per cent of respondents, who studied at an average of 1.4 different locations.
- Graduate or postgraduate study was undertaken by 40 per cent of musicians. Disciplines included music performance (36%), music education (39%) and non-related fields (16%).
- The most common course of study is an undergraduate degree in music, which was undertaken by 62 per cent of musicians.
- Using a Likert scale from Ineffective (1) to Highly effective (10), musicians rated the effectiveness of their formal education and training in terms of their careers. Musicians who had undertaken graduate level education and training gave a mean rating of eight, and those who had undertaken undergraduate level education gave a ranking of seven.
- Musicians were asked what changes they would make to the education and training that they had undertaken. Responses embraced numerous themes, the three most common curriculum areas being: (1) the inclusion of career education and industry experience (20%); (2) instrumental pedagogy (18%); and (3) business skills (15%). Career education and industry experience also arose as major concerns. In particular, say musicians, students need to be made aware of the potential for them to achieve their goals, and should plan and study accordingly.
- Performance, pedagogy and business practices arose as: (1) the curriculum areas for which educational change was most often recommended; (2) the skills most used by participants; and (3) the most commonly pursued informal education and training.

- Effective curriculum should include, as core components, small business skills including communication and career development studies, pedagogy, psychology of performance, language (particularly for conductors) and physical wellbeing.
- Experience within the profession is an important way for student musicians to learn about the potential for engagement in a variety of roles, and to understand the skills that they would need to take advantage of available opportunities.
- The most common reason (33%) for non-completion of formal study was an early transition to work.
- Almost 70 per cent of respondents had engaged in informal education and training. The three most common activities were performance (58%), pedagogy (36%) and activities through professional networks (35%).
- Entry requirements for undergraduate performance degrees were criticized by musicians, who suggest that students should be directed towards realistic streams of study at the commencement of their programmes. Musicians also suggest that undergraduate degrees should be of longer duration in order for graduates to be able to create sustainable careers.

Index